The Code of the Warrior

THE CODE OF THE WARRIOR

Exploring Warrior Values
Past and Present

SHANNON E. FRENCH

ROWMAN & LITTLEFIELD PUBLISHERS, INC.
Lanham • Boulder • New York • Oxford

ROWMAN & LITTLEFIELD PUBLISHERS, INC.

Published in the United States of America
by Rowman & Littlefield Publishers, Inc.
4720 Boston Way, Lanham, Maryland 20706
www.rowmanlittlefield.com

PO Box 317
Oxford
OX2 9RU, UK

British Library Cataloguing in Publication Information Available

Library of Congress Cataloging-in-Publication Data

French, Shannon E., 1970-
    The code of the warrior : exploring warrior values past and present /
Shannon E. French
        p. cm.
Includes bibliographical references and index.
    ISBN 0-8476-9756-8 (cloth : alk. paper)
    1. Soldiers.   2. Military art and science.   3. Sociology, Military.
I. Title.
    U104 .F68   2003
    355.02—dc21

                                                2002011868

Printed in the United States of America

⊗™ The paper used in this publication meets the minimum requirements of
American National Standard for Information Sciences—Permanence of Paper
for Printed Library Materials, ANSI/NISO Z39.48–1992.

To U.S. Navy SEAL Chad S.,
my warrior alter-ego,
and to my "Advanced Warriors"
Alex, Andy, Ben, Brad, Cade, Casey, Chris, Chuck,
Clint, Colette, Dan, David, Dennis, Derek, Donnie,
Dusty, Genevieve, Greg, Ian, Jerick, Jerry, Justin,
Kevin, Lew, Lisa, Liz, Lora, Mario, Matt, Michael,
Nathan, Nick, Richard, Rob, Russ, Scott, Steven, Ted,
Thom, Tim, William, and Wilson,
and to *all* of my student warriors, past and present,
serving here and around the world
to defend our freedom

Come back with your shields!

Contents

Foreword

Senator John McCain

I know the character of Americans who take up arms to defend our nation's interests and to advance our democratic values. I know of all the battles, all the grim tests of courage and character, that have made a legend of our military's devotion to duty.

"Character," said the nineteenth-century evangelist Dwight Moody, "is what you are in the dark."

I have always found that the most difficult choices between honor and dishonor occur when no one is watching. For a politician, that presents something of a dilemma. We like to have our virtue affirmed in the public spotlight. But no matter how clever you are in crafting a public image of integrity, if it is a false image, the truth will emerge, and usually sooner than expected.

The lessons I learned as a young man and officer have sometimes helped me withstand the temptations of public life to cut a few corners here and there for the sake of ambition. And sometimes not. I wouldn't want anyone to be fooled into thinking that I am the example of rectitude I pretend to be to my children. But events I have witnessed and the example of others have taught me that it is far preferable in one short time to stick by truths that give more meaning to life than fame and fortune.

Bad people can occasionally do good things. Good people can occasionally do bad things. But those things are anomalies in a life that is defined by opposing acts. People of bad character will never reach the end of life satisfied with the experience. People of good character will never waste their life, whether they die in obscurity or renown. They will know a happiness far more sublime than pleasure.

God grants us all the privilege of having our character tested. The tests come frequently, as often in peace as in war, as often in private as in public.

For me, many of those tests came in Vietnam. I knew no one there who ever chose death over homecoming. But I knew some men who preferred death to dishonor. The memory of them, of what they bore for us, helps me see the virtue in my own humility. It helps me understand that good character is self-respect, and courage and humility are its attributes.

Many years have passed since I learned that lesson. But the comforts and privileges of my present life don't obscure the memory of what I witnessed then. And in recent years when I have faced difficult decisions and chosen well, the choice was made easier by the memory of those who once made harder choices and paid a much higher price for it. And when I chose poorly, their example made me ashamed and left me no explanation for my failure other than my own weakness.

Shannon French's book is useful in explaining, reinforcing, and helping to impart these ideals. As one of my heroes, Theodore Roosevelt, once said, "To educate a person in mind and not in morals is to educate a menace to society."

It has been commonplace for a very long time that military professionals are held to a higher standard of integrity than is insisted upon in other professions. The public generally holds that view. And officers themselves take pride in claiming the distinction. Our officer corps takes pride in embracing the higher expectations that our country has of their character and conduct, even if there are occasional and perhaps inevitable failures to meet those expectations.

Shannon French writes: "In many cases this code of honor seems to hold the warrior to a higher ethical standard than that required for an ordinary citizen within the general population of the society the warrior serves. The code is not imposed from the outside. The warriors themselves police strict adherence to these standards."

Military units cannot function well, especially in combat environments, if the members of the unit are not scrupulously honest with each other. Officers will not be able to do their jobs if they are not, to a certain degree, selfless. If they are not, it will be hard to endure even the ordinary hardships of military life, much less be willing to risk their lives for their country's cause.

A man I love and admire, Vice Admiral William P. Lawrence, USN, who as a midshipman developed the present Honor Concept at the Naval Academy, once said the academies "must graduate special persons—officers who will place the interests of the country and the welfare and safety of their subordinates above their own."

I believe that young men and women join the armed forces to serve a cause greater than self-interest. They must make the most of their patriotism. They must foster virtues of courage, obedience, loyalty, and conscientiousness. To have a military that functions as well as it can, it must be fully committed to endorsing these virtues and behaviors in military professionals. It requires a sense of honor that demands as the price of self-respect the sacrifice of self-interest. What a poor life it is that has no greater object than itself.

Those who claim their liberty but not their duty to the civilization that ensures it live a half-life. Success, wealth, and celebrity gained and kept for private interest is a small thing. It makes us comfortable, eases the material hardships our children will bear, and purchases a fleeting regard for our lives, yet not the self-respect that in the end will matter to us most. But have the character to sacrifice for a cause greater than self-interest and invest in life with the eminence of that cause, and self-respect is assured.

In this book, Shannon French captures the essence of the military's core values, history, traditions, the benchmark of its leadership, and the raison d'être of servicemembers' development of character and honor. She writes: "The code of the warrior not only defines how he should interact with his own warrior comrades, but also how he should treat other members of his society, his enemies, and the people he conquers. The code restrains the warrior. It sets boundaries on his behavior. It distinguishes honorable acts from shameful acts." Nothing more needs to be said.

Acknowledgments

I would never have been able to finish this project without the love, encouragement, and unflagging support of my future husband, Doug Brattebo (who lends me his strength and always has more faith in me than I do); my parents, Peter (who taught me philosophy at his knee and continues to challenge and inspire me daily) and Sandra (my greatest fan and patient, indefatigable editor extraordinaire) French; newest supporters and loyal readers Don and Pat Brattebo; and my wonderful friends Marianne "Tae" Makar (who promised she would still love me even if I missed *every* deadline), Jennifer and Scott Senko (who encouraged me constantly and fed me home-cooked meals during my most intense writing binges), Laurissa "Missy" James (who generously typed up the first draft of chapter 4 for me in her own few hours of free time), Greg Mac-Donald (the philosopher-Marine who for motivation lent me the anchor and globe he earned at Parris Island), Christian "Zen" Nix (without whom I might never have completed my Ph.D. and gone on to teach at the United States Naval Academy [USNA]), Sue Dwyer (an amazing role model, mentor, and occasional dog-sitter), Wyn Hilty and Bob Settles, and all those dear to me with whom I have spent much too little time over the past three years because I had to work on The Book.

This work also would never have been possible without the help and guidance of my friends and colleagues at USNA, especially my incredible "skippers," George Lucas and Capt. Corky Vazquez, USN, for whom it has truly been a joy to work; my first advocates, Capt. Betsy Holmes, USN, Dave Johnson, and Capt. Mark Clemente, USN; the extraordinary USNA historians, political scientists, psychologists, and fellow philosophers who have given me sources, comments, constructive criticism, and encouragement, including Ernie Tucker, Steve Wrage, Rich Abels, Brad Johnson, Doug Marlow, Dave Garren, Larry Lengbeyer, Chris Eberle, and the members of the Naval Academy Research Council; all the outstanding "Luce Hall Warriors"; always on-target war movie/war literature critic,

Lt. Col. Bill Stooksbury, USMC; and authors/warriors Cmdr. (ret.) Ward "Mooch" Carroll, USN, and Cmdr. Bob "Sprout" Proano, USN. I would also like to thank all of "my" NE203 instructors for their patience, timely pats on the back, and words of wisdom, especially Adm. (ret.) Bud Edney, Adm. (ret.) Hank Chiles, Capt. (ret.) Rick Rubel, USN, and Col. (ret.) Bob Blose, USMC.

I am deeply indebted to the extremely supportive leadership at USNA, including division directors Capt. Red Smith and Capt. Bob Wells; character development director Capt. Jim Campbell; commandants Adm. Gary Roughhead and Col. John Allen, USMC (who writes and speaks most eloquently about the warrior ethos himself); Dean William Miller (who sat in on my "Code of the Warrior" course and now knows more about Bushido than most deans alive); Deans Michael Halbig, Frederick Davis, and David Vetter (who all made time to show an interest in my work); Capt. James Grant, USN; and superintendent Adm. John Ryan. In addition, I must thank the organizers of JSCOPE (the Joint Services Conference on Professional Ethics) and my colleagues in character development and the philosophy department at the United States Air Force Academy (USAFA), including Col. Mark Hyatt, Maj. Cheryl Soat, Col. (ret.) Bill Rhodes, Charlie Hudlin, J. Carl Ficarrotta, and Carlos Bertha. The opportunities I was given to present my work-in-progress at JSCOPE and at two successive years of NCLS (the Air Force Academy's impressive annual National Character and Leadership Symposium) were vital to the refinement of my central thesis, as were the comments and questions I received from my civilian and military colleagues and from the midshipmen and cadets in attendance from ROTC and NROTC units, United States Military Academy (USMA) USNA, USAFA, United States Coast Guard Academy, and the United States Merchant Marine Academy. My thanks, too, to editors Bard Maeland and James Turner Johnson of the *Journal of Military Ethics* and John Kekes of *Public Affairs Quarterly* for publishing some of my earlier warrior ethics pieces. I would also like to thank philosophers Felicia Ackerman and Margaret Urban Walker; Martin Cook and Col. Robert H. Taylor of the Army War College; Don Snider of USMA; Laurent Murawiec, civilian Pentagon consultant; Capt. (ret.) Karl Hasslinger, formerly of the Office of the Secretary of Defense/Net Assessment; and Pat Barrows, Andy Hines, Neil Duffy, and Adm. (ret.) Jerry Miller for believing in and boosting this project.

Last but not least, I'd like to thank all the folks at Rowman & Littlefield Publishers; my copyeditor, Cheryl Hoffman; and my outstanding editors, Maureen MacGrogan, without whom I would never have started this book, and Eve DeVaro, without whom I might never have finished it.

1

Why Warriors Need a Code

At the United States Naval Academy I teach a military ethics course called "The Code of the Warrior." My students are all midshipmen preparing for careers as officers in the U.S. Navy or Marine Corps. Each semester, on the first day the class meets, I ask the midshipmen to reflect on the meaning of the word "warrior" by giving them an exercise that requires them to identify whether any of a list of five words are perfect synonyms for warrior. They are then asked to write a brief explanation of why each word succeeds or fails as a synonym. The time constraints keep their responses relatively raw, yet they are often surprisingly earnest and at times even impassioned.

The words I offer my students for their consideration are "murderer," "killer," "fighter," "victor," and "conqueror." I have found that most of them reject all five. The reasons that they give to account for why they wish to dismiss each of these as synonyms for warrior consistently stress the idea that a true warrior has to be morally superior in some way to those who might qualify for the other suggested epithets. Consider these representative comments from a variety of midshipmen:

> *Murderer:* "This word has connotations of unjust acts, namely killing for no reason. A warrior fights an enemy who fights to kill him."

> *Killer:* "A warrior may be required to kill, but it should be for a purpose or cause greater than his own welfare, for an ideal."

> *Fighter:* "Simply fighting doesn't make a warrior. There are rules a warrior follows."

> *Victor:* "Warriors will lose, too—and the people who win aren't always what a warrior should be."

> *Conqueror:* "A conqueror may simply command enough power to

overcome opposition. He can be very lacking in the ethical beliefs that should be part of a warrior's life."

Almost without exception, my students insist that a warrior is *not* a murderer. They can even become emotional in the course of repudiating this (intentionally provocative) potential synonym. It is very important to them that I understand that while most warriors do *kill* people, they never *murder* anyone. Their remarks are filled with contempt for mere murderers:

- "Murder is committed in cold-blood, without a reason. A warrior should only kill in battle, when it is unavoidable."

- "Murderers have no noble reason for their crimes."

- "While a murderer often kills innocent or defenseless people, a warrior restricts his killing to willing combatants. He may stray, but that is an error, not the norm."

- "A murderer is someone who kills and enjoys it. That is not a warrior."

- "This term has very negative connotations associated with it because a murderer is one who usually kills innocent, unarmed people—while a warrior has honor in battle and does not take advantage of the weak."

- "A murderer murders out of hate. A warrior does not. He knows how to control his anger."

- "A warrior is not a murderer because a warrior has a code that he lives by which is influenced by morals which must be justified."

- "Warriors fight other warriors. Therefore they kill, not murder."

- "'Murderer' lacks any implication of honor or ethics, but rather calls to mind ruthlessness and disregard for human life."

- "A murderer kills for gain, or out of anger. He does not allow victims a fair fight."

- "The term 'murder' represents an act done with malice. Warriors kill people in an honorable way."

- "A murderer has no honor."

Clearly, my students do not regard the distinction between a warrior and a murderer as a trivial one. Nor should they. In fact, the distinction is essential, and understanding it is one of the primary aims of this text.

Murder is a good example of an act that is cross-culturally condemned.

Whatever their other points of discord, the major religions of the world agree in the determination that murder (variously defined) is wrong. According to the somewhat cynical seventeenth-century philosopher Thomas Hobbes, the fear of our own murderous appetites is what drove us to form societies in the first place. We eagerly entered into a social contract in which certain rules of civilized behavior could be enforced by a sovereign power in order to escape the miserable, anarchic state of nature where existence is a "war of every man against every man" and individual lives are "solitary, poor, nasty, brutish, and short."[1] In other words, people want to live under some sort of system that at least attempts to make good the guarantee that when they go to sleep at night, they will not be murdered in their beds.

Unfortunately, the fact that we abhor murder produces a disturbing tension for those who are asked to fight wars for their tribes, clans, communities, cultures, or nations. When they are trained for war, warriors are given a mandate by their society to take lives. But they must learn to take only certain lives in certain ways, at certain times, and for certain reasons. Otherwise, they become indistinguishable from murderers and will find themselves condemned by the very societies they were created to serve.

Warrior cultures throughout history and from diverse regions around the globe have constructed codes of behavior based on their own image of the ideal warrior. These codes have not always been written down or literally codified into a set of explicit rules. A code can be hidden in the lines of epic poems or implied by the descriptions of mythic heroes. One way or another, it is carefully conveyed to each succeeding generation of warriors. These codes tend to be quite demanding. They are often closely linked to a culture's religious beliefs and can be connected to elaborate (and frequently death-defying or excruciatingly painful) rituals and rites of passage.

In many cases this code of honor seems to hold the warrior to a higher ethical standard than that required for an ordinary citizen within the general population of the society the warrior serves. The code is not imposed from the outside. The warriors themselves police strict adherence to these standards, with violators being shamed, ostracized, or even killed by their peers. One historical example comes from the Roman legions, where if a man fell asleep while he was supposed to be on watch in time of war, he could expect to be stoned to death by the members of his own cohort.

The code of the warrior defines not only how he should interact with his own warrior comrades but also how he should treat other members of his society, his enemies, and the people he conquers. The code restrains the warrior. It sets boundaries on his behavior. It distinguishes honorable acts from shameful acts. Achilles must seek vengeance for the death of his friend Patroclus, yet when his rage drives him to desecrate the corpse of his arch nemesis, he angers the gods. Under the codes of chivalry, a

medieval knight has to offer mercy to any knight who yields to him in battle. In feudal Japan, samurai are not permitted to approach their opponents using stealth but rather are required to declare themselves openly
before engaging combat. Muslim warriors engaged in offensive jihad cannot employ certain weapons, such as fire, unless and until their enemies
use them first.

But why do warriors need a code that ties their hands and limits their
options? Why should a warrior culture want to restrict the actions of its
members and require them to commit to lofty ideals? Might not such
restraints cripple their effectiveness as warriors? What's wrong with
"All's fair in love and war"? Isn't winning all that matters? Why should
any warrior be burdened with concerns about honor and shame?

One reason for such codes may be to protect the warrior himself (or
herself) from serious psychological damage. To say the least, the things
that warriors are asked to do to guarantee their culture's survival are far
from pleasant. There is truth in the inescapable slogan "War is hell." Even
those few who, for whatever reason, seem to feel no revulsion at spilling
another human being's guts on the ground, severing a limb, slicing off a
head, or burning away a face are likely to be affected by the sight of their
friends or kinsmen suffering the same fate. The combination of the warriors' own natural disgust at what they must witness in battle and the fact
that what they must do to endure and conquer can seem so uncivilized,
so against what they have been taught by their society, creates the conditions for even the most accomplished warriors to feel tremendous self-
loathing.

In the introduction to his valuable analysis of Vietnam veterans suffering from post–traumatic stress disorder (PTSD), *Achilles in Vietnam: Combat Trauma and the Undoing of Character,* psychiatrist and author Jonathan
Shay stresses the importance of "understanding . . . the specific nature of
catastrophic war experiences that not only cause lifelong disabling psy-
chiatric symptoms but can *ruin* good character."[2] Shay has conducted
countless personal interviews and therapy sessions with American combat veterans who are part of the Veterans Improvement Program (VIP).
His work has led him to the conclusion that the most severe cases of PTSD
are the result of wartime experiences that are not simply violent but that
involve what Shay terms the "betrayal of 'what's right.'"[3] Veterans who
believe that they were directly or indirectly party to immoral or dishonorable behavior (perpetrated by themselves, their comrades, or their commanders) have the hardest time reclaiming their lives after the war is over.
Such men may be tortured by persistent nightmares; may have trouble
discerning a safe environment from a threatening one; may not be able to
trust their friends, neighbors, family members, or government; and may
have problems with alcohol, drugs, child or spousal abuse, depression, or
suicidal tendencies. As Shay sorrowfully concludes, "The painful paradox
is that fighting for one's country can render one unfit to be its citizen."[4]

Warriors need a way to distinguish what they must do out of a sense of duty from what a serial killer does for the sheer sadistic pleasure of it. Their actions, like those of the serial killer, set them apart from the rest of society. Warriors, however, are not sociopaths. They respect the values of the society in which they were raised and which they are prepared to die to protect. Therefore it is important for them to conduct themselves in such a way that they will be honored and esteemed by their communities, not reviled and rejected by them. They want to be seen as proud defenders and representatives of what is best about their culture: as heroes, not "baby-killers."

In a sense, the nature of the warriors' profession puts them at a higher risk for moral corruption than most other occupations because it involves exerting power in matters of life and death. Warriors exercise the power to take or save lives, order others to take or save lives, and lead or send others to their deaths. If they take this awesome responsibility too lightly—if they lose sight of the moral significance of their actions—they risk losing their humanity and their ability to flourish in human society.

In his powerful work, *On Killing: The Psychological Cost of Learning to Kill in War and Society*, Lt. Col. Dave Grossman illuminates the process by which those in war and those training for war attempt to achieve emotional distance from their enemies. The practice of dehumanizing the enemy through the use of abusive or euphemistic language is a common and effective tool for increasing aggression and breaking down inhibitions against killing:

> It is so much easier to kill someone if they look distinctly different than you. If your propaganda machine can convince your soldiers that their opponents are not really human but are "inferior forms of life," then their natural resistance to killing their own species will be reduced. Often the enemy's humanity is denied by referring to him as a "gook," "Kraut," or "Nip."[5]

Like Shay, Grossman has interviewed many U.S. veterans of the Vietnam War. Not all of his subjects, however, were those with lingering psychological trauma. Grossman found that some of the men he interviewed had never truly achieved emotional distance from their former foes, and they seemed to be the better for it. These men expressed admiration for Vietnamese culture. Some had even married Vietnamese women. They appeared to be leading happy and productive postwar lives. In contrast, those who persisted in viewing the Vietnamese as "less than animals" were unable to leave the war behind them.

Grossman writes about the dangers of dehumanizing the enemy in terms of potential damage to the war effort, long-term political fallout, and regional or global instability:

Because of [our] ability to accept other cultures, Americans probably committed fewer atrocities than most other nations would have under the circumstances associated with guerrilla warfare in Vietnam. Certainly fewer than was the track record of most colonial powers. Yet still we had our My Lai, and our efforts in that war were profoundly, perhaps fatally, undermined by that single incident.

It can be easy to unleash this genie of racial and ethnic hatred in order to facilitate killing in time of war. It can be more difficult to keep the cork in the bottle and completely restrain it. Once it is out, and the war is over, the genie is not easily put back in the bottle. Such hatred lingers over the decades, even centuries, as can be seen today in Lebanon and what was once Yugoslavia.[6]

The insidious harm brought to the individual warriors who find themselves swept up by such devastating propaganda matters a great deal to those concerned with the warriors' own welfare. In a segment entitled "Clinical Importance of Honoring or Dishonoring the Enemy," Jonathan Shay describes an intimate connection between the psychological health of the veteran and the respect he feels for those he fought. Shay stresses how important it is to the warrior to have the conviction that he participated in an *honorable* endeavor:

Restoring honor to the enemy is an essential step in recovery from combat PTSD. While other things are obviously needed as well, the veteran's self-respect never fully recovers so long as he is unable to see the enemy as worthy. In the words of one of our patients, a war against subhuman vermin "has no honor." This is true even in victory; in defeat, the dishonoring absence of human *themis* [shared values, a common sense of "what's right"] linking enemy to enemy makes life unendurable.[7]

Shay finds echoes of these sentiments in the words of J. Glenn Gray from Gray's modern classic on the experience of war, *The Warriors: Reflections on Men in Battle.*[8] With the struggle of the Allies against the Japanese in the Pacific theater of World War II as his backdrop, Gray brings home the agony of the warrior who has become incapable of honoring his enemies and thus is unable to find redemption himself:

The ugliness of a war against an enemy conceived to be subhuman can hardly be exaggerated. There is an unredeemed quality to battle experienced under these conditions, which blunts all senses and perceptions. Traditional appeals of war are corroded by the demands of a war of extermination, where conventional rules no longer apply. For all its inhumanity, war is a profoundly human institution. . . . This image of the enemy as beast lessens even the satisfaction in destruction, for there is no proper regard for the worth of the object destroyed. . . . The joys of comradeship, keenness of perception, and sensual delights [are] lessened. . . . No aesthetic reconciliation with one's fate as a warrior [is] likely because no moral purgation [is] possible.[9]

By setting standards of behavior for themselves, accepting certain restraints, and even "honoring their enemies," warriors can create a lifeline that will allow them to pull themselves out of the hell of war and reintegrate themselves into their society, should they survive to see peace restored. A warrior's code may cover everything from the treatment of prisoners of war to oath keeping to table etiquette, but its primary purpose is to grant nobility to the warriors' profession. This allows warriors to retain both their self-respect and the respect of those they guard.

Some may prefer to establish the importance of a warrior's code without reference to the interests of the warriors themselves. It is in fact more conventional to defend the value of a warrior's code by focusing on the needs of society rather than the needs of warriors as individuals. These are well-intentioned attempts to provide warriors with an external motivation to commit to a code. One such approach has been presented in military ethics circles as "the function argument."

Lt. Col. (ret.) J. Carl Ficarrotta, USAF, provides an extremely lucid exposition of the function argument in his essay "A Higher Moral Standard for the Military."[10] The central thesis of the function argument, whose proponents include Sir John Winthrop Hackett and Malham M. Wakin, is that men and women of bad character cannot function well as soldiers, sailors, airmen, or marines.[11] This claim is based on the unique demands of military service. Those who support the function argument point out that comrades-in-arms must be able to trust one another in order to be effective; they must be willing to behave selflessly and sacrifice themselves for the good of the mission; and they must embody "the virtues of courage, obedience, loyalty, and conscientiousness" when the stakes are at their highest.[12] In other words, "if one thinks (for whatever reason) that it is important to have a military that functions as well as it can, one also is committed for these same reasons to thinking military professionals are more strictly bound to exhibiting these functionally necessary virtues and behaviors."[13]

The function argument is useful, as far as it goes. It highlights the unique demands of military service that seem to require special virtues or moral commitments. Ficarrotta argues persuasively, however, that the range of valid conclusions that can be derived from the function argument is limited. Because it links the motive for ethical behavior to military effectiveness, the function argument cannot, by itself, provide reasons for the warrior to behave well in situations where bad behavior does not seem to have a negative impact on the function of the military:

> All this argument leads us to are higher standards *in the military context*. Military people must be scrupulously honest with each other when there is some military issue at hand. They must be selfless when it comes to the demands of military work. They must be courageous when there is some military task to be performed.

What the function line does *not* establish is that the military professional has special reasons to be "good" through and through. The argument gives a soldier who would never even think about lying in his unit no special reason not to lie to his spouse or cheat on his income tax. The military function will be no worse off if a sailor always puts the needs of the service above her own, but still gives nothing to charity. As long as a pilot is courageous in combat or in dealing with his fellow professionals, he might just as well be a coward with a burglar for his father or his wife. We might well be (and should be) disappointed about these non-military moral failures, but the function line doesn't give us *special* reasons to be strict outside the military context.[14]

To stretch this objection even further, the function argument (again, considered *by itself*) gives no guarantee against the conclusion that it makes no difference how warriors behave *even in the military context,* so long as their behavior does not in fact cause them to fail to function effectively in their specific martial roles. That moral failings such as selfishness or a tendency to manipulate the truth could lead to functional failure is irrelevant. Only the actual consequences matter. The argument does not hinge on the acceptance of specific concepts of good character or moral absolutes. It is contingent upon the validity of certain empirical claims about the real world. If a particular warrior were to prove that he can function effectively and get his job despite having despicable character flaws, the function argument alone would not present him with any reason to improve himself.

The ancient Greek philosopher Aristotle, writing about the virtue of courage in the fourth century B.C., speculated that military effectiveness might indeed be distinct from personal virtue. "It is quite possible," he wrote, "that the best soldiers may be not men [who possess virtues such as courage] but those who are less brave but have no other good; for these are ready to face danger, and they sell their lives for trifling gains."[15] Regrettably, the answer to the question "Can warriors still get the job done if they do not have a code?" might be yes.

Suppose we allow that the function argument is enough to prove that warriors need to maintain at least some moral standards and exhibit certain virtues, in site-specific ways (e.g., to be courageous on the battlefield, not to lie to peers when doing so could jeopardize their safety or cause them to lose faith in you). Even so, it cannot ensure against the very moral failings that most worry those who want warriors to have a code for society's sake. It is possible, for instance, that the U.S. military might function more effectively if those in uniform routinely misled Congress (perhaps to manipulate them into increasing the defense budget or to maintain the secrecy of covert operations, as in the Iran-Contra scandal). Nor would such behavior necessarily erode trust within the ranks, if it were seen as a case of "us" versus "them."

The counterclaim could be that since the overriding function of the U.S.

military is to uphold and defend the Constitution, strictly speaking, any unconstitutional behavior—and intentionally subverting legitimate congressional authority over the military certainly qualifies as that—would be prohibited, if one were reasoning along the lines of the function argument. This suggests that a code derived from the function argument could be construed to require the warrior to commit to a wider range of values, all stemming from the Constitution. These would include respecting the rights of individuals; treating persons equally regardless of race, gender, ethnicity, or religious beliefs; supporting a system of checks and balances to prevent abuses of power; and promoting democratic ideals such as liberty and justice for all.

One potential pitfall to this otherwise appealing argument for American warriors upholding constitutional values is that it might lose force for the warriors themselves when they believe the actual survival of their nation is threatened. When asked whether they would hesitate to violate the Constitution if their country's very continued existence as an independent power were on the line, I have heard several of my students respond, "We've all taken an oath to uphold and defend the Constitution of the United States, but what is the point of upholding and defending the Constitution if the United States itself no longer exists?" In other words, if the choice were between staying true to the values of the Constitution and seeing the nation fall, and violating the Constitution in order to save the country from annihilation, they would choose to commit the violation, save the nation, and try to restore constitutional order when peace returned. It would be vanity to assume no crisis so extreme could ever face a superpower like the United States. What is evident from this is that if we are going to link warriors' moral obligations to their function, we need to be very clear about what that function is. Warriors who think their job is to defend the nation, understood in terms of preserving territorial integrity and protecting the population, will have a different code than those who think their duty is to preserve constitutional values at all costs (including the cost of the nation itself), even if both subscribe to the function argument.

A further concern I have regarding the function argument is that it considers warriors only as means to an end, namely, the end of protecting the nation. I realize that this is due to the argument's structure and not the result of any lack of compassion on the part of its authors or proponents. Yet it is a fault nonetheless. The highly influential eighteenth-century German philosopher Immanuel Kant charged that every rational being is bound by a categorical imperative "to treat humanity, whether in your own person or in the person of another, always as an end in itself and never merely as a means."[16] The word "merely" in this formulation must not be overlooked. Of course warriors are the means by which the nation is defended. To treat them as *mere* means, however, would be to fail to recognize that they are also citizens of the nation and human beings whose value is not limited to their utility as warriors. Although they may enjoy fewer liberties than their civilian counterparts, warriors retain their inalienable rights and deserve to be granted a full measure of dignity and respect.

Both the leaders and members of the general population of a nation that shows no concern for what price its warriors must pay for its defense stand in violation of the categorical imperative. It is possible to show proper respect for individuals whom you intend to send into harm's way or even to certain death. This requires first of all acknowledging the profundity of their sacrifice. Warriors are not mere tools; they are complex, sentient beings with fears, loves, hopes, dreams, talents, and ambitions—all of which may soon be snuffed out by a bomb, bullet, or bayonet. Second, those who send them off to war must make an effort to ensure that the warriors themselves fully understand the purpose of, and need for, their sacrifice. Those heading into harm's way must be given sincere assurances that their lives will not be squandered, and their leaders must not betray their trust.

Finally, the state must show concern for what will happen to its warriors after the battles are won (or lost). The dead should be given decent burials (if it is possible) and appropriate memorials. Those wounded in body should be given the best medical care, and treatment should be made available for those with psychological wounds. Former warriors must be welcomed back into the communities that spawned them and sent them away to do what needed to be done. If these conditions are met, even those warriors who lose their lives for the cause were not *mere* means to an end.

This brings us back to my earlier line of reasoning. It is not enough to ask, Can our warriors still get the job done if they do not have a code? We must also consider the related question, What will getting the job done do to our warriors if they do not have a code? Accepting certain constraints as a moral duty, even when it is inconvenient or inefficient to do so, allows warriors to hold on to their humanity while experiencing the horror of war—and, when the war is over, to return home and reintegrate into the society they so ably defended. Fighters who cannot say, "This far but no farther," who have no lines they will not cross and no atrocities from which they will shrink, may be effective. They may complete their missions, but they will do so at the loss of their humanity.

Those who are concerned for the welfare of our warriors would never want to see them sent off to face the chaotic hell of combat without something to ground them and keep them from crossing over into an inescapable heart of darkness. A mother and father may be willing to give their beloved son or daughter's *life* for their country or cause, but I doubt they would be as willing to sacrifice their child's soul. The code is a kind of moral and psychological armor that protects the warrior from becoming a monster in his or her own eyes.

Nor is it just "see-the-whites-of-their-eyes" frontline ground and special forces troops who need this protection. Men and women who fight from a distance—who drop bombs from planes and shoot missiles from ships or submarines—are also at risk of losing their humanity. What threatens them is the very ease with which they can take lives. As technology separates individuals from the results of their actions, it cheats them of the chance to absorb and reckon with the enormity of what they have done. Killing fellow human beings, even for the noblest cause, should never feel like nothing more than a game played using the latest advances in virtual reality.

In his book *Virtual War: Kosovo and Beyond,* the highly regarded international journalist and author Michael Ignatieff airs his concerns about the morality of asymmetric conflicts in which one side is able to inflict large numbers of casualties from afar without putting its own forces at much risk (e.g., by relying primarily on long-range precision weapons and high-altitude air assaults). In such a mismatched fight, it may be easy for those fighting on the superior side to fail to appreciate the true costs of the war, since they are not forced to witness the death and destruction firsthand. Ignatieff warns modern warriors against the "moral danger" they face if they allow themselves to become too detached from the reality of war:

> Virtual reality is seductive. . . . We see war as a surgical scalpel and not a bloodstained sword. In so doing we mis-describe ourselves as we mis-describe the instruments of death. We need to stay away from such fables of self-righteous invulnerability. Only then can we get our hands dirty. Only then can we do what is right.[17]

I have argued that it can be damaging for warriors to view their enemies as subhuman by imagining them like beasts in a jungle. In the same way, modern warriors who dehumanize their enemies by equating them with blips on a computer screen may find the sense that they are part of an honorable undertaking far too fragile to sustain. Just as societies have an obligation to treat their warriors as ends in themselves, it is important for warriors to show a similar kind of respect for the inherent worth and dignity of their opponents. Even long-distance warriors can achieve this by acknowledging that some of the "targets" they destroy are in fact human beings, not demons or vermin or empty statistics.

More parallels can be drawn between the way that societies should behave toward their warriors and how warriors should behave toward one another. Societies should honor their fallen defenders. Warriors should not desecrate the corpses of their enemies but should, whenever possible, allow them to be buried by their own people and according to their own cultural traditions. Among his therapy patients, Jonathan Shay found several veterans suffering from "the toxic residue left behind by disrespectful treatment of enemy dead."[18] And while societies must certainly show concern for the aftereffects of war on their own troops, victorious warriors can also maintain the moral high ground by helping to rebuild (or in some cases create) a solid infrastructure, a healthy economy, an educational system, and political stability for their former foes.

These imperatives I have put forward apply to relations among warriors and nations defended by warriors. The moral requirements become much murkier when warriors must battle murderers. This is a topic I will tackle in the concluding chapter of this book (chapter 9, "The Warrior's Code Today: Are Terrorists Warriors?").

There seems little need to advise warriors from within the same culture to treat each other as ends—at least, not after they have fought together against a common enemy. The motif that echoes in nearly every war memoir or veteran's interview is that comrades-in-arms come to feel an intense love for one another. In his outstanding war novel, *Gates of Fire*, chronicling the courageous stand by the Spartans at Thermopylae, Steven Pressfield makes a compelling case that "the opposite of fear is love."[19] The love a warrior has for his comrades is what gives him the strength to stand against the dreadful tide of a heavily armed, charging host of enemies. Pressfield presents this point eloquently through the words of a character named Suicide, a slave fighting beside the Spartan peers:

> "When a warrior fights not for himself, but for his brothers, when his most passionately sought goal is neither glory nor his own life's preservation, but to spend his substance for them, his comrades, not to abandon them, not to prove unworthy of them, then his heart truly has achieved contempt for death, and with that he transcends himself and his actions touch the sublime. This is why the true warrior cannot speak of battle save to his brothers who have been there with him. This truth is too holy, too sacred, for words."[20]

Writing about his own experiences in World War II, renowned biographer William Manchester conveys matching sentiments in his memoir *Goodbye, Darkness:*

> I understand, at last, why I jumped hospital that Sunday thirty-five years ago and, in violation of orders, returned to the front and almost certain death.
> It was an act of love. Those men on the line were my family, my home. They were closer to me than I can say, closer than any friends had been or ever would be. They had never let me down, and I couldn't do it to them. I had to be with them, rather than let them die and me live with the knowledge that I might have saved them. Men, I now knew, do not fight for flag or country, for the Marine Corps or glory or any other abstraction. They fight for one another. Any man in combat who lacks comrades who will die for him, or for whom he is willing to die, is not a man at all. He is truly damned.[21]

Warriors' willingness to fight alongside their comrades and perhaps die for them is the most undeniable evidence there can be for their mutual love and respect. In the famous St. Crispin's Day speech from *Henry V*, the ever perceptive William Shakespeare has his King Henry acknowledge his shared humanity with even the most "vile" commoners among those warriors with whom he intends to make a stand at Agincourt:

> [H]e which hath no stomach to this fight,
> Let him depart; his passport shall be made,
> And crowns for convoy put into his purse:
> We would not die in that man's company,
> That fears his fellowship to die with us.
> This day is call'd—the feast of Crispian:
> He that outlives this day, and comes safe home,
> Will stand a tip-toe when this day is nam'd,
> And rouse him at the name of Crispian.
> He that outlives this day, and sees old age,
> Will yearly on the vigil feast his friends,
> And say, To-morrow is saint Crispian:
> Then will he strip his sleeve, and show his scars,
> And say, These wounds I had on Crispin's day.
> Old men forget; yet all shall be forgot,
> But he'll remember, with advantages,
> What feats he did that day. Then shall our names,
> Familiar in their mouths as household words, —
> Harry the king, Bedford and Exeter,
> Warwick and Talbot, Salisbury and Gloster, —
> Be in their flowing cups freshly remember'd.
> This story shall the good man teach his son;
> And Crispin Crispian shall ne'er go by
> From this day to the ending of the world,
> But we in it shall be remembered, —
> We few, we happy few, we band of brothers;
> For he to-day that sheds his blood with me,
> Shall be my brother; be he ne'er so vile,
> This day shall gentle his condition.
> And gentlemen in England, now a-bed,
> Shall think themselves accurs'd, they were not here;
> And hold their manhoods cheap, whiles any speaks,
> That fought with us upon saint Crispin's day.[22]

Sharing a code, along with the sheer force of shared experience, is what binds warriors together in the crucible of combat. That is why most warriors' codes come from within the warrior culture itself; they are not imposed upon it by some external source (such as a fearful civilian population). Of course, there are many rules that govern the lives of modern warriors that were put in place by the societies that they serve. Some of these exist to protect against abuses of military power. Others are to make sure a given nation's warriors do not violate international standards of conduct. In the United States, specific rules of engagement (ROE) and the Uniform Code of Military Justice (UCMJ) spell out much of what is expected of our warriors. But a code is much more than rules of this type.

In his critical analysis of the problem of motivating ethical behavior among combat troops, *Obeying Orders: Atrocity, Military Discipline, and the Law of War,* Mark Osiel, a law professor at the University of Iowa, wrestles with the complex subject of how to control warriors' conduct in the "fog of war." His research goes beyond traditional academic and legal scholarship to include firsthand interviews with war criminals and their victims.

The central thesis of *Obeying Orders* is that "the best prospects for minimizing war crimes (not just obvious atrocity) derive from creating a personal identity based on the virtues of chivalry and martial honor, virtues seen by officers as constitutive of good soldiering."[23] In other words, Osiel asserts that the best way to ensure that, for instance, a young U.S. Marine will not commit a war crime even if given (illegal) orders to do so by a superior officer is not to drill the said Marine on the provisions of international law and the UCMJ, but rather to help him internalize an appropriate warriors' code that will inspire him to recognize and reject a criminal direction from his officer.

He tells the story of a young enlisted Marine in the Vietnam War whose judgment concerning the distinction between combatants and noncombatants was compromised after he had seen one too many of his buddies blown away. An officer found the youth "with his rifle at the head of a Vietnamese woman."[24] The officer could have tried barking out the relevant provisions of military law. Instead, he just said, "Marines don't do that." Jarred out of his berserk state and recalled to his place in a longstanding warrior tradition, the Marine stepped back, and lowered his weapon. As Osiel notes, the statement "Marines don't do that" is "surely a simpler, more effective way of communicating the law of war than threatening prosecution for war crimes, by the enemy, an international tribunal, or an American court-martial."[25]

Osiel makes a strong case for this psychologically powerful code- and character-based approach to the prevention of war crimes. He connects it to Aristotle's virtue ethics, which stresses the importance of positive habituation and the development of certain critical virtues, such as courage, justice, benevolence, and honor, over the rote memorization of specific rules of conduct. Simply staying within the bounds of a rule book, as Osiel observes, can often be less demanding than consistently upholding high standards of character and nobility:

The manifest illegality rule merely sets a floor, and a relatively low one at that: avoid the most obvious war crimes, atrocities. It does not say, as does the internal ideal of martial honor: always cause the least degree of lawful, collateral damage to civilians, consistent with your military objectives. By taking seriously such internal conceptions of martial honor, we may be able to impose higher standards on professional soldiers than the law has traditionally done, in the knowledge that good soldiers already impose these standards upon themselves.[26]

Osiel comments on the importance of shaming tactics (especially so-called reintegrative shaming, which aims to reform, not permanently ostracize, the offender) to motivate modern warriors' dedication to the ideals of martial honor. He also defends the value of presenting persons entering the military culture with role models who remained true to their codes of honor even in the face of nearly overwhelming challenges or temptations. As further support for his position, he points out that this approach of reinforcing desirable character traits among military professionals in no way undermines a rule-following approach but rather provides additional motivation to obey rules when they are clear ("bright-line rules") while giving much-needed guidance when the rules are not enough:

> In cases that are legally easy (but otherwise stressful, dangerous, or physically demanding), then, martial honor contributes to having the proper inclinations and emotions, those conducive to skillful performance of one's duties. In legally hard cases, however, professional character reveals itself more in virtuosity of perception, deliberation, and choice.[27]

A warrior's code of the type advocated by Osiel cannot be reduced to a list of rules. "Marines don't do that" is not merely shorthand for "Marines don't shoot unarmed civilians; Marines don't rape women; Marines don't leave Marines behind; Marines don't despoil corpses," even though those firm injunctions and many others are part of what we might call the Marines' Code. What Marines internalize when they are indoctrinated into the culture of the Corps is an amalgam of specific regulations, general concepts (e.g., honor, courage, commitment, discipline, loyalty, teamwork), history and tradition that adds up to a coherent sense of *what it is to be a Marine.* To remain "Semper Fidelis," or forever faithful to the code of the Marine Corps is never to behave in a way that cannot be reconciled with that image of what it is to be a Marine.

What it is to be a Marine is not the same as what it is to be an Air Force pilot or what it is to be an Army Ranger. For this reason, specific subcultures within the U.S. military, though equal under the UCMJ, have different warriors' codes. Their codes necessarily have some common ground, given that they are all American warriors, sworn to uphold and defend the values of the Constitution. This shared foundation notwithstanding, even within the U.S. Navy, for example, the code that governs the Navy

SEAL community is quite distinct from the code of a naval aviator, and neither could be confused with the code of a surface warfare officer (SWO) or that of a submariner.

A code that encompasses all of what it is to be a particular kind of warrior may help the warrior who has internalized it determine the proper course of action in a situation the rule writers could never have foreseen. The motivation for individual warriors to remain true to their code often comes from their desire not to betray the memory of the warriors who came before them, as well as from their determination not to let down the warriors alongside whom they are now fighting. When future U.S. Army officers attend the U.S. Military Academy at West Point, they are taught to remember the "Long Gray Line" of former cadets that stretches back through the centuries and includes such giants as Generals Robert E. Lee, Ulysses S. Grant, Dwight D. Eisenhower, Omar Bradley, George S. Patton, and Roscoe Robinson Jr. (the first African American four-star general). At times, the reverence modern warriors feel for their illustrious predecessors almost resembles the ancestor worship that is found in so many of the world's older religions. Warriors are proud to receive the legacies of the past and wish to remain worthy of them.

While unique aspects of the codes of each warrior's own culture or subculture provide the final flourishes to his or her self-definition, most warriors also feel themselves a part of an even longer line, a line of men and women from diverse cultures throughout history who are deserving of the label "warrior." This is a legacy that spans not just centuries but millennia.

When the warriors of today want to improve their understanding of what it is to be a warrior, they naturally seek out the most accurate information about the harsh realities of war. But in addition they are often drawn to war-themed poetry, literature, and myth. These sources can convey the emotional dimension of the warrior's existence more profoundly than purely factual accounts of battles, tactics, casualties, and military careers. And the inspiration to strive for high ideals can come even from a culture's unrealized visions of the perfect warrior. When a television recruiting advertisement for the U.S. Marine Corps shows a knight in shining armor morphing into a Marine in dress blues, the specter of medieval chivalric perfection it evokes may never have existed in the flesh, yet this in no way reduces the impact.

In the following chapters, I will offer a sampling of some of the most influential interpretations of the code of the warrior and constructions of warrior archetypes from around the globe that have helped shape our broader conceptions of what it is to be a warrior. Though my selections do have some breadth—ranging from the Romans to Native Americans to Chinese warrior monks—this is by no means an exhaustive survey. Even restricting myself to the historical rather than the current, I found the number of significant warrior cultures available for study absolutely staggering. In the end, my selections were dictated by several considerations.

First of all, I wanted to give examples that were likely to be familiar but that might not have been considered in this context or in relation to one another. A number of my students, when asked to conjure up an archetypal warrior picture a knight of the Round Table. Others see a samurai, still others a Viking in a horned helmet (although a few already know it was the Celts, not the Vikings, who wore horned helmets). These are at least a small selection of the cultures with which a modern Western warrior might identify. Second, I tried to avoid too much overlap. The culture of the Spartans is deeply fascinating, but it contains key elements that I have explored here by looking at Homeric Greek warriors and the soldiers of the Roman legions. Each of the warrior cultures I touch upon introduces features that are not seen in the others I cover, although those distinctive features can be found in many additional cultures that I was not able to consider in this volume. Finally, I confess to simply having a personal interest in the particular warrior values and ideals featured in this book.

A gentleman I have been honored to call my friend, Andrew H. Hines Jr., was once a B-17 navigator for the U.S. Army Air Corps in World War II. Andy flew several successful missions out of Foggia air base in Italy, including raids over Belgrade, but was eventually shot down and spent the remainder of the war in German prison camps Stalag Luft III (site of the notorious "Great Escape") and Moosburg before being liberated by Patton's Third Army. Many years later, as a retired businessman and poet, Andy tried to capture in verse the experience of what it was, for him, to be a warrior. One of his poems, entitled "The Somme, 1914–1918," contains his reflections on the meaning of a warrior's life, and death:

> We drove across the Somme today
> Where war's flail once struck hard,
> And all was peaceful and serene
> But graves stood as on guard.
>
> The endless rows of sugar beets
> Bespoke a fertile earth
> But richer dust is buried here
> Beneath the dark green turf.
>
> And battles sometimes futile seem
> Not worth the heavy cost,
> But each must stand in his own time
> Or see his freedom lost.[28]

Why do warriors fight? What is worth dying for? How should a warrior define words like "nobility," "honor," "courage," or "sacrifice"? What are the duties and obligations of a warrior and to whom are they owed? How can you measure a warrior's commitment? What should bring a warrior honor, and what should bring a warrior shame? As we look at each warrior culture in the following chapters, we will seek the answers to these questions. My hope is that this will give you the opportunity to critically evaluate and compare different warriors' codes, so that you can judge which aspects of them should be rejected and which should be preserved or revived for the future to create an ideal code of the warrior for this new millennium.

NOTES

1. Thomas Hobbes, *The Leviathan* (New York: Collier Books, 1962), 100.
2. Jonathan Shay, *Achilles in Vietnam: Combat Trauma and the Undoing of Character* (New York: Simon & Schuster, 1994), xiii.
3. Shay, *Achilles in Vietnam*, xiii.
4. Shay, *Achilles in Vietnam*, xx.
5. Dave Grossman, *On Killing: The Psychological Cost of Learning to Kill in War and Society* (Boston: Little, Brown, 1996), 161.
6. Grossman, *On Killing*, 163.
7. Shay, *Achilles in Vietnam*, 115.
8. J. Glenn Gray, *The Warriors: Reflections on Men in Battle* (New York: Harper & Row, 1970), 152–53.
9. Gray, *The Warriors*, 152–53.
10. J. Carl Ficarrotta, "A Higher Moral Standard for the Military," in *Ethics for Military Leaders*, ed. George R. Lucas, Paul E. Roush, Lawrence Lengbeyer, Shannon E. French, and Douglas MacLean (Boston: Pearson Custom Publishing, 2001), 61–71.
11. John Winthrop Hackett and Malham M. Wakin, *War, Morality, and the Military Profession* (Boulder, Colo.: Westview Press, 1986).
12. Ficarrotta, "Higher Moral Standard," 64.
13. Ficarrotta, "Higher Moral Standard," 64.
14. Ficarrotta, "Higher Moral Standard," 65.
15. Aristotle, *Nicomachean Ethics*, 1117b. 15–20, in *Introduction to Aristotle*, ed. Richard McKeon (Chicago: University of Chicago Press, 1973), 406.
16. Immanuel Kant, *Foundations of the Metaphysics of Morals*, trans. Lewis White Beck (Indianapolis: Bobbs-Merrill Educational Publishing, 1959).
17. Michael Ignatieff, *Virtual War: Kosovo and Beyond* (New York: Henry Holt), 2000), 214–15.
18. Shay, *Achilles in Vietnam*, 117.
19. Steven Pressfield, *Gates of Fire: An Epic Novel of the Battle of Thermopylae* (New York: Bantam, 1998), 380.
20. Pressfield, *Gates of Fire*, 379.
21. William Manchester, *Goodbye, Darkness: A Memoir of the Pacific War* (New York: Dell, 1979), 451.
22. William Shakespeare, *Henry V*, 4: 3, in *The Globe Illustrated Shakespeare: The Complete Works*, ed. Howard Staunton (New York: Greenwich House, 1986), 850.
23. Mark Osiel, *Obeying Orders: Atrocity, Military Discipline, and the Law of War* (New Brunswick, N.J.: Transaction Publishers, 1999), 23.

24. Osiel, *Obeying Orders*, 23.

25. Osiel, *Obeying Orders*, 23.

26. Osiel, *Obeying Orders*, 32.

27. Osiel, *Obeying Orders*, 37.

28. Andrew H. Hines Jr., *Time and The Kite* (St. Petersburg, Fla.: author, 1989), 23.

2

The Homeric Hero:
A Hector Who Wins?

The classical Western image of the ideal warrior is that of a man whose astounding prowess in battle earns him power and respect among his peers. His display of skill, courage, and brute strength entitles him to recognition and favor within his community. A beautiful wife (or "prize woman"), gold, and land are some examples of the rewards that may be bestowed upon him by his grateful society for services rendered in conflicts against their enemies.

Are such material rewards really sufficient to motivate a man to face the sustained horrors of war? Certainly, the promise of wealth, women, and property may inspire an untried youth to gird his loins, take up his sword, and march off against a fearsome foe, but what happens once he has felt hot blood splatter in his face, been deafened by the din of clanging weapons, and experienced the terrifying chaos of a melee? Will status symbols really seem worth dying for then?

The question of what is reason enough to drive men into battle (and back into it again and again) is one of the central themes of Homer's epic poem the *Iliad*. A stunningly complex work of warrior literature, the *Iliad* presents events from the Trojan War, a legendary Bronze Age conflict between temporarily united Greek states and the wealthy Asian city-state of Troy (or Ilion). It also offers some of the most compelling and believable accounts of warriors' struggles to find meaning in their martial existence that have ever been captured in the pages of fiction. Any attempt to dissect the values of Western warrior cultures that does not include an examination of the Homeric tradition must be considered incomplete.

Assigning a date to the composition of the *Iliad* is a matter vigorously debated by classical scholars. As Michael Wood explains in *In Search of the Trojan War*, the poem that we have today is most likely derived from a work that was first written down sometime in the sixth century B.C. and attributed to a possibly mythical eighth-century B.C. blind poet named Homer. However, the work may have originally been composed even centuries earlier as an oral poem that was then passed down generation to generation by ancient Greek bards or storytellers. As Wood notes:

> [S]o-called formulas, or repeat phrases[,] show that the Homeric poems are . . . characteristically oral poems. But in what sense were they composed? Was there one act of composition, or a gradual accretion of a poetic tradition? Did Homer exist? When were the poems written down, and what relation does the written text we have bear to that first written text, let alone to the orally composed poem(s) which may have preceded it? These are the problems which for the last two centuries have been at the centre of what scholars call the "Homeric Question."[1]

Also hotly disputed is the historical accuracy of the epic.[2] Archaeological evidence from Bronze Age sites in modern Turkey and Greece that were uncovered in the late 1800s through the audacious efforts of wealthy European entrepreneur-turned-archaeologist Heinrich Schliemann suggests that a great battle between the Trojans and an invading Greek army that ended with the total destruction of Troy did in fact take place some time around 1250 B.C. What are believed to be the ruins of Homer's Troy can be found at Hisarlik in northwest Turkey. And Mycenae, identified by Homer as the home of High King Agamemnon, the supreme commander of the Greek expeditionary force against Troy, is located in southern Greece, where archaeologists have revealed the ruins of a great palace inhabited by a wealthy royal dynasty throughout the Bronze Age. Finds of martial equipment and artistic depictions of warriors headed off to battle discovered at Hisarlik, Mycenae, and other Bronze Age sites such as Knossos, Tiryns, and Orchomenos actually match specific descriptions in Homer, despite the fact that Homer himself, if he existed at all, probably lived at least four centuries after the time when such items were created and used:

> [T]here are descriptions of actual Mycenean objects in Homer. The tower-shaped body shield usually associated with Ajax [is] represented on the Thera frescoes. . . . The figure-of-eight shield occurs on thirteenth-century frescoes from Mycenea, Tiryns and probably Knossos. The "silver-studded sword" is known from sixteenth- and fifteenth-century finds. The leg greaves indicated in Homer's epithet about the "well-greaved Achaians" likewise have been found in Bronze-Age tombs and not in the succeeding Iron Age. The boar's-tusk helmet, perhaps the most famous of all (carefully described in *Iliad* X, 261) has been found on numerous representations, with a full example from Knossos; Homer even notes how the tusks are laid in rows with the curves alternating. . . . The technique of metalwork inlay

described in the making of Achilles' shield is exemplified in the shaft grave daggers. . . . There is also the question of Homer's references to a thorax, or suit of body armour, made of bronze plates: such a suit has now been found at Dendra. Add to these examples the almost universal assumption in Homer that bronze is the metal for swords and tools, and you have an impressive collection of detail in the military sphere which suggests that Homer is preserving descriptions from long before his time. [3]

We may never know for certain just how much historical fact is woven into Homer's fiction. But whether we view the Homeric heroes as pure literary invention or as characters sketched from life, their influence as an example of ideal warriors within the Western tradition cannot be overstated. The legendary figures of Achilles, Hector, Patroclus, Ajax, Odysseus, King Priam, and King Agamemnon have stirred martial imaginations from pagan times to the present day.

Alexander the Great reportedly slept with a copy of the *Iliad* under his pillow and claimed to be a direct descendant of the Greek champion, Achilles. Julius Caesar visited what was then believed to be the site of Troy in 48 B.C. and claimed the Trojan prince Aeneas as his ancestor. The story of Troy was popular throughout the Dark Ages of medieval Europe and was revived yet again by Elizabethan poets who promoted the fanciful belief that the British royal family of the Tudors sprang from Trojan lineage.[4]

Nineteenth- and twentieth-century authors have not only referenced and retold Homer's tale but have also related it directly to their own wartime experiences. Perhaps the most moving example of a modern warrior reaching back to Homer for comfort and inspiration is found in a poem by Patrick Shaw-Stewart, a British soldier in World War I who fought and died in the blood-soaked battle of Gallipoli near the original site of the city of Troy. As Michael Wood recounts, Stewart "reread the *Iliad* on the way to Gallipoli, [and] felt a dreadful sense of *déjà vu* at the sight of Imbros, of Troy and these 'association-saturated spots.'"[5] Facing the terror of going "over the top" and rushing the Turkish machine guns, Stewart yearned for the strength and insight of the godlike Achilles:

O hell of ships and cities
Hell of men like me,
Fatal second Helen,
Why must I follow thee?

Achilles came to Troyland
And I to Chersonese:
He turned from wrath to battle,
And I from three days' peace.

Was it so hard, Achilles,
So very hard to die?
Thou knowest and I know not—
So much the happier I.

I will go back this morning
From Imbros over the sea;
Stand in the trench, Achilles,
Flame-capped, and fight for me.[6]

Why would a modern soldier on the brink of battle want to conjure up flame-capped Achilles to fight by his side? What enduring wisdom is woven into the words of the *Iliad* that has allowed its characters to maintain a meaningful connection with those who have taken up arms across at least three millennia? Who are the Homeric heroes? What warrior values do they represent? Why did they fight? How did they fight? What brought them honor and what brought them shame? What, for them, was worth dying for?

To answer the question, Why did they fight? I am tempted to borrow the succinct response of some of my students: "women."[7] The *Iliad* picks up its narrative in the tenth year of a war that began over the seduction of the most beautiful woman in the world. And the earliest seeds of the conflict were sown at the wedding of a mortal king to a goddess.

According to Greek mythology, Zeus, the ruler of all the gods, fell in love with a beautiful sea goddess named Thetis. However, before he could make her one of his many wives, Thetis warned Zeus that it had been prophesied that if she ever bore a son, that son would be greater than his father. Zeus certainly did not want to help produce a young god who could eventually overthrow his power, so he decided to set aside his own desires for Thetis and marry her off to a mere mortal. The husband he chose for her was King Peleus of Phthia, a small but prosperous state in Thessaly.

Thetis was less than delighted at the prospect of marrying a mortal, but she was somewhat consoled by Peleus's good looks, status, and reputation and by the promise that her wedding would have the tremendous distinction of being attended by nearly all the gods and goddesses of the Greek pantheon. Only one significant goddess would not be invited: Eris, the goddess of discord and strife. It was reasoned that her particular gifts would not be a welcome addition to such a festive occasion.

The wedding ceremony proceeded smoothly enough, but the celebration of the unusual union was thrown into sudden chaos when the uninvited guest, Eris, crashed the party and tossed a "gift" among the mortal and divine revelers. A mortal woman, one of Thetis's attendants, stooped to retrieve what Eris had thrown. It was a solid gold apple inscribed with a simple message. But when the woman read the message, she quickly dropped the glittering fruit as if it had stung her.

The apple rolled to the feet of Hera, queen of the gods. Naturally curious, she, too, picked it up and read the inscription. Her reaction was quite different from that of the mortal woman. "Why, it's a present for me," she said. "How sweet!"

Athena, goddess of wisdom, was intrigued. "May I see that?" she asked, quickly snatching the apple from Hera's hand. As she read the words delicately carved upon it, she turned and smiled at the other goddess. "My dear Hera," she said. "You seem to have made a mistake. This apple reads, 'For the Fairest.' The mortal who first touched it was wise not to claim it in a room full of so many goddesses. But surely *you* must see that this apple was intended for me."

Hera certainly did not see things Athena's way, and before long the two goddesses were shouting such angry words at one another that the walls of Peleus's palace began to shake and all of his mortal wedding guests started to flee in terror. Aphrodite, goddess of love, stepped up to the enraged immortals. "Goddesses, please," she spoke soothingly, "you are scaring the mortals. What is the source of this fierce quarrel?" Athena sheepishly held up the apple, and Aphrodite plucked it from her hand. She examined its shiny perfection carefully. "This is indeed a pretty little present. But why should you two fight over it so? It must be obvious to both of you that this trinket was meant . . . for *me*." Now there were three goddesses bitterly contesting the apple's proper ownership. The goddess Eris threw back her head and laughed. The reception hall quickly emptied, Peleus and Thetis retired to their bridal chamber, and Zeus led all the gods and goddesses up through the clouds to their divine home on Mount Olympus.

Zeus could not stand hearing the three goddesses bicker over the apple of discord, but he also knew that if he gave the apple to any one of them, the other two would be furious with him. Rather than face two goddesses' wrath, he decided to pass off the problem to some poor unsuspecting human. Reasoning that beauty is the best judge of beauty, he looked across all the world's kingdoms for the handsomest man he could find. Finally, his gaze settled on Paris, prince of Troy.

Paris was relaxing in a sunlit field outside the walls of his royal city when Hera, Athena, and Aphrodite suddenly appeared before him in all their glory. A golden apple marked, "For the Fairest" fell into his hands, and the booming voice of Zeus struck his ears: "*You* must choose!" Paris was terrified. For many moments he could not move or speak. But as the significance of his situation slowly washed over him, he gradually began to appreciate the opportunity that it presented. He gathered his wits about him and turned on all of his charm.

"I gather that I am being asked to decide which of you is the most fair," he said to the three divine beauty contestants. "Such a task is far beyond my power. Each of you is a goddess, unique, incomparable, and exquisite. How can I choose between you? Is a rose lovelier than a lily? It is a judgment no man could make. But perhaps there is another way I can award this apple to one of you. Tell me, how would each of you show your appreciation if I gave the prize to you?"

Hera spoke first. "I am the queen of the gods. If you give the apple to me, I will make you the most powerful king the world has ever seen. All of Asia will be yours to command, the rest of the world yours to conquer."

"That is a generous offer, indeed," said Paris. "But I must hear the others."

Athena stepped forward. "I am the goddess of wisdom, young Paris. Give me the prize, and I will make you the wisest man who ever lived. All your questions will be answered, and men everywhere will honor your advice."

"Very interesting," said Paris. "But there is still Aphrodite."

The goddess of love gave a gentle sigh. "Ah, Paris. How can I compete against such bids as these? I cannot make you a ruler or a sage. I control very little with my small powers. The only thing I have to offer you is . . . the most beautiful woman in the world."

Paris slapped the apple into her hand. "Sold!"

What Aphrodite neglected to mention was that the most beautiful woman alive at that time was, in fact, already married. Her name was Helen, and she was the wife of King Menelaus of Sparta, a very powerful Greek ruler. Helen (whose real father was the god Zeus himself) was so astonishingly lovely that her mortal father, King Tyndareus, at first despaired of ever choosing a husband for her. Every eligible man in Greece had tried to woo Helen, and like Zeus with the golden apple, Tyndareus feared that if he gave his daughter's hand to one, all the other suitors would rise up against him.

Eventually, the problem was solved by Odysseus, the clever young king of the island nation of Ithaca. Odysseus had been a suitor of Helen himself until the crazed competition drove him to withdraw from the running and instead take as his bride Penelope, Helen's lovely, intelligent, and gentle-tempered cousin. He then recommended to Tyndareus that all of Helen's remaining suitors be required to take an oath that they would respect the king's decision regarding his future son-in-law and would even fight on behalf of Helen's new husband if anyone ever tried to steal her away. All the suitors willingly took the oath, each hoping to be the one who would get Helen, and all went peacefully away when the match between Helen and Menelaus was announced. Menelaus's brother, Agamemnon, powerful sovereign of the wealthy city-state of Mycenae, doubled the family connection by marrying Helen's sister, Clytemnestra.

Having been promised Helen's love by the goddess of love herself, Paris rashly ignored the fact that Helen's husband, Menelaus, and her brother-in-law, Agamemnon, were extremely formidable figures to whom many other great chieftains and warriors of Greece owed allegiance. Paris sailed off to Sparta and presented himself at Menelaus's court as the son of King Priam of Troy on a visitor's tour of Greece. Menelaus graciously welcomed Paris into his home, shared a fine supper with him, and introduced him to his gorgeous wife. Just as Helen looked at Paris, Aphrodite's mischievous little son, Eros, shot an arrow of love into her heart. That night, she agreed to run off with the handsome young prince and sail with him back to Troy. As a kind of second dowry, she brought with her stores of treasure from her husband's palace.

Paris's crime of abducting Menelaus's wife would have been disturbing to ancient Greek culture on many levels. It is easy to grasp the injury of stealing another man's wife. But to Menelaus, Helen was more than an object of affection. She was a symbol of his rank among his peers. Tyndareus had chosen him from a field of suitors for the hand of Helen because of his family position (he and Agamemnon were heirs to the distinguished and enormously wealthy House of Atreus), not because Helen expressed any preference for the Spartan king. Romantic feelings were irrelevant. Helen was simply Menelaus's most prized possession.

Add to this the fact that when Paris took Helen (and other palace treasures) from Sparta, he violated the guest-host relationship, which the Greeks viewed as sacred. Although Paris was a stranger and a foreigner, Menelaus had accepted Paris into his home on the strength of his noble blood (the royal house of Troy). It was an unspeakable insult for Paris to have accepted Menelaus's hospitality and then so grossly violated his trust.

Greek culture at this time hovered somewhere between tribal and feudal, consisting of many city-states ruled by a small number of aristocratic families who could afford to maintain small armies to defend their borders. Weaker city-states would align themselves with strong city-states, committing their military resources in return for protection against rival states. The guest-host rules formed one of the supports that stabilized this system.

A prince from any city-state could visit any other city-state with which he was not at war and request hospitality. If his request was granted, his host guaranteed that no harm would come to him while under the host's roof. The guest, in turn, was required not to harm his host or his host's household in any way during his stay. This pleasant, common-sense arrangement, staked on the honor of the parties concerned, allowed members of the ruling families of Greece to travel comfortably across the country and safely meet with one another to forge or strengthen military and political ties.

Though not a Greek, Paris was accorded the same courtesy as a Greek prince when he presented himself at Menelaus's door. Thus, when he so egregiously violated the guest-host relationship, he set himself up not merely as an enemy of Sparta but as an enemy of Greece. His infamous behavior was an insult to the Greek way of life.

Many of the prominent rulers of Greece were drawn to support

Menelaus's grievance against Paris, not only because they abhorred the Trojan's blatant disregard for their traditions, but also because they had each personally pledged their honor to defend Menelaus's rightful claim to Helen when they took the oath required of all of Helen's original suitors. Others who had never vied for Helen's hand (and so had not taken the oath required by her father) were nevertheless bound by equally strong obligations to Menelaus or Agamemnon, as allies of Sparta and Mycenae. One way or another, the theft of Helen committed almost the whole of Greece against the doomed city of Troy.

On the macro scale, then, the Homeric Greeks went to war primarily to defend King Menelaus's honor and their own. There would also be material benefits to a successful campaign, for Troy was very prosperous, as were the lands and towns around it (which would be seized and sacked for plunder to fulfill the needs of so great an invasion force). But the storytellers of ancient Greece made an obvious effort to attach a cause to the Greek assault on Troy other than the mere pursuit of riches.

Sympathy for the principal characters in the tale must have depended at least in some measure on the idea that the Greeks fought in a noble cause. Clearly, the attack on Troy was not a defensive action. Paris stole possessions belonging to the king of Sparta (including his wife), but he did not try to seize any Spartan territory. No Greek blood was spilled in the Trojan prince's escapade. But naturally the Greek poets, propagandists and apologists for their own people, resisted painting the Greeks as instigators of the Trojan War, as greedy aggressors laying siege to a wealthy foreign fortress. Rather, they portrayed their warriors as reluctantly compelled to fight to defend their laws and traditions and remain true to their oaths and treaties. Thus the warriors of the *Iliad* are handed down to us not as brutes and thugs who fought only for gold but as the noble guardians of Bronze Age Greek values. Perhaps a version of the story of the Trojan War that did not give this attention to the question of justification on the Greek side would not have survived so many generations or held so much interest for those who would like to find some nobility amid the brutality of war.

While Paris is branded an inexcusable villain, Homer's epic does not by any means present a wholesale condemnation of the Trojans. On the contrary, Homer makes a point of reviewing the conflict from the Trojan perspective with no little amount of sympathy. After all, once Paris has brought the bitter Greeks to their doorstep, the Trojan people have no choice but to defend their city. It is well understood that once the Greeks conquer the Trojan resistance, they will show no mercy to the people of Troy. All men of fighting age will be killed, as will all elderly citizens and many helpless infants. The Trojan women will be raped and forced to become the slaves or concubines of the Greek commanders. Troy will be destroyed, and all of its treasures parceled out among the triumphant Greek warriors.

Homer places the most disturbing predictions about the future of Troy in the mouth of Priam, king of Troy, who confides his fears to his favorite son, Prince Hector:

"O pity me, a poor old man, not yet by grief deprived of sense and reason. Me, who on the brink of helpless age now trembling soon will [Zeus], the father of the gods, to ruin doom. Complete in depth of misery, many sights of horror [have I] seen: my sons around me slain, my daughters ravished, burnt their palaces, my little children dashed against the ground in dire massacre by the ruthless Greeks; and my sons' wives by their accursed hands to slavery dragged! Myself, the last perhaps, a ghastly carcass, stiff and pale, by sword or javelin butchered, maybe thrown without my palace-gates, to feed the devouring dogs."[8]

Since the Trojan people stood to lose so much in their struggle with the Greeks, it is reasonable to ask why they ever accepted Paris into their city with the stolen Helen. The answer appears to involve grudging loyalty and pride. Homer makes it plain that the Trojans are not at all pleased with Paris for bringing the wrath of Greece down on their heads. All but Paris's brother Hector and their father, King Priam, also seem to blame Helen for her part in the affair. But despite their anger toward the miscreant couple, the Trojans do not expel them because Paris is still a prince of their generally honored and beloved royal house. And they cannot bring themselves simply to hand over one of their own to his enemies. Nor will their pride allow them to admit their fear of Greek domination.

In book 3 of the *Iliad*, Prince Hector, berating his brother Paris for turning away from the sight of fierce Menelaus on the battlefield, comments bitterly on the Trojan decision to support Paris against the Greeks:

"Paris, you pretty boy," he shouted at him, "You woman-struck seducer; why were you ever born? . . . How the long-haired [Greeks] must laugh when they see us make a champion of a prince because of his good looks, forgetting that he has no strength of mind, no courage. . . . And now are you too cowardly to stand up to the brave man whom you wronged? You would soon find out the kind of fighter he is whose lovely wife you stole. Your lyre would not help you at all, nor Aphrodite's gifts, those locks of yours and your good looks, when he had made you bite the dust. But the Trojans are too soft. Otherwise you would have been stoned to death long ago for the evil you have done."[9]

In an attempt to make the cause of the trouble be the end of it, Hector, with the support of the other Trojan warriors, shames Paris into agreeing to fight Menelaus in a single combat that would decide the entire conflict and stop the Greek siege. A pact is drawn between the two sides that all other fighting will cease while the two chiefly interested parties settle their dispute over Helen. If Paris wins, he will keep Helen and the treasures he stole from the Spartan palace and the Greek forces will leave

Trojan lands and sail home to Greece. If Menelaus wins, the Trojans will return Helen and the Spartan treasure and, again, the Greeks will depart. The odds are heavily in Menelaus's favor, as he ranks among the best warriors of Greece. Paris, on the other hand, is a lover, not a fighter.

The duel between Helen's two mates begins, with Menelaus quickly gaining the upper hand. But before Paris can be killed, the goddess Aphrodite, still grateful to the handsome Trojan prince for giving her the golden apple, creates a thick mist to confuse Menelaus. Then she magically whisks Paris back to the safety of his bedroom, where he rejoices in his escape and makes love to the beautiful Helen. Meanwhile, both the Trojans and the Greeks declare Menelaus the winner of the combat (since he was clearly "ahead on points" when Paris left the match unfinished), and the Trojans prepare to hand over the Spartan queen and treasure.

Sadly, peace is not what the gods have in mind for Troy. Hera and Athena, still bristling over their golden apple slights, conspire to reignite the conflict. Athena, disguised as a warrior, goes to the side of a Trojan named Pandarus and persuades him to break the current truce by taking a potshot at Menelaus:

> "Pandarus, my lord, will you use your wits and take a hint from me? If you could bring yourself to shoot Menelaus with an arrow, you would cover yourself with glory and put every Trojan in your debt, Prince Paris most of all. He would be the first to come forward with a handsome gift, if he saw the great Menelaus, son of Atreus, struck down by a shot from you and laid out on a funeral pyre."[10]

Pandarus wounds, but does not kill, the Spartan king, and the fragile peace between the Greeks and the Trojans is permanently shattered.

On the Homeric view, the people of Troy may be guilty of excessive pride and misplaced loyalty, but they are by and large the tragic victims of a few bad characters whose selfish and immoral actions anger the gods and place the Trojans in a truly no-win situation. With the exception of Paris, Homer portrays the Trojans and their allies as honorable men who are motivated primarily by the desire to preserve the beautiful city of Troy and its inhabitants from sack and sword. Their suffering and deaths come as part of the sweeping punishment meted out against Paris for violating the guest-host relationship, Helen for betraying her husband, and Pandarus for breaking a solemn truce. Zeus, the Greek god of justice, chooses to let the many suffer for the crimes of the few.

So far I have focused primarily on the big picture. But Homer clearly recognizes that knowing the reasons why nations (or city-states) go to war may not tell us anything about why individual warriors from those nations go to war or continue to fight. He therefore takes the time to show us inside the soul of each of his main characters, from both sides of the battle, to expose the personal motives behind their frenzied charges. Most wonderfully, Homer gives each warrior in his epic a unique and complex personality. These characters are not mere two-dimensional fighting machines. Homer imbues them all with internal life and emotional depth so that their struggles to adhere to their warriors' codes can genuinely engage our sympathy.

When my Naval Academy students have finished reading the *Iliad*, I often ask them to tell me which of Homer's characters they admire most, and why. A popular reply is Hector, prince of Troy, and the reasons they give most concern their sense of why he fights. It may surprise some to learn that competitive young American students would favor a character who champions the losing side of the battle. But it is Hector's humanity and nobility of character, not his unhappy fate, to which they are drawn.

Homer's Prince Hector is a man who fights with tremendous ferocity on the battlefield but who is not driven by rage or bloodlust. Although he relishes his moments of small-scale victory, we are given the impression that Hector fights not because he wants to but because he has a duty to his people. He would rather be at home with his wife and young son, Astynax, but he is the greatest warrior that the Trojans have. If he does not defend the city, it will certainly fall to the Greeks. His exceptional physical prowess and martial skills, combined with his standing in the community as a respected member of the royal family, create special responsibilities for him. By rights, his brother Paris (the cause of the crisis) should have offered himself up for the protection of Troy. However, since Paris chooses not to live up to his obligations, the burden shifts to Hector's more capable (and unshirking) shoulders. The defense of the city is placed in his hands, and all the hopes of the Trojan people are pinned on his performance as a fighter and a leader.

There are several moving scenes in the *Iliad* that fill in the details of Hector's character and expose his warrior's code. In book 6 we see him step away from the ever raging battle and slip inside the still secure stone walls of Troy. His aims are to visit the obnoxious Paris in his bedchamber and shame him out of Helen's arms and back onto the battlefield and to encourage the women of Troy to make special offerings to the gods to request divine support for the Trojan cause. (Throughout the *Iliad*, Hector is portrayed as a very pious man.) These missions accomplished, Hector tries to steal a moment alone with his wife. He rushes to their private chambers, but

[f]inding not within his blameless wife, he on his threshold stood, and of his servants thus inquiry made: "Be quick, and tell me truly, whither went my lovely consort, fair Andromache?" . . . his household's faithful governess replied: ". . . she is gone to Ilion's lofty tower, urged by the direful news that in the field the Trojans suffered much and Greeks prevailed. Alarmed and seemingly frantic, to the walls she hurried, and the nurse her infant bore."[11]

Touched by his wife's concern, Hector heads immediately to the tower, and when Andromache catches sight of him, she runs into his arms. They speak together for some time, and Andromache pours out her fears for her husband's safety and the ultimate fate of herself and their son, Astynax, should the worst occur. Weeping, she takes her husband's hand and speaks "with anxious fondness":

> "Ah! Rashly brave! Thy courage will thyself destroy. Nor dost thou pity this thy son, in helpless infancy, and me thy wife, unhappy, doomed a widow soon to be. For soon the Greeks will slay thee, all combined assailing. But for me, of thee bereft, better it were to sink beneath the ground. For no relief or solace will be mine when thou art dead, but unremitting grief."[12]

Hector does not dismiss his wife's concerns. Rather, he is sincerely sympathetic to them. He has no illusions about the job he has taken on and the likelihood of failure. His response is not false bravado but grim determination. He honestly acknowledges the pain he feels when he realistically contemplates his family's bleak future. He predicts the fall of Troy, with all the suffering and loss that must entail, and admits that nothing he imagines hurts him more than the thought of his beloved wife being dragged off as a slave after he is dead and no longer able to protect her. He then defends his commitment to the battle:

> "[F]rom the Trojans much I dread reproach, and Trojan dames whose garments sweep the ground, if, like a coward, I should shun the war. Nor does my soul to such disgrace incline, since to be always bravest I have learned, and with the first of Troy to lead the fight; asserting so my father's lofty claim to glory, and my own renown in arms."[13]

Both internal and external factors and influences motivate Hector. For the external, he is certainly aware that the people of Troy are counting on him and will brand him a coward if he avoids the conflict. Also, because he is a prince of Troy, his royal family's reputation is partly staked on his performance. Any perceived lack of mettle in his son would reflect badly on King Priam, as well as on Hector himself.

It is significant that these same external pressures exist for Prince Paris, too, and yet are not enough to keep him from choosing Helen's sweet kisses over the sting of Menelaus's sharp spears. What distinguishes Hector from his brother is a question of character. What makes Hector noble and Paris ignoble is that Hector chooses to make courage one of his defining virtues. He voluntarily links his very identity to the virtue of bravery on the battlefield. What others demand of him matters because it matches precisely what he demands of himself.

Hector's image as "the brave Prince Hector, Defender of Troy" is reinforced by public opinion, but it was created and is maintained by his own efforts to shape his character to fit that mold. He cannot now, in the midst of such a dreadful conflict, allow himself to be anything other than Troy's bravest defender without losing his self-respect and all sense of identity, meaning, and purpose in his life. He cannot be Hector and be a coward.

Paris, on the other hand, does not like to be *judged* a coward or *called* a coward by the people of Troy, but he does not really care whether or not he is, in fact, a coward. He faces external pressure to act like a warrior, but he has no personal commitment to a warrior's code. If he could spend the entire war hiding away with Helen and suffer no public condemnation for it, he would not hesitate to do so.

Hector, however, cannot allow himself to stay hidden away with his wife. So after explaining to her his reasons for returning to the battle, he moves to say good-bye to his little son, cradled nearby in his nurse's arms. This is one of Homer's most timeless moments. As the great warrior bends toward his baby's face, the boy begins to cry, frightened by his father's massive war helmet. Hector exchanges smiles with his wife, removes the menacing helmet, and takes the boy in his arms. He tosses Astynax playfully in the air until the baby laughs gleefully. He then prays aloud that his son will be allowed to grow up as a free man and become a great warrior like his father. And with final words of love and consolation for his wife, he places the baby in her arms, puts his helmet on his head, and walks back to the war.

It is a touchingly human scene that could have been set in the home of almost any warrior from any age who experienced the surreal transposition of bloody battle scenes and tender family moments. Homer forces us to confront the fact that it is possible for the same man to be gentle with his child, compassionate with his wife, respectful to his aging parents, brave and loyal to his comrades, yet also utterly vicious and merciless to his enemies. The hand that is dipped in blood can also be the hand that rocks the cradle. Hector is an excellent warrior, but he lives in many other roles as well, including brother, son, father, and husband.

In contrast to an all-too-human Hector, Homer presents us with the godlike Achilles. Achilles, too, is a vivid, three-dimensional character. But unlike Hector, he is exclusively a warrior. Every part he plays in life is directly related to his prowess on the battlefield, and every relationship he has is shaped by his martial experience. We can imagine Hector's happy home life before the Greek ships sailed over the horizon. There is a pre-war Hector. By contrast, Achilles' entire existence is wrapped up in the events of the Trojan War.

Recall that Achilles is the son of King Peleus and the sea goddess Thetis, into whose wedding reception the golden apple of discord was tossed, precipitating the Greek-Trojan conflict. After the chaotic events of their actual union settled down, Thetis became quite content with her mortal husband; that is, she was content until it occurred to her that any children she might have with Peleus might not inherit her immortality.

There are several versions of the myth detailing Thetis's treatment of her children by Peleus. One of the most popular versions states that after each child was born, Thetis would hold the baby over the fire in an attempt to burn away its mortal half and make it divine. Not surprisingly, none of the children survived this experiment in postnatal eugenics, and Thetis hid the true cause of their deaths from her increasingly suspicious (and bereft) husband. Finally, when young Achilles arrived, Peleus sent servants to spy on his wife. These servants saw Thetis place the child over the fire and snatched him away before he could be burnt. Frustrated, Thetis attempted another method. She stole out of her husband's palace with the child and carried him to the river Styx, which borders Hades (the Greek underworld) and therefore has magical properties. Holding baby Achilles by his heel, she dipped him into the river to purge him of his mortal taint. This procedure was actually effective, but, unfortunately, she forgot to splash any water on the heel by which she had held the child. The result was that Achilles turned out completely invulnerable except for his heel. A blow to no other part of his body could harm him, but any wound to his heel would be fatal. (It is from this myth that we inherit the expression his/her "Achilles' heel" to describe a person's primary weakness or fatal flaw.)

Shortly after failing to fry but successfully dipping her child, Thetis had Achilles' fate read by an oracle. The oracle foretold that Achilles would have to select from two very distinct potential lives. On one path, he would become a glorious warrior, the greatest Greece had ever seen, who would accomplish great deeds during the Trojan War that would never be matched or forgotten. That life, however, would be a short one. Soon after slaying his greatest enemy, he would fall dead on the field. Nor would he be given time to enjoy the experiences of being a husband, a father, or the inheritor of his father's kingdom of Phthia. On the other path, Achilles would lead a long and peaceful life, marry, have children, and rule over Phthia. But he would never win glory or renown, never taste victory, never know how it felt to be heralded as the greatest living warrior, first among all the Greek champions against Troy.

Achilles had been too young to vie for fair Helen's hand and so never took the suitor's oath to protect or retrieve her from any kidnapper or seducer. Nevertheless, once Helen was stolen by Paris, Thetis knew that the Greek leaders, having heard the predictions about her son's potential military prowess, would soon come to Phthia to collect him for their expedition to Troy. In an effort to detour Achilles away from his shorter, more painful possible life path, Thetis packed Achilles (who was presumably a teenager by this time) off to the island of Skyros to live with his female cousins.[14] Thetis insisted that Achilles dress like a woman while on Skyros, so that no rumor of the young prince's true whereabouts could reach the force marshaling around Agamemnon and Menelaus.

Achilles is not the only character to attempt "draft dodging" in the myth of the Trojan War. To help persuade the other suitors to take the oath to protect Helen (which he had suggested to Helen's father, King Tyndarus), Odysseus also made the pledge himself, even though he had already withdrawn his own request for Helen's hand in order to court her clever and faithful cousin, Penelope. When Helen was kidnapped, Odysseus knew that he would be called upon to journey with the others to Troy. But he was loath to make that trip, since it had been prophesied to him that if he went to the war, he would not be able to return to the shores of his homeland of Ithaca for at least twenty years.

Odysseus was very happy in Ithaca with his "like-minded" wife, Penelope, and their newborn son, Telemachus. So when an embassy from the brothers Agamemnon and Menelaus arrived at his royal estates to demand that he make good on his oath, Odysseus tried to convince the men that he had gone mad. He dressed himself in filthy rags, hitched himself to a plow, and began plowing the same furrow over and over again. This might have worked, except for the suspicious nature of Palamedes, one of the ambassadors. Palamedes forced Odysseus to give up the ruse by grabbing the baby Telemachus away from his mother and placing him in the path of his father's plow. Naturally, Odysseus stopped his plow before hitting the child and tenderly lifted his son into his arms. This proved that he was not truly out of his mind, and he was required to join the expedition.

Having failed to avoid the war altogether, Odysseus made it his personal mission to make the campaign as short as possible. He knew that the godlike Achilles would be a blessing for the Greek cause, so he set out to search for the missing youth. Arriving eventually on the island of Skyros, Odysseus quickly saw through Achilles' drag disguise. But rather than just demand that he reveal his true nature, Odysseus decided to trick Achilles into blowing his cover, even as he had been made to do back in Ithaca. To that end, Odysseus sent presents to Achilles and all of his female cousins: beautiful scarves, rich jewelry, fine dresses, and also a well-made spear and shield. While these gifts were being opened, Odysseus hid behind a column, blew a warning blast on his war horn, and shouted that the palace was under attack. The girls cried out in panic, but Achilles, without thinking, snatched up the shield and spear and ran to defend the palace gate. Odysseus met him there and led him off to war.

Achilles is drawn into the conflict with Troy, not because his own honor is at stake (he is not bound by any oath to participate) or because he feels that justice demands that he support the Greek cause, but because fighting at Troy is simply his destiny (or at least one of his two possible destinies). Achilles is not motivated to fight against the Trojans for duty's sake or to defend his home and family. He kills Trojans because his fellow Greeks ask him to, he is good at it, and for his trouble he receives accolades, respect, and high-status plunder such as gold and beautiful prize women. For no more than this, he battles day after day outside the Trojan city for ten long years.

In the original Greek, the first word of Homer's *Iliad* is "wrath" or "rage." Homer begs the nine Muses, goddesses of creativity, to sing through him, not about the Trojan War, but about the rage of a single warrior: Achilles. Achilles' anger, in its various forms, drives the plot of the entire epic. To understand what Homer hopes to convey, therefore, we have to ask, why, exactly, is Achilles angry?

The key to Achilles' wrath is wrapped up in the issue of what brings honor and what brings shame to the heroes of Homer's epic. In the opening scenes of the *Iliad*, we learn that King Agamemnon has been forced to give up his beautiful prize woman, Chryseis, because her father, Chryses, is a priest of Apollo who has the power to summon a plague that could destroy the whole Greek army. Since he and his brother Menelaus are the leaders of the force against Troy, Agamemnon considers it an outrage that he, of all people, should be deprived of any status symbol. Also, he much preferred the company of his captive woman to that of his own wife, Clytemnestra. He had already turned down a generous offer of gold for her.

Agamemnon expresses his outrage over the loss of Chryseis to the Greek champions and demands that they make it up to him with the award of some other prize. Achilles, who is usually a man of few words (noted for his battle skills, not his diplomacy), tries to point out that all the spoils of war that have so far been gathered by the Greeks are already divided amongst the commanders. For Agamemnon to receive a new prize, some other commander must forfeit one. It would not be fair, Achilles argues, for Agamemnon to take someone else's reward away just because he was unlucky enough to have chosen as a concubine a woman whose father has a direct line to the sun god, Apollo. Consolingly, he points out that there will be plenty of prizes for Agamemnon and everyone else when they finally conquer Troy.

Achilles' speech enrages Agamemnon. He cannot bear the idea of being left with fewer status symbols than the other Greek commanders because he believes that his wealth and power entitle him to a greater, let alone equal, share of the plunder. For a modern analogy, imagine a powerful politician being told that he must give up his Lexus luxury sedan in order to save his party from some disastrous scandal and simply to do without private transportation until the next election is won. Meanwhile, all of his campaign staffers will still be driving around town in Mercedes, Porsches, Land Rovers, and Cadillacs. Even though the loss of his own car in no way alters his staffers' claims to their own vehicles, the politician will no doubt have a serious "What's wrong with this picture?" reaction and demand that someone from his staff pony up a replacement vehicle for him, even if it means giving up his or her own.

For having spoken out, Achilles finds himself the focus of Agamemnon's indignation. Agamemnon decides that Achilles himself should recompense the Mycenean king for his sacrifice of Chryseis by giving the king his own prize woman, Briseis. So Briseis is led from Achilles' tent and over to the encampment of Agamemnon's household.

Agamemnon's action is an enormous insult to Achilles. Although Agamemnon has greater wealth and political power than Achilles, it is Achilles who has done the most damage by far to the Trojans on the battlefield. He is, without question, the best fighter that the Greeks possess. He has kept the Greek cause alive for ten years without having any personal commitment to it to motivate him. And the material rewards he has already received seem insufficient compared with his efforts. He bitterly explains this when Agamemnon first threatens to appropriate his prize:

> "Not for wrongs to me came I so far from home, this war to wage against the Trojans. They had never driven my steeds or cattle, nor laid waste the fields of fertile Phthia, my well-peopled realm; . . . But thee, . . . we have followed, for thy pleasure, here, to win revenge for Menelaus, and for thee, . . . a favor now repaid with base ingratitude and reckless scorn! For thou hast threatened to usurp my prize, the precious meed of many bloody toils; . . . Compared with thine, my share is always small, . . . the greater part of war's laborious task these hands perform; but, when the spoil is shared, thine are the richest prizes!"[15]

Unlike Hector, who has his home and family to defend, Achilles has only a slender commitment to the war. His feelings can be compared to those captured so poignantly by W. B. Yeats in his famous World War I–era poem, "An Irish Airman Foresees His Death":

> I know that I shall meet my fate
> Somewhere among the clouds above;
> Those that I fight I do not hate,
> Those that I guard I do not love;
> My country is Kiltartan Cross,
> My countrymen Kiltartan's poor,
> No likely end could bring them loss
> Or leave them happier than before.
> Nor law, nor duty bade me fight,
> Nor public men, nor cheering crowds,
> A lonely impulse of delight
> Drove to this tumult in the clouds;
> I balanced all, brought all to mind,
> The years to come seemed waste of breath,
> A waste of breath the years behind
> In balance with this life, this death.[16]

Achilles has no reason to hate the Trojans, and their defeat will not affect his countrymen back in Phthia. Nor does he particularly love his fellow Greeks. The only man in his camp with whom he shares a close bond is his companion, Patroclus. As a boy, Patroclus accidentally killed a friend while playing a game and was forced to flee with his father from their native land of Opus. They were taken in and given sanctuary in Phthia by King Peleus, and Patroclus was raised alongside Prince Achilles to be his playmate and squire.[17] The two became the best of friends and, ultimately, devoted comrades-in-arms. So it is that in book 16 of the *Iliad*, Achilles reveals that his perfect dream for the conclusion of the war would be for every other warrior, Trojan and Greek alike, to kill each other off, leaving only him and Patroclus alive to pull down the walls of the conquered city. Clearly, Achilles did not really love the other Greek champions, Patroclus excepted, any more than their Trojan counterparts.

Homer puts a wonderful speech into the mouth of the character of Sarpedon, a Lycian prince and Trojan ally, addressing his best friend and fellow warrior, Glaucus, which neatly reveals what motivates men like the Homeric heroes to fight and how fragile and insufficient those reasons can sometimes seem:

> "O Glaucus, . . . why are we honored most in Lycia, with high seats of dignity, with plenteous feasts and ever-flowing bowls? There all admiring gaze, as we were gods, and on the banks of Xanthus we enjoy a large domain, by public suffrage given, purple with vineyards, rich with waving wheat. Now, therefore, 'tis our duty in the front to stand of all the Lycians, breasting first the fiery brunt of battle; that of us our mail-clad warriors may with plaudits say, 'Not without glory do our [leaders] maintain their royal state; not merely do they feast on dainties, and drink wine abundantly, as honey sweet, but are distinguished, too, by valor, and conspicuous in the van[guard] of Lycia's heroes!'—O my friend! Could we, shunning this war, forever be exempt from feeble age and death, I would not then among the foremost in the field advance, nor to the glorious combat thee exhort. But since the fates press on us nevertheless, and death, from causes numberless, impends, which man by care or flight can never evade, now let us march, to give some foe renown, if fall we must, or glory win ourselves."[18]

Given the choice between a long, largely uneventful life concluding with old age, decline, and death, and a shorter but more passionate existence highlighted by fame, glory, material rewards, and a dramatic death, Sarpedon and Glaucus, just like Achilles, are drawn to select the latter. At the same time, they wish there were some third alternative open to them in which they could enjoy the benefits of their warrior status without necessarily sacrificing their futures and dooming themselves to an agonizing death. (One can imagine them in the modern world happily pursuing careers as high-paid professional athletes, where the sacrifices exchanged for such status generally fall short of a spear thrust through the chest.) Reviewing their limited options, their attitude is the ancient equivalent of "it's better to burn out than fade away." Like Yeats's Irish airman, they judge the warrior's life and the warrior's death to be preferable to more peaceful options, but they are not so gung-ho as not to genuinely regret the fate that leaves them with no better alternatives. When they pause before a battle, they find that the scales that measure what they have to gain and lose tilt in favor of returning to the fight, but not by much.

So it is understandable that when Achilles is stripped of his prize, Briseis, and the respect from his peers that she represents, his scales suddenly tip the other way. Furious with Agamemnon and disdainful of his colleagues who allowed this public insult to proceed unchecked, Achilles withdraws his followers (an army of hardened warriors known as the Myrmidons) and himself from the war and goes off to sulk in his tent. He vows that he will not return to the field of battle until Briseis is returned to him, unmolested and accompanied by profuse apologies and abundant compensatory gifts from King Agamemnon. Otherwise, he will not lift a weapon at all unless the Trojans are about to burn his own ships (his only means to return home to Phthia).

Shortly after deciding to remove himself from the conflict, Achilles walks to the shoreline and calls out from the beach for his sea goddess mother, Thetis:

"O dearest mother! Since thy son was born to life so short, Olympian [Zeus], the god who thunders from on high, was bound, at least, to give me glory; but his promise now is utterly forgotten. Shame and scorn attend me, for my fame is stained with wrong by Atreus' son, wide-ruling Agamemnon! He holds my prize, by lawless power usurped."[19]

Thetis, after hearing her son's grievances in detail, agrees to visit Zeus and beg him to punish the Greeks for failing to show Achilles proper respect. She accomplishes this mission, and under Zeus's direction the gods see to it that the Greeks fighting without Achilles begin to suffer setbacks and serious defeats at the hands of the Trojans. Eventually, things become so bad for the Greeks that all of their primary commanders are dead or wounded and the Trojan army is on the verge of overrunning their encampment and destroying their ships anchored off shore.

It is at this point (book 16 of the *Iliad*) that Patroclus, who appears to have more sympathy for the Greek cause and more loyalty to the Greek forces than Achilles, decides to visit his great warrior friend in his tent and try to persuade him to return to the fray and rally the Greek warriors. Patroclus employs several distinct approaches in his attempt to sway Achilles from his stubborn course. All appeal, in one way or another, to Achilles' sense of honor and warrior's code.

Patroclus's first tactic is simply to explain the Greeks' dire predicament to Achilles. His hope seems to be that the thought of a Trojan victory will be so abhorrent to Achilles that his concern to avert it will overcome his anger against Agamemnon. Patroclus names all the Greek champions who have recently fallen on the field and are now wounded or dying. He describes the fierce onslaught of the Trojans under the command of Prince Hector and warns that the enemy may soon be in a position to cut off any possible Greek retreat by burning the Greek ships at anchor.

Patroclus's moving account of impending Greek failure falls on deaf ears. For, as we have already observed, Achilles was never motivated to fight by patriotic zeal or the Greek cause or a sense of esprit de corps with his fellow Greeks. Achilles particularly does not feel that he owes any duty to an army of soldiers who suffer their supreme commander to insult the one man who was the primary agent behind all of their previous victories and the only warrior among them capable of defeating their greatest enemy, Prince Hector.

Trusting to the strength of their friendship, Patroclus then shifts to the riskier strategy of trying to shame Achilles into action. Hoping to change his perspective, he asks Achilles to consider how other people (his peers, the Myrmidons who fight for him, the citizens back in Greece) will judge his decision to remain outside the conflict because of a quarrel over a woman. He asks, "What will future generations have to thank you for, if you will not help the [Greeks] in their direst need?"[20]

But, again, Patroclus's approach fails to show an understanding of what Achilles really cares about and what considerations drive his decisions. Achilles is seldom influenced by the views of others, while the Trojan prince, Hector, uses the opinions of his fellow Trojans to calibrate his moral compass and set his standard for honorable behavior. Achilles keeps his own counsel and holds himself apart from other men. It is important to him that the other Greeks show him the level of respect due to a man of his lineage and martial accomplishments, but he decides for himself what that proper level of respect is. He does not think, "Because the Greeks honor me this much, it is clear that I have done well and I am a worthy man." He thinks, "I know myself that I have done well and I am a worthy man, therefore the Greeks should honor me this much." The idea that other warriors may mock him or future generations condemn him could only make him contemptuous of those who could evaluate him so wrongly. Knowing the opinions of others will not make him modify his behavior to fit their standards.

Frustrated beyond any fear of losing Achilles' love or protection, Patroclus resorts to insults, calling Achilles a man without pity and even questioning his parentage. Then a softening thought occurs to him concerning what could account for his friend's intractable resistance to all threats and entreaties. He speculates that Achilles' real reason for staying away from the fray may be that his goddess mother has informed him of some horrible prophecy regarding his fate if he once again asserts his dominance on the fields of Troy. Expressing his concern should such a paralyzing prediction exist, Patroclus offers to put on Achilles' distinctive armor and, so disguised, rally the Greeks himself.

As Homer has by this point already revealed, there is, in fact, a prophecy hanging over Achilles' head; he knows that his own death will follow shortly after the death of Hector. But Achilles insists to his friend Patroclus that it is not any fear of his untimely death that keeps him from reengaging the enemy. Rather, he will not fight because of King Agamemnon's insult to his honor:

> "I am not influenced by any oracle, or word from [Zeus] brought by my honored mother; but my heart and soul indignant are with anguish stung, that thus a tyrant, flushed with power and pride, has robbed a chieftain equal to himself, even of his rightful prize. . . . The lovely maid, my valor's glorious [reward], assigned me by the [Greeks], whom I won by my own javelin, . . . even her the tyrant Agamemnon, Atreus' son, snatched from my arms, as from an exiled wretch, contemptible and base! . . . My wrath, indeed, I said should not abate, till war and shouts of fight my ships should reach."[21]

Achilles feels that he would be further shamed if he reneged on his fierce declaration that he would not fight again unless it were to defend his own ships. He and Agamemnon are engaged in a battle of wills, and Achilles does not want to be the first to crack under that pressure, especially since he judges Agamemnon to be beyond question the one in the wrong. However, he does yield somewhat to Patroclus's persuasion, for he allows his friend to attempt the trick of putting on Achilles' famous armor to frighten the Trojans and inspire the Greeks.

While he is donning Achilles' armor, Patroclus receives a stern warning from Achilles that he must not allow himself to get carried away if the ruse is successful. He must not attempt to defeat Hector and take Troy himself. To do so would be to exhibit undue arrogance and excessive pride, or what the Greeks termed "hubris." In its most extreme form, hubris is thinking oneself equal to the gods, master of one's own destiny, answerable to no one. Although reasonable pride in one's talents and accomplishments is expected among the Homeric warriors, the gods always punish hubris.

Wearing Achilles' armor, Patroclus prepares to lead the Myrmidons into battle. Before he does, Achilles stands before the troops and delivers an unusual sort of pep talk. First, he stresses that his conviction that he has been acting as an honorable warrior should is unassailable and that he is utterly immune to the criticism of others. Then he challenges his followers to prove that they are honorable, as well, by living up to their claims that they have been aching to return to combat and slaughter more Trojans:

> "Valiant Myrmidons! Let none of you forget your menaces against the Trojans, all the time my wrath continued, and ye loitered at my ships. Then every man reproached me, and ye said: 'Relentless son of Peleus! Sure with

gall thy mother fed thee! Cruel! Thus to keep thy friends, repining vainly, at thy ships! Home let us go, . . . since fruitless wrath so occupies thy mind.' Such were the words, ye, oft assembling, spake. But now, before you lies the mighty work of war, so long, so ardently desired. Let every soldier, therefore, bravely now the battle wage."[22]

Patroclus and the Myrmidons then charge into battle, and both sides do in fact believe that it is the great Achilles himself who has retaken the field. Mowing men down like grass, Patroclus pushes the Trojans back from the Greek encampments and away from the Greek fleet. But instead of stopping with that small victory, as Achilles advised, he presses on, relishing his own success and savoring the borrowed status bestowed on him by Achilles' armor. He take on enemy after enemy, advancing toward the walls of Troy.

One of those to fall beneath Patroclus's thrusting spear is the Lycian prince, Sarpedon, whose powerful words to his friend Glaucus before an earlier battle were noted above. Homer presents the death of Sarpedon in a particularly poignant manner in two respects. First of all, he shows us the anguish of the god Zeus, who is Sarpedon's real father (as the result of an affair with Sarpedon's beautiful mother, the queen of Lycia, years before). Since he truly loves his son, Zeus is tempted to alter Sarpedon's destiny and rescue him from death. And, as the ruler of all the gods, he has the power to do so. However, as he contemplates that interference, the other Olympic gods (especially the goddess Hera, his sister and wife) warn him against it. Hera points out that if Zeus steps in to change the fate of one mortal, the other gods will feel licensed to use their powers to reshape the futures of all their mortal favorites as well:

"A man, by nature mortal, doomed by old established laws to certain death, wouldst thou deliver from his doleful fate? Do so; but be assured not all the gods thy conduct will approve. Another thing I tell thee; thou, attentive, weigh it well. If to his home, with life, thou shouldst restore Sarpedon, may not other deities their offspring wish to save from deadly fight? For many children of immortals wage this war around old Priam's lofty town; in whom excessive ire thou wouldst provoke! But though the chief be dear to thee, and grief thy bosom rend, permit him now to fall in glorious combat, by the warlike hands of brave Patroclus; and when life has left his noble body, give it, thou, in charge to death and gentle sleep, to bear it thence to wide-spread Lycia. There his mournful friends and brethren shall perform his funeral rites, and to his memory tomb and column raise: such honors are appointed for the dead."[23]

Zeus accepts Hera's rebuke, thus consigning his beloved son to a brutal death. And by this instrument Homer reveals his heroes' attitudes toward fate and divine intervention. All of Homer's key characters generally embrace fatalism, although they occasionally, in a fit of hubris, try to alter or escape their destinies. And their relationship with their gods is not much marked by love or trust, but rather by fear, anger, or frustration. Although the gods frequently play a role in the progress of the war, they do not, as Hera argues, cross the line into rewriting the basic, preset plot-lines of the primary players. So the Homeric warrior believes that if it is his fate to suffer death or defeat, no amount of pious devotion to his gods will persuade them to rescue him.

The second way in which Sarpedon's death is made more affecting than others within the epic is the part played in the final moments by Sarpedon's comrade, first cousin, and best friend, Glaucus. When the then unstoppable Patroclus assails Sarpedon, Glaucus is a distance away, fighting other Greek champions. Across the raging battlefield, Glaucus hears Sarpedon call out, knowing even as he does that Glaucus cannot possibly get to his side in time to save his life. As Sarpedon groans out his last breaths, he begs Glaucus to take command of the Lycians and fight with them to retrieve his corpse from their enemies, so that at least his body may be given a proper burial and not just stripped of his armor and fed to the Greek dogs:

> So, by Patroclus slain, indignant still the leader of the mail-clad Lycians groaned, and to his friend he cried: "Glaucus, my friend, brave combatant of heroes, greatly thee it now behooves to be a spearman bold, a dauntless warrior. . . . Speeding through the field, extort the chiefs of Lycia to contend for slain Sarpedon's corpse, and thou with them, for my sake, combat bravely. Grief and shame eternal would be thine, if me the Greeks despoil of armor. . . . Be valiant, then, and all our people to the conflict urge." As this he said, the last cold touch of death his eyes and nostrils closed. Upon his breast Patroclus trod, and from his body pulled the reeking spear; adhesive to the spike his heart-strings followed, and with them came forth his noble spirit.[24]

Glaucus himself has just been badly wounded by an arrow in his shoulder, but upon hearing his comrade's final words, he prays to the god Apollo for just enough strength to fulfill Sarpedon's dying request and retrieve his mangled corpse. Glaucus rips the arrow from his own flesh, and Apollo takes his pain away so that he can stand and summon not only the Lycians but also Prince Hector and other Trojan champions to battle for his cousin's body. The Greeks manage to strip off Sarpedon's bronze armor as a trophy for Patroclus, but while the Lycians and the Trojans put up a strong defense around the remains of the Lycian prince, Zeus sends Apollo down to whisk Sarpedon's body out of harm's way. Glaucus is therefore not allowed to comply fully with his friend's final directions, but it is clear that he was prepared to do so, even at the cost of his own life.

Now that Hector has entered the melee, it is past time for Patroclus to withdraw, given Achilles' specific entreaty that he not test himself against the Trojan prince. He ought to know that only Achilles has the necessary skills to stand a chance against Hector, but Patroclus is still buoyed by his defeat of Sarpedon and blinded by hubris. Ignoring the threat of Hector, he tries to scale the walls of Troy and is rebuffed three times by the god Apollo, who tells him it is not his fate to orchestrate the fall of Troy. Finally, he comes face-to-face with Hector, the greatest fighter among the Trojans.

Apollo cracks Patroclus's disguise by causing his borrowed armor to fall off, so that Hector and the other Trojans can see that they are not really up against the godlike Achilles. The contest that ensues between Hector and Patroclus is not true single combat, because before it is even clear how the two will match up, a Trojan youth named Euphorbus lobs a lucky spear at Patroclus, piercing him through the back. Hector then runs up and finishes the job by ramming his own spear deep into Patroclus's belly.

Patroclus dies because of his hubris, but he remains proud to the last. Trying to diminish Hector's sense of superiority, Patroclus with his dying breath taunts the Trojan prince, pointing out that he only managed to kill Patroclus after he was helped along by a god and a spear-wielding boy. In this way, he tries to diminish the credit (and status) that Hector can receive for slaying Achilles' closest companion.

The news of Patroclus's death comes as a devastating blow to the once proud Achilles. He blames himself, his anger with Agamemnon, and his concern over his own personal honor (in the sense of the respect due him from his peers) for producing the conditions that led to Patroclus's downfall. Balanced against the slaughter of his beloved friend, Agamemnon's seizure of Briseis means nothing to him. The only things that had really made life worth living for Achilles at Troy were the honor he received for his accomplishments on the battlefield and his friendship with Patroclus. The former was soured for him when Agamemnon treated him with such blatant disrespect. Losing Patroclus as well reduces his existence to a life without meaning, fulfillment, or purpose, except for the suddenly all-consuming desire to seek revenge for his friend's death by killing Prince Hector.

Achilles has no armor (since the armor he had lent to Patroclus was taken away by Hector), but to retrieve his friend's corpse from the field, Achilles strides naked from his tent, stands in the Greek trenches dug on the edge of their encampments, and bellows out such a terrifying war cry that the Trojans are temporarily driven off, allowing Patroclus's body to be duly collected and taken back to Achilles' tent. Achilles then asks his mother, Thetis, to commission new armor for him from the metalworking god, Hephaestus, so that he can challenge Hector as soon as possible. Thetis is heartbroken by this request, knowing that Hector's death will herald her son's, but she complies with his wishes after she hears his agonized expression of the despair that has overtaken him:

[W]ith tears quick-falling, Thetis spake: "Thy life, my son, will . . . be brief indeed; for after Hector's fate, thy own is near." With high disdain, Achilles, answering, said: "That moment let me die; since t'was my doom not to defend my comrade slain in fight! Unaided in his dying hour, he fell, far distant from his country; . . . my prowess needed to repel the blow. . . . I . . . was no light in darkness, to Patroclus, and the rest of my unhappy countrymen, of whom such multitudes by Hector's arm have fallen; but here, a fruitless burden to the ground, sit idly at the ships; though such as I am in martial prowess as no Greek can match, while in the council others me excel. Ah! May fell discord perish utterly from gods and men extinct, with cruel wrath, which even the wisest to destruction leads. So Agamemnon, king of men, to rage me fatally excited! But to this, as done and past, and not to be recalled, we must submit, through sad necessity, our aching hearts repressing. Now to war I go to meet the murderer of my friend. And death I will embrace whenever decreed by [Zeus] and the other blessed immortal gods. For, lo! Not even the strength of Hercules could death escape, though most of all mankind he was beloved of [Zeus]. . . . So also I, if fate like his be mine, must low be laid by death, the grim destroyer! Glory now, the [reward] of heroes let me reap. . . . Stay me not, though fondly thou entreat me, even thou canst not persuade!"[25]

Since his heart is no longer in their quarrel, Achilles makes peace with Agamemnon. The Mycenean king, for his part, finally complies with Achilles' initial demands, returning Briseis (whom he swears not to have touched) along with treasure as compensation. Rather than taking full responsibility for his actions, however, Agamemnon, ever the politician, delivers a slick speech in which he blames his bad behavior on uncontrollable passions inflicted on him by the gods.

Achilles is so enraged against Hector that as soon as his divinely smithed armor arrives, he wants the Greeks to charge the field and help him destroy the Trojan army. Achilles' interest in this battle is, as ever, entirely personal. He still does not really care about the Greek cause or the condition of the Greek troops. It is Odysseus, always the cleverest of the Greek champions, who gently points out to the furious Phthian prince that the men he wants to commit immediately into combat have already fought long and hard for Patroclus. They should be allowed to eat and rest so they can recover the strength to do their side any credit in battle. Grudgingly, Achilles agrees to wait while Odysseus ensures that the urgent needs of the troops are met.

When all is prepared and he is finally encased in his new armor, Achilles rushes onto the field, screaming for Hector's blood. He slaughters many Trojan warriors as he presses toward their prince. Hector, meanwhile, has his own fateful decision to make. Elated when he slew Patroclus, he soon afterward absorbs the fact that he may have signed his own death warrant (and that of every citizen in Troy) by killing the great Achilles' best friend. He knows that Achilles will be coming after him, and he does not know whether he should make a stand and face the enraged Phthian *mano-a-mano* or retreat back within the walls of Troy to defend his people there from a reenergized Greek siege.

The advancing Greek army with Achilles at its head quickly decimates a significant portion of the Trojan forces, making a withdrawal seem most advisable. Some of the Trojan leaders criticize Hector for not having ordered a retreat as soon as Achilles took the field. But Hector hesitated, and the Trojans were badly hit before they were finally able to pull back and regroup. Hector knows that if he could defeat Achilles, all of his critics would be silenced and the Greeks would probably be completely demoralized. Hector's royal parents, King Priam and Queen Hecuba, urge him to stay inside the high, protective walls of the city. They beg him not to fight Achilles while he is in his murderous rage. They point out that inside the royal palace, Hector's wife and son need his protection. To avoid the direct challenge of Achilles, however, still feels like the coward's choice to this man who has so far proudly worn the mantle of Troy's last, best hope for salvation.

As Hector agonizes over this conflict of duties, torn between his obligation to safeguard the future of Troy and the demands of his warrior's honor (which requires him to embrace his fate without fear and answer Achilles' challenge), Homer allows us a glimpse inside Hector's mind. An internal monologue exposes his reasoning and emotions at this critical juncture:

> Against a jutting turret he reclined his radiant shield, and sorrowfully thus debated with his own heroic mind: "Unhappy that I am! Should I, indeed, enter the gates and skulk behind the wall, shame would attend me! Chiefly just reproach Polydamas would vent, who counseled me to draw the troops within the sheltering town, that fatal night when great Achilles rose. But then, I yielded not! Ah! Surely, then, yielding had been the wiser course! But now, since my temerity has slaughter caused, and ruin of my people, much I dread the scornful taunts of Trojan men and dames. . . . Some envious wretch, inferior far to me, may now exult, and say: 'Proud Hector, rashly confident of his own strength, destroyed the host of Troy.' Such clamors will they raise. And better far it would be to return, Achilles slain, triumphant, or a glorious death endure in battle for my country. But, suppose, I lay aside my bossy shield and helm, and, leaving here my spear against the wall, go now myself to meet the brave Achilles! What if I offer Helen to restore to Atreus' sons, with all the treasures brought by Paris, in his fleet, from Greece to Troy; Helen, the cause of war; and yield, besides, (to be divided by [the Greek] host), whatever hidden treasures in our town may yet remain; compelling strictly for the Trojan chiefs to pledge a solemn oath that nothing is concealed, but all produced for distribution, all the wealth within our much-loved city's walls? But why these thoughts, fondly and vainly, do I thus indulge? Such meeting cannot be. He would not pity, nor in the least respect, but slay me straight, unarmed and unresisting, woman-like! For

now I cannot from an oak's high bough or rock's tall summit, conference hold with him in safety. . . . Better it is to try the glorious fight, and quickly ascertain whether to him or me [Zeus] will glory give."[26]

It is easy to sympathize with Hector. His judgments as a commander have been questioned, leaving him uncertain whether he has done all that he could to avert disaster for his city. Unlike Achilles, he worries what his peers and countrymen (and women) say of him; their evaluations of him affect how he regards himself. Ideally, he would like to put an end to the war and save the Trojans from slavery or the sword. But he does not see that option placed before him. In reality, there is no way for him to appease Achilles now that the Phthian is consumed by rage, grief, and guilt at the death of Patroclus. No matter what decision he makes, Hector's defense of Troy is inescapably doomed. But since he cannot know that for certain, he decides to grasp at his only chance for an eleventh-hour save (or the classic "Hail Mary pass"). If he faces Achilles, either he will be killed, in which case Troy will fall, as it most likely will anyway, or he will triumph and become the savior of Troy after all. If he has to die, he judges that it would be better to be killed by the greatest Greek warrior who ever lived than to be caught in the general slaughter as Troy's defenses crumble.

Is Hector less admirable than Achilles because he has qualms about their impending duel and sincerely wishes it could be avoided? A point that should not be overlooked is that Hector has a lot more to live for than Achilles does. By the time Achilles is scouring the battlefield for Hector, he has lost everything in life that he once prized. He is a truly tragic figure, saturated by despair but kept alive by his need for revenge, fueled by his intense guilt and shame over having failed to protect the life of his dearest friend, closest companion, and comrade-in-arms. Hector, too, is somewhat ashamed of his past conduct. He worries that, like Patroclus, he may have allowed hubris to derail his most crucial decision making as a Trojan leader. But he has a lot more to live for than Achilles: he is truly committed to the welfare of his city; he has an affectionate, respectful relationship with his royal parents; he has strong ties of friendship and loyalty with the other Trojan leaders, many of whom are his own brothers (for King Priam had no fewer than fifty sons when the Trojan War began); and he truly loves his devoted wife, Andromache, and their infant son, Astynax.

Hector stands to lose a great deal if he falls to Achilles, and the odds are clearly not in his favor. Achilles is, after all, godlike: invulnerable except for his heel. And he is coming after Hector full of rage and clothed in impenetrable armor fashioned by a god. Who, in Hector's place, would not be afraid and wish for an honorable way out of the situation?

Addressing the subject of courage in book 3, chapter 9 of the *Nico-*

machean Ethics, the fifth-century B.C. Greek philosopher Aristotle speculates that facing the likelihood of death in battle will be more difficult for
a noble man who generally lives a happy and virtuous life than for one
who is less fortunate:

> [D]eath and wounds will be painful to the brave man and against his will,
> but he will face them because it is noble to do so or because it is base not to
> do so. And the more he is possessed of excellence in its entirety and the hap-
> pier he is, the more he will be pained at the thought of death; for life is best
> worth living for such a man, and he is knowingly losing the greatest goods,
> and this is painful. But he is none the less brave, and perhaps all the more
> so, because he chooses noble deeds of war at that cost. . . . it is quite possi-
> ble that the best soldiers may be not men of this sort but those who are less
> brave but have no other good; for these are ready to face danger, and they
> sell their life for trifling gains.[27]

In light of these ideas, we might, on the one hand, give Hector high marks
for having the nobility of character to accept the great risk of combat with
Achilles when to do otherwise would seem base.

On the other hand, it might also be possible to criticize Hector for being
concerned with whether he *appears* noble or base in the eyes of others.
From his private debate it is not entirely clear whether Hector is, as I have
suggested before, primarily concerned with sticking to the honorable path
because he genuinely wants to be an honorable man, or whether he is
only interested in ensuring that public perception regards him as an honorable man (whether that perception is accurate or not). If we give him the
benefit of the doubt, we may speculate that Hector's character includes
what Aristotle describes as "a kinship to excellence, loving what is noble
and hating what is base."[28] If we are skeptical, we may imagine that Hector does not truly hate baseness but only fears being thought base and
being shamed for his base behavior (where cowardice would be an example of base behavior).

Whatever his ultimate motivation, Hector resolves to stand and face
the wrath of Achilles. However, when Achilles actually spots Hector
across the battlefield and comes rushing toward him with his powerful
warrior's frame wrapped in shimmering armor that makes him appear
wreathed in flame, Hector's will temporarily snaps and he simply runs
away in a panic. It was one thing for Hector to steel himself to the idea
of facing the godlike Achilles; it was quite another for him to have the
man himself come charging at him like a god of war, bellowing for his
blood.

Achilles immediately pursues Hector, and the two men run a bizarre,
high-stakes footrace of three complete laps around the wide outer walls
of Troy. Finally, the goddess Athena, disguised as Hector's brother Dei-
phobus, appears beside Hector and calms him down, helping him to
regain his senses and his resolve. Comforted by the divine being at his

elbow whom he takes to be his brother, Hector stops running and assumes a combat stance opposite Achilles:

"No longer will I fly thee, Peleus' son! Round the great city of the Trojan king thrice have I fled, and could not thy approach abide. But now my ardent soul persuades firmly to stand, to slay thee, or be slain. Come, there-fore, let us both invoke the gods, for they will see and hear attentively, and solemn compacts faithfully attest: thy [corpse] I will not treat with foul dis-grace if [Zeus] shall grant me victory, and I take thy life, Achilles; but of arms despoiled, I will restore thee to the sons of Greece. Now, promise thou to do the like for me."[29]

Hector addresses his dreaded enemy respectfully, trying to establish some terms with him before they come to blows. But Achilles is not inter-ested in treating Hector with any degree of respect. To him, theirs cannot be a civilized, though deadly, contest between well-matched opponents. In his rage, Achilles has become a vicious animal, devoid of all humanity, thinking only of the kill:

The fierce Achilles, with disdainful look, infuriate, answered: "Hector, hate-ful wretch, abhorrent to my soul, talk not to me of compacts. As by lions with mankind no treaties can be made; as wolves and lambs no concord hold, but everlasting hate; so friendship cannot be between us two, nor oath, nor covenant, till one shall fall."[30]

The fight begins with the two men standing some yards apart, armed with shields and spears. Achilles hurls his spear at Hector, but, to Hec-tor's astonishment and delight, Achilles' aim is too high and the weapon sails harmlessly over Hector's swiftly ducked head. Hector's confidence surges, and in that moment he imagines himself actually capable of bring-ing down the great Achilles. He throws his spear with terrific strength and perfect aim, striking Achilles squarely. But what might have been a fatal blow simply bounces off Achilles' barely dented shield, provided to him by Hephaestus, the divine smith. Hector reaches back to where he believed his brother to be standing in order to request another spear. But Deiphobus (Athena) has disappeared.

Slowly the realization dawns on Hector that he is not fated to win this fight:

"Ah me! The gods have called me to my death! I thought that the brave Dei-phobus was here, but him the walls encompass. In his shape, [Athena] has deceived me! Surely, now, inevitable death must be my doom. Ah, certain-ly, such always was the will of [Zeus] supreme, and his far-shooting son [Apollo], who yet, with liberal favor, hitherto have guarded me; but fate overtakes me now. Yet I will not, without an effort, fall inglorious, but attempt a mighty feat, to be remembered even in distant times." As thus he spake, he drew the [sword], keen, heavy and huge, that from his shoulders hung, and like an eagle, bird of loftiest flight, stooping, precipitate, through sable clouds, to pounce a tender lamb or timid hare, he rushed impetuous, with uplifted sword, against his mighty foe.[31]

Achilles takes up another spear, and the two great warriors clash in close combat. Hector is wearing Achilles' old armor, taken off the body of Patroclus, and at first Achilles cannot find anywhere to strike with his spear. But then he observes that Hector's neck is exposed and he drives his weapon home, sending Hector sprawling in the dust:

> And stern Achilles gloried over him: "When thou, O Hector, didst the [corpse] despoil of slain Patroclus, doubtless all thy thoughts were confident of safety for thyself, regardless then of me, so far remote! Ah, foolish prince! . . . Behold I come, and thou art low in death!" . . . With feeble voice and tremulous [Hector], so great in battles once, now faintly spake: "By thy own life, and by thy knees, I pray, and by thy parents, O! Permit me not, when dead, to be the prey of Grecian dogs. Accept the abundant heaps of brass and gold, my sire and honored mother will present, and to their house my lifeless [corpse] restore, from Trojan men and matrons to receive the mournful tribute of a funeral flame." With unrelenting eye, the furious [Achilles], revengeful, answered: "Dog, implore not me for mercy, for my own or parents' sake! I wish that hatred could induce me even to feast on bloody morsels of thy flesh, so dire the griefs to me that thou hast caused! No mortal from the dogs shall save thy head, though bringing hither for thy ransom ten or twenty times thy worth and promising yet more to bring! Should Priam offer me thy weight in gold, he should not thee redeem. Thy mother shall not lay thee on a bier, bewailing thee, her offspring; but by dogs and birds thou shalt be utterly devoured." Him Hector, gasping, dying, answered thus: "Alas! I knew thee, and expected not to move thy heart to pity! Hard it is as iron. But consider, for thyself, lest I may bring upon thee from the gods some just chastisement, on that . . . day when, . . . great as thou art, thee Paris and Apollo shall destroy." As this he said, the fated moment came, and death in darkness wrapped him. From his limbs the disembodied spirit took its flight to Hades, moaning its too early loss of manly energy and youthful bloom. Him then, though dead, Achilles thus addressed: "Die thou, and fate I will myself accept, whenever such may be the will of [Zeus], and other deathless gods!"[32]

Achilles shows his worthy opponent no mercy, not even in the limited sense of agreeing to let Hector's bereaved parents buy back his body for a proper burial. Even when Hector is dead, Achilles is more interested in pursuing some further revenge against the Trojan prince's corpse than in considering the warning of Hector's final words: the prediction that Prince Paris will soon, with the help of the god Apollo, engineer Achilles' own death. Achilles' wrath against the Trojan is no less overpowering after inducing Hector's demise than when the Phthian was first given the news of his friend Patroclus's death.

Rejoicing in Achilles' victory, all the other Greek champions gather around Hector's corpse, stab it with their weapons, and make mocking comments. It is as if they feel that by gloating over the fallen Hector and dipping their swords and spears in his blood, they can share some portion of the high-status kill. At least they can say that they were there when a Greek brought down the greatest warrior of the Trojans. But, in truth, it is only Achilles whose status is assured for having delivered the deadly blow.

Achilles' triumph is quickly tainted by his utter disregard for basic decency and decorum. Not content with killing Hector, he proceeds next to desecrate the body by piercing Hector's ankles and tying them with a leather strap to the back of his chariot. He then races the chariot around the fields of Troy with the dead prince's head bouncing behind in the dust. Seeing this dreadful sight, King Priam, Queen Hecuba, and all the people of Troy shriek and weep for Hector, their last, best defender, while Hector's devoted wife Andromache faints dead away. Even the gods are horrified by Achilles' treatment of Hector's body. Remembering all the sacrifices Hector had made to them, they take steps to preserve his body magically so that it is not disfigured or allowed to decay.

Achilles, for his part, does not care what any mortal or immortal may think of him or his behavior. Nothing matters to him but the memory of Patroclus, the friend and comrade he let down, whose elaborate funeral he orders arranged. As a blood offering to his dead companion, Achilles slits the throats of twelve Trojan prisoners of war and throws their bodies on Patroclus's funeral pyre. Meanwhile, the other Greeks celebrate with feasts and Olympic-style games.

The death of Hector brings Achilles no peace, nor does Patroclus's funeral. Night after night, he is barely able to eke out any sleep. Seeking some release, every morning he gets up and again drags Hector's corpse behind his chariot, circling Patroclus's funeral mound. But nothing gives him any satisfaction or closure. He is a warrior with no cause he truly embraces, far from his own country, with no beloved comrades left to fight for or revenge. He no longer has any appreciation for his own glory or fame. Hector, dying, knew that he died for his family and for Troy. Achilles, though alive, has nothing to live for and nothing left worth dying for.

Book 24, the final chapter of the *Iliad*, recounts the redemption of the great Achilles and the quieting, at long last, of his terrible rage. After some debate, the gods ultimately decide that the Trojans should be allowed to give the body of brave Hector an appropriate burial. Consequently, Hermes, the messenger god, is dispatched to Troy to lead King Priam safely into the Greek camp so that he can confront Achilles in person and offer him a ransom of treasure in exchange for Prince Hector's corpse. Before he leaves on this mission, Priam has harsh words for his nine surviving sons, underlining the Trojan warrior ethic and the standard set by men like Hector:

> His nine remaining sons their hapless sire sternly reproved: ". . . ye worst of sons, ye scandal to my name! O, that ye all had perished at the ships in Hector's stead! Wretch that I am! My children were the best in fertile [Troy] once; now all are gone! Mestor, the mighty chieftain; Troilus, conspicuous in the fight, . . . And Hector last, who was a deity among the sons of men, for not of man he seemed the progeny, but of a god! . . . none are left me now but these, my ignominy, liars and dancers, great in nothing, save in beating time to music's wanton sound, and common plunderers of my people's wealth!"[33]

Just like Achilles, Priam has, in the course of this awful war, seen all the joy go out of his life. He, too, has nothing left to look forward to but his own preordained death.

The scene in which King Priam confronts Prince Achilles is truly extraordinary. Homer asks us to imagine how the Trojan king feels, having to go down on his knees and beg Achilles to accept a rich ransom for Hector's corpse. For modern readers, an imperfect but still useful analogy would be to a bereaved father being forced to visit his son's murderer on death row to entreat him to reveal where he stashed the boy's body before, by the murderer's execution, the victim's family loses all chance of ever recovering their loved one's remains:

> By all unseen came in the [Trojan] king, a tall, majestic form, and clasped Achilles knees, and kissed his hands. The parent kissed those dreadful murderous hands, by which so many of his sons were slain. . . . [S]o Achilles was amazed, beholding godlike Priam; while the rest looked at each other, wondering! Low on earth the wretched man implored his pity thus: "O great Achilles, equal to the gods! Remember now thy father, old like me, and tottering on the verge of doleful age. . . . no friend at hand. . . . Yet he has comfort when good tidings come, that thou art living still. Daily he hopes to see, from Troy returned, his much-loved son. But I, completely wretched, once, alas! Was happy, in a race of gallant sons, excelling all in [Troy's] widespread realm! Not one of them is left! When hither came [the Greek] host, full fifty sons were mine; one mother bore nineteen; the rest were born of other dames. Now cruel [Ares, god of war] of these by far the greater number has destroyed. And one who stood alone, my hope, my joy, defender of my city, and of all, him (fighting for his country) thou hast slain; my Hector! For his sake, hither I come, even hither, to the hostile fleet of Greece, to ransom him of thee; and presents bring of boundless price. O reverence the gods, Achilles, and commiserate me; persuaded by memory of thy father. I, indeed, am much more wretched. Truly, I have borne what never man on

earth before myself has undergone, the hand of him who slew my children, humbly to my lips to raise!"[34]

Seeing the proud, aging king, so like his own father, kneeling before him in supplication is such a wrenching sight that it penetrates even Achilles' armor of rage and pierces his stern heart. He sees Priam no longer as an enemy but as a noble and honorable man who, like himself, has been crushed beneath the heel of fate. Shutting out the rest of their companions, with whom they have less in common than they have with each other, the two great warriors, old and young, take a moment to mourn their respective losses.

[T]aking Priam's hand, [Achilles] gently turned the poor old man away, together both sobbing aloud! One for his godlike son, heroic Hector, poured a flood of tears, and prostrate lay before Achilles' feet. The other wept for father and for friend, alternatively. Their groans were heard afar, and echoed from the tent's high roof. At length, when great Achilles satiate was with grief, and in his breast and limbs convulsive throbs of anguish thrilled no longer, from his seat he rose, and, kindly raising by the hand the venerable king, with pity viewed his hoary head and beard all white with age. Then thus he soothed his woe: "Unhappy man! What ills hast thou endured! How couldst thou come hither alone, amidst our hostile fleet, even to the presence of the man who slew thy gallant sons, so many, and so brave? Surely, of tempered steel thy heart is framed! But now be seated: let us, for a time, permit our sorrows in our hearts to rest, however keenly felt; for sighs and tears no benefit can bring."[35]

When their emotions have settled down, Achilles shares his philosophy of life: the belief that humans are the playthings of the gods, subject to divine whims and meted out fixed shares of joy and suffering. The judgments of the gods are seemingly random. The good or noble are not always rewarded, the wicked or base not always punished. There is no real justice, only fate:

"Such is the thread spun by the gods for miserable men, that we must live in trouble, [while] they on high [are] free from care and woe. Two urns are placed on [Zeus's] exalted threshold; filled with gifts of natures opposite; with evil one, with good the other. He to whom is dealt a mingled draught of both, sorrow endures, and bliss enjoys, successive. But the wretch to whom the bad is without mixture given is doomed to infamy and horrid want; by meagre famine through the world pursued, he restless wanders, scorned by gods and men! What signal honors did the powers divine decree to Peleus, in his natal hour! With joyful splendor and abundance blessed, he shone preeminent among mankind, and bravely ruled the warlike Myrmidons. To him, besides, a mortal though he was, the bounteous gods a goddess gave to wife. Yet even him has [Zeus's] all-ruling will afflicted. From his bed no princely race of gallant sons to regal sway succeeds. One only son is his, to early death predestined! Nor, while living, do I now cherish his age, but from my country far, continue here, a deadly bane to thee and thy unhappy sons. Thou, too, old man, as we have heard, hast been for bliss renowned. . . . And thou in children and in riches all the people of thy kingdom didst excel. But since the gods this dire calamity have brought upon thee, war and blood of men surround thy city. But to heaven submit, and yield not thou to sorrow uncontrolled, fruitless and vain. Thou canst not from the dead recall thy son: Ah! Sooner must thou feel thyself some other stroke of cruel fate.[36]

Achilles' sage reflection on the human condition is cut off when Priam suddenly recollects his mission and, banking on his fragile new bond with the Phthian prince, essentially demands to be shown Hector's corpse without further delay. Here Homer shows us that however much Achilles may have softened his heart and released his rage against the Trojan king, he is still acutely aware of their relative positions in the present conflict. No amount of sympathy for Priam can cause Achilles to abandon completely his immense pride and conviction of Greek superiority. His newfound respect for Priam does not blind Achilles to the fact that he still holds all the cards. He quickly reprimands Priam for taking a commanding tone with him and trying to insist where he ought to request humbly.

Then, having reasserted his dominance, demonstrating that he, and not Priam, is in control of the situation, Achilles sees to it that Hector's body is prepared for transport back to Troy. In doing so, he suffers a temporary pang of conscience regarding Patroclus. He worries that, even after all he has done to seek vengeance for his slain friend, Patroclus's shade (spirit or ghost) still may not approve of his making even temporary peace with Priam by allowing the ransom of Hector's remains. Here is the scene as Homer unfolds it:

To him majestic Priam thus replied: "Ah! Give me not a seat, . . . while Hector lies neglected in thy tent; but grant him quickly to my longing eyes, and take the ransom we have brought. Mayst thou enjoy that ransom, and return in peace to thy dear native land; since thou hast now permitted me to live and view the light." The stern Achilles, with a wrathful glance eyed him, and said: "Provoke me not, old man! I have determined Hector to release. . . . I know, nor canst thou hide it, some one of the gods conducted thee, O Priam, to the ships. No mortal would have dared, though young and bold, to penetrate, alone, [our] camp. Nor could, unnoticed by the guard, have passed, nor easily removed the ponderous beam and bolts, access preventing to my doors. Now, therefore, with thy sorrowful complaints urge me no farther, lest I suffer not even thee, a sacred suppliant, in my tent, and so infringe the dread commands of [Zeus]," he said; the monarch trembled and obeyed. Then, like a lion, from his tent rushed forth the fierce [Achilles]; not alone; with him, his warlike servants went. . . . [They], from the wain, removed the ransom of great Hector's head, ines- timably rich. Two cloths they left to shroud the dead, a splendid tunic, too, that covered decently the lifeless chief . . . that old Priam should not view his ghastly son; lest, agonized at heart, he might not wrath restrain, but irri- tate Achilles, who might slay him in his rage, infringing even the dread commands of [Zeus]. When now the maidens had the body bathed and well anointed, they around it drew the snow-white shroud and vest. Achilles' self, uplifting, laid it on the funeral bed. . . . Then, with a cry of lamentation, he the name invoked of his beloved friend: "Patroclus! Now, be not offended, if in [Hades] hall the tidings thou shalt hear, that I restore heroic Hector to his father's arms! For he a ransom not unseemly brings; of which a portion large, and worthy thee, I dedicate to thy lamented shade!" he said; and, thence returning to the tent, resumed his seat with carvings rich adorned, just opposite to Priam: then, again, he kindly thus the mourn- ful king addressed: "Thy son, old man, according to thy wish, is now restored. Upon the funeral bed he lies, and, with Aurora's early dawn, thou shalt behold him on his way to Troy. But let us now be mindful of repast; for even Niobe, unhappy dame, renounced not food when, in her palace, dead, all her twelve children lay: six blooming sons, and six fair daughters, slain together! . . . Come, then, let us, divine old man, to nourishment attend. Again hereafter, mayst thou mourn thy son, conveyed to [Troy]: many tears for him will then be shed, not without ample cause."[37]

After the two men dine together, they take the opportunity to size one another up, and both are impressed by what they see. They may be on opposite sides of the war, but assessing one another simply as men they find much to admire:[38]

When of meat and wine they had enough, and appetite had ceased, then Priam, son of Dardanus, admired Achilles, gazing over his manly shape and beauty; for he seemed a present god, in majesty and grace! Achilles, too, with admiration viewed the [Trojan] king; his noble aspect comely and benign, and charmed with listening to his sweet discourse. When each, delighted had the other viewed, the godlike senior said: "Now, loved of [Zeus], dismiss me to repose, that we the boon of sleep refreshing, may at last enjoy. For never have my sorrowing eyelids closed in slumber, since my hapless son was slain; but, groaning constantly, with boundless grief, prone have I lain on earth, groveling in dust, before my palace-gate. Now, also, food I first have tasted, and have swallowed wine, which, till this moment, never touched my lips," he said. Achilles bade forthwith his friends and captive maidens to prepare the beds.[39]

It is a scene that brings to mind the words of the stirring Rudyard Kipling poem "The Ballad of East and West," which also plays on the theme that even in the throes of conflict two men can recognize their shared humanity and respect one another's martial skills, commitment, and character. The poem tells the tale of Kamal, leader of nomads who regularly raid horses and provisions from a British army outpost in the British Indian Empire. After the British colonel's prized mare is ridden away by Kamal, the colonel's son mounts another horse (a dun) and rides off after the thief:

> They have ridden the low moon out of the sky, their hoofs drum up the dawn,
> The dun he went like a wounded bull, but the mare like a newroused fawn.
> The dun he fell at a watercourse in a woeful heap fell he,
> And Kamal has turned the red mare back, and pulled the rider free.
> He has knocked the pistol out of his hand small room was there to strive,
> "'Twas only by favour of mine," quoth he, "ye rode so long alive:
> There was not a rock for twenty mile, there was not a clump of tree,
> But covered a man of my own men with his rifle cocked on his knee.
> If I had raised my bridlehand, as I have held it low,
> The little jackals that flee so fast were feasting all in a row:
> If I had bowed my head on my breast, as I have held it high,
> The kite that whistles above us now were gorged till she could not fly."
> Lightly answered the Colonel's son: "Do good to bird and beast,
> But count who come for the broken meats before thou makest a feast.
> If there should follow a thousand swords to carry my bones away,
> Belike the price of a jackal's meal were more than a thief could pay. . . .
> But if thou thinkest the price be fair, thy brethren wait to sup,
> The hound is kin to the jackalspawn, howl, dog, and call them up!
> And if thou thinkest the price be high, in steer and gear and stack,
> Give me my father's mare again, and I'll fight my own way back!"
> Kamal has gripped him by the hand and set him upon his feet.
> "No talk shall be of dogs," said he, "when wolf and gray wolf meet.
> May I eat dirt if thou hast hurt of me in deed or breath;
> What dam of lances brought thee forth to jest at the dawn with Death?"
> Lightly answered the Colonel's son: "I hold by the blood of my clan:
> Take up the mare for my father's gift by God, she has carried a man!"
> . . . They have looked each other between the eyes, and there they found no fault,
> They have taken the Oath of the BrotherinBlood on leavened bread and salt:
> They have taken the Oath of the BrotherinBlood on fire and freshcut sod,
> On the hilt and the haft of the Khyber knife, and the Wondrous Names of God. . . .
> Oh, East is East, and West is West, and never the twain shall meet,
> Till Earth and Sky stand presently at God's great Judgment Seat;
> But there is neither East nor West, Border, nor Breed, nor Birth,
> When two strong men stand face to face, tho' they come from the ends of the earth![40]

Achilles not only returns Hector's corpse but also, as an added mark of respect, agrees to arrange a twelve-day cease-fire between the Greeks and the Trojans to allow time for the Trojans to give their dead defender a lavish funeral befitting his stature and heroic demise. As Priam leads the body back to Troy on a cart, his approach is spotted first by Cassandra, Hector's sister, who then gathers the other citizens of the doomed city together to honor their fallen champion:

> They to the town, with doleful cries and groans, the coursers drove, and mules, with Hector, dead. Their coming none perceived, of [Troy's] sons or lovely daughters, save Cassandra, fair as golden [Aphrodite]. . . . On the funeral bed she saw the lifeless corpse, and, with loud shrieks, proclaimed it through the town: "Ye Trojan men and Trojan women, hither come, and see your Hector dead, if ever ye rejoiced to meet him, glorious from the field of fame! For he was, erst, the glory and delight of [Troy] and his people!" Not a man or woman then was left within the town. All, by intolerable anguish driven, poured from the gates, and crowded round . . . in throngs tumultuous. Foremost of them all, the wife affectionate and mother fond embraced their Hector's head, and over him rent their hair in agony. Around them stood the multitude in tears. They would have wept and wailed their hero slain, there standing, sad, before the gates, even till the sun had set, if Priam, . . . had not restrained the sorrowing crowd: "Give way, and let the mules now pass. Hereafter ye may have your fill of mourning, when the dead is carried home."[41]

Although the entire city is in mourning, when Hector's body is laid out in state in the royal palace, it is the women of Troy who put their sorrow into words. So in the final scene of the *Iliad* the last descriptions of Hector, tamer of horses, come not from his fellow warriors but from three women who truly loved him: his wife, Andromache, his mother, Hecuba, and his erstwhile sister-in-law, Helen. Surely it is not insignificant that Homer gives the final speech in his epic to Helen of Troy, the beautiful woman so highly prized by two societies that her seduction brought them to war.

All three women praise Hector's character and nobility, but it is from Helen that we hear of his generous spirit. She speaks of Hector not as a warrior or a prince but as a gentle, understanding man who refused to blame others for his troubles. Even though the war that ripped his family apart and ended his hope for a happy, peaceful future was started when she ran off with Paris, Hector was one of the few people in Troy who always treated Helen with kindness and respect. Here are the lamentations made over Hector by the Trojan women:

> At the royal dome arrived, they laid great Hector on a splendid couch, and round him stationed masters of the song, singing a mournful dirge, in measured strains, with sounds of heartfelt woe. And, while they sang, the females' plaintive cries, responsive, rose. Among them, fair Andromache began her lamentation; in her snow-white arms clasping heroic Hector's

clay-cold cheek. "My husband! Thou hast fallen in thy prime of manhood, leaving me disconsolate, a helpless widow in thy lonely house. Our little son, a tender infant now, his days of manly strength will never attain. Long ere that time, this city overthrown will lie in ruins; thou, her only hope and guardian, thou, who bravely didst protect her matrons, and their infants, being gone! Ah! Soon those matrons must be forced away in Grecian ships, myself among the rest! Thou, too, my hapless boy, must go with me, condemned, a wretched slave, in servile tasks to labor, for some hard unfeeling lord. Or else, a ruthless Greek may hurl thee down from [Troy's] lofty tower,[42] tremendous death avenging so his brother or his sire or son beloved, whom Hector may have slain. For many of the Greeks, by Hector's arm, have bit the ground; for, in the cruel fight, thy father, o my son, was ever fierce. And therefore, now, his country mourns him dead! O Hector! Thou, unutterable grief and agony hast on thy parents brought. But woes exceeding all to me hast left! For, in thy dying moments, thy dear hand was not extended, from thy bed, to me. Nor didst thou speak one last momentous word which I had always treasured in my heart, remembering, night and day, with pensive tears." Weeping, she spake. The matrons wailed around, and Hecuba, among them, vents her grief: "O Hector! Dearest to my heart, by far, of all my children! Surely, when alive, thou wast a favorite of the gods; for now, when cold in death, thy corpse has been their care. My other sons, by stern Achilles seized, were sold by him, beyond the barren main, to Samos, Imbras, and the bleak, rough coast of rocky Lemnos. But, bereaving thee of life by ruthless steel, he dragged thee oft, with unrelenting rage, around the tomb of him thy valor slew; disgraceful act, which did not him restore to life; yet fresh thou still continuest, like one newly dead, whom [Apollo's] silver bow, with arrows mild, has gently slain." So spake the weeping dame, exciting in the multitude around ungovernable grief. Among them next unhappy Helen, thus her woe expressed: "Hector! Beloved most by me, of all my consort's brethren! Paris, truly, graced with godlike beauty, is my consort now, who brought me from my home! Ah! Would to heaven that I had died before that fatal day! This, now, I count the twentieth tedious year since first I hither came, and left, alas, my native country. Yet no angry word or scornful have I ever heard from thee! And if, at any time, another's tongue reproached me; of thy brothers or their wives or sisters clad in robes with sweeping trains, or else thy mother; for thy sire has been indulgent still, as if his child I were, thou didst rebuke them, and their wrath disarm by thy benignity and soothing speech. I therefore weep, with aching heart, for thee, and mourn, with thine, my own unhappy fate. For no one now, in spacious Troy, remains a friend to me, but all abhor me quite." So spake the lovely mourner. Groan for groan the crowd immense reechoed.[43]

Although the *Iliad* begins with the rage of Achilles, it ends with an account of the Trojan's funeral for their fallen prince, Hector:

Nine successive days they toiled, and brought, from Ida's hills, huge heaps of wood. When the tenth morning rosy light from heaven to men displayed, they, weeping, carried forth what once was valiant Hector. On the pile they laid that breathless body; kindling soon aspiring flames; and, when appeared again the rosy-fingered daughter of the dawn, Aurora, then all [Troy] was convened around the pyre of Hector, chief of men. When they had met, and full the concourse, first they quench with dark-red wine, the glimmering fire and glowing embers, next his brethren sad and fond associates carefully collect his snow-white bones, bemoaning as they toiled and bathing with abundant tears their cheeks, these they deposit in a golden urn, which purple cloths, of texture glossy smooth, from eyes of mortals hid. Then in the grave they laid it, covered thick with heavy stones, and over it diligently raised a tomb; while, stationed all around were watchful guards, lest, ere the work was done, the warlike Greeks should, unawares, assail them. Having heaped the lofty mound, they thence to Troy returned, and there, assembled in the splendid halls of Priam, . . . enjoyed a sumptuous banquet. So the funeral rites they finished, to illustrious Hector due.[44]

The rest of the tale of the Trojan War, including the death of Achilles (shot in the heel with an arrow by Paris, whose aim was aided by Apollo) and the famous trick of the wooden horse, are recounted elsewhere but do not figure in Homer's poem (at least as it has been handed down to us). Homer's second epic, the *Odyssey*, is set after the fall of Troy and follows the adventures of the homeward-bound Odysseus, trying to return at last to his faithful wife, Penelope, and now young adult son, Telemachus.

The themes of the *Odyssey* are different from those of the *Iliad*, and Odysseus is an entirely new kind of warrior, quite distinct from either the fierce and passionate Achilles or the kind and honorable Hector. Odysseus uses his wits, not just his strength, to conquer his opponents. He relies on trickery, luck, imagination, and the patronage of the goddess Athena to whisk him, with varying success, through the rough spots of his journey. He is a transitional figure, taking Greek culture from the warrior ethic of the Trojan War era into a new age in which the city-state of Athens (whose citizens, like Odysseus, are devoted to Athena), acting under a new code, will come to forge a small empire using intelligence and strategy instead of size and strength.

The symbolic importance of Odysseus is only heightened by the fact that after the death of Achilles it is Odysseus, and not the more traditional warrior Ajax, who is awarded Achilles' splendid armor, saved from Trojan plunder. When Achilles is killed, Odysseus fights off the Trojans so that Ajax can carry the Phthian prince's body back to the Greek encampment. Once there, Ajax tries to claim the armor, as Achilles' natural heir on the battlefield. The other Greeks protest that while Ajax carried the corpse, it was Odysseus who protected it with his sword. After they award the armor to Odysseus on those grounds, Ajax commits suicide.

Ajax seems second only to Achilles for sheer fighting ability but, like Achilles, is never noted for his wit or eloquence. In fact, Homer mocks Ajax by having him trip (thanks to some interference by Athena) and fall face-down into a pile of dung while competing in a footrace against

Odysseus. It may not be stretching the symbolism to say that Ajax stumbles owing to his lack of wisdom, while Odysseus, the new breed of intelligent warrior, carries the day. While Odysseus, like Hector, has a family he loves and a full life waiting for him beyond the war, Ajax, like Achilles, cannot find any meaning in his existence once he has been stripped of his honor on the Trojan field. There is no future after Troy for his type of warrior, whose only cause is the quest for glory and the recognition of his peers.

The two central figures of the *Iliad*, Hector and Achilles, embraced similar beliefs about the role of fate in directing human lives and the importance of maintaining honor and avoiding shame. But their characters sustain many more contrasts than comparisons. Achilles sets his own standards of conduct and relies exclusively on his own internal judgments of when he is deserving of honor and when he should feel shame. Hector derives his code from the collective judgment of his culture and his peers. Both had great martial prowess, but Achilles fought for personal reasons and was not concerned with the welfare of others (except his friend Patroclus), while Hector fought to defend Troy and her people from harm. Achilles dreamt of no future beyond the battlefield, while Hector longed for a peaceful life at home with his beloved family. Achilles was consumed by rage, Hector driven by duty.

Which man is the more ideal warrior? Which embodies a more noble code? Is the lesson of the *Iliad*, as I have heard a fair number of my students insist, that the greatest warrior would be a Hector who wins? Homer leaves these questions unanswered. Achilles is the victor when the two men clash on the dusty plains of Troy, but when Troy falls at last, neither warrior is alive to see it. Achilles' death is not recorded by Homer, yet in the *Odyssey* Homer arranges for the wandering Odysseus to encounter the very bitter ghost of Achilles, who declares his disdain for the empty glory he sought in life. And in the closing pages of the *Iliad*, it is Hector who receives final honors from his own mortal enemy as well as from the city, and in particular the women he tried so desperately to defend.

NOTES

1. Michael Wood, *In Search of the Trojan War* (New York: Penguin, Plume Books, 1985), 124.

2. For a clear summary and excellent discussion of this debate, again I recommend Michael Wood's *In Search of the Trojan War.*

3. Wood, *Trojan War*, 130.

4. Wood, *Trojan War*, 30–36.

5. Wood, *Trojan War*, 35.

6. Patrick Shaw-Stewart, "Untitled," cited in Wood, *Trojan War*, 35.

7. Midshipman Richard Alderson was the first of my students to give this response.

8. Homer, *Iliad*, trans. William Munford (Boston: Little & Brown, 1846), 22.58–70. All references are to this translation unless otherwise noted.

9. Homer, *Iliad*, trans. E. V. Rieu (Harmondsworth, England: Penguin Books, 1950), 3.38–57.

10. Homer, Iliad, trans. Rieu, 4.93–99.

11. Homer, *Iliad*, 6.374–89.

12. Homer, *Iliad*, 6.406–13.

13. Homer, *Iliad*, 6.441–46.

14. Sofia Souli, *Greek Mythology* (Athens: M. Toubis, 1995), 131.

15. Homer, *Iliad*, 1.203–22.

16. William Butler Yeats, *Selected Poems: Lyrical and Narrative* (London: Macmillan, 1930), 141.

17. Edward Tripp, *The Meridian Handbook of Classical Mythology* (New York: Penguin, New American Library, 1970), 449.

18. Homer, *Iliad*, 12.421–46.

19. Homer, *Iliad*, 1.460–67.

20. Homer, *Iliad*, trans. Rieu, 16.31–32.

21. Homer, *Iliad*, 16.67–85.

22. Homer, *Iliad*, 16.267–81.

23. Homer, *Iliad*, 16.600–621.

24. Homer, *Iliad*, 16.661–81.

25. Homer, *Iliad*, 18.94–127.

26. Homer, *Iliad*, 22.140–86.

27. Aristotle, *Nicomachean Ethics*, in *A New Aristotle Reader*, trans. J. L. Ackrill, (Princeton: Princeton University Press, 1987), 3.9.7–20.

28. Aristotle, *Nicomachean Ethics*, 10.9.30–31.

29. Homer, *Iliad*, 22.351–63.

30. Homer, *Iliad*, 22.364–71.

31. Homer, *Iliad*, 22.413–31.

32. Homer, *Iliad*, 22.460–510.

33. Homer, *Iliad*, 24.345–60.

34. Homer, *Iliad*, 24.650–700.

35. Homer, *Iliad*, 24.695–720.

36. Homer, *Iliad*, 24.720–61.

37. Homer, *Iliad*, 24.762–859.

38. Outside of the *Iliad*, Greek mythology tells the story that Achilles, shortly after the death of Hector, literally finds love with an enemy on the battlefield when he falls for the Trojan ally Penthesilea, an Amazon queen. Unfortunately, the consistently ill-fated Achilles only recognizes his love for her *after* he has struck her a mortal blow in single combat. Once again, the joy of life is denied him.

39. Homer, *Iliad*, 24.869–90.

40. Rudyard Kipling, "Ballad of East and West," in *Collected Verse* (Garden City, N.Y.: Doubleday, 1907), 136–41.

41. Homer, *Iliad*, 24.963–92.

42. This is in fact the fate of Hector's infant son, according to legend.

43. Homer, *Iliad*, 24.994–1074.

44. Homer, *Iliad*, 24.1083–111.

3

The Two Faces of Rome: Stoicism and Hedonism

From the year 31 B.C. when the first official emperor of Rome, Augustus Caesar, assumed power until the great civilization slowly toppled and fell four centuries later,[1] the legionaries of the Roman Empire set the gold standard for martial excellence across the ancient world. Many books have been written about the history of the Roman Empire, and I will not attempt to summarize that lengthy history here. Our interest is in the *values* of ancient Rome and the philosophical perspectives that influenced her warrior class: the soldiers of the Roman legions.

A popular household god among the pagan, polytheistic citizens of Rome was Janus, the two-faced god. Janus was thought to be an ideal guardian for the Roman home, since his double set of eyes allowed him to keep a close watch in two directions at once. But the image of Janus also provides a useful analogy for the discussion of Roman values, for in Roman culture we find vivid illustrations of two extremes: self-discipline and self-indulgence.

The Romans adopted many of the religious beliefs of the Greeks, including their Olympic gods. These gods were given Roman names (Zeus became Jove, Hera became Juno, Aphrodite became Venus, Ares became Mars, Athena became Minerva, and so on), but they retained the Greek conceptions of their powers and attributes. Greek traditions of worship were assimilated as well, such as shrines, offerings, and animal sacrifices. Many Romans accepted the Greek belief that after death their souls would journey to a sad, gray underworld ruled by the gloomy god Hades (called Pluto by the Romans) and his reluctant queen, Persephone (Proserpine). Some thought that a lucky few—great warriors or leaders, perhaps—might be taken up to Olympus itself to live with the gods or else be allowed to enjoy eternity in an Eden-like setting known as the Elysian fields.

The Romans took great pride in their practical achievements. They were successful and efficient architects, engineers, soldiers, administrators, and statesmen. For many educated Romans, the more romantic or spiritual aspects of the accepted Greco-Roman religion, including its vision of life after death, were difficult to swallow. In addition, there was little moral guidance to be found in the behavior of the Olympic gods and goddesses. So for those who wished to wrestle further with questions of ethics and the meaning of human existence, the Roman philosophical community offered alternative schools of thought.

Two of these schools of thought made available to disenchanted Romans were again Greek imports: Stoicism and hedonism. Both philosophies rejected the tenets of the standard Greco-Roman religion, including the belief in life after death. They focused instead on how to live the good life here on earth. However, beyond their aim and earthly focus, these views had little in common. Like those of the god Janus, these two faces of Rome looked in very different directions for the answers that they sought.

For the purposes of trying to reconstruct the Roman code of the warrior, we should first follow Janus's gaze toward the precepts of Stoicism. In his book *The Romans,* historian R. H. Barrow comments that "the Romans were natural Stoics long before they heard of Stoicism."[2] He notes that Roman philosophers generally did not attempt to create their own original theories but rather had a tendency to shop around established doctrines, selecting and assembling points that appealed to them:

> No Roman adopted the whole of any philosophy; some parts did not interest him, other parts he adapted to his own instinctive beliefs and found in them a statement of what he had never clearly articulated for himself. It may perhaps be an exaggeration to say that the Roman adopted only what suited his Roman ideals, for undoubtedly philosophical studies did influence the conduct and outlook of many. But certainly the Roman was not greatly interested in the coherence of a system, or in pursuing the fundamental questions of metaphysics. He was interested primarily in action and its springs and justification. Hence Roman philosophy is largely eclectic, and it is concerned chiefly with morals.[3]

Given the Roman habit of evaluating moral theories by the "gut-check" method, it may help us to understand their attraction to Stoicism if we begin with a sketch of the Roman character. In a valuable summary of Roman ideals, Barrow highlights the qualities of character that the Romans most admired:

> *Gravitas* means a 'sense of the importance of the matters in hand', a sense of responsibility and earnestness. It is a term to apply at all levels—to a statesman or a general as he shows appreciation of his responsibilities, to a citizen as he casts his vote with consciousness of its importance, to a friend who

gives his advice based on his experience and on regard for your welfare. . . . It is the opposite of *levitas*, a quality the Romans despised, which means trifling when you should be serious, flippancy, instability. *Gravitas* is often joined with *constantia*, firmness of purpose, or with *firmitas*, tenacity; it may be seasoned with *comitas*, which means the relief given to over-seriousness by ease of manner, good humour, and humour. *Disciplina* is the training which provides steadiness of character; *industria* is hard work; *virtus* is manliness and energy; *clementia*, the willingness to forgo one's rights; *frugalitas*, simple tastes.[4]

Keeping in mind this construction of Roman virtues, let us now consider the central points of Stoic ethics as they may have appealed to the Roman mind.

The philosopher Zeno, who taught in Athens until his death in 263 B.C., is credited with having founded the Stoic school of philosophy. Zeno had a habit of lecturing to his students from the front porch, or *stoa*, and it is from this that the word "Stoicism" is derived. By all accounts Zeno was a charismatic teacher who persuaded many followers to adopt Stoic principles. Along with his most famous pupil, Cleanthes, Zeno was viewed by his contemporaries as something of a political or religious activist.[5]

Zeno challenged the conventional wisdom, which held that any human being's hope for happiness rested entirely in the hands of fate or some other unyielding and amoral divine power. It was thought by some that Zeus himself, ruler of all the Olympic gods, whimsically parceled out unequal portions of joy and sorrow to all the poor, helpless mortals who were his playthings. (Recall that this was the Homeric view expressed by the character Achilles in the final book of the *Iliad*.)

While Zeno did believe firmly in fate, he did not believe it, or the callousness of any imagined deity, to be responsible for an individual's happiness. He told his students that only they themselves could be held responsible for their emotional experience of life. He taught that the key to both happiness and virtue lay in understanding the nature of control.

As rational creatures, we naturally want to control our lives and organize our world so that we get to enjoy as many pleasant moments as possible while avoiding that which is unpleasant. Generally speaking, we all want to possess the same sorts of goods, such as health, love, friendship, success, wealth, and respect, while avoiding the evils of pain, illness, death, loneliness, failure, poverty, and ignominy. We tend to envy the man or woman who is presented with the many opportunities for delight and pity the one who seems overburdened with occasions for sorrow.

Unfortunately, we seem to exercise little control over the goods that we crave. I can try to take care of my physical self, but no amount of healthy living will shield me from all injury or disease, and my eventual death is a certainty. Nor can I protect the people whom I love from illness, injury, or death. I cannot be certain that those I love will love me back or that I will ever find a mate with whom I am well matched. The ultimate success of many of my projects depends on factors beyond my control, as does my financial status. Even my reputation can be ruined through no fault of my own if my enemies choose to malign me.

Rather than concluding from these dismal points that my happiness is completely out of my own hands, Zeno would have urged me to reconsider where and on what I have chosen to pin my happiness. The central tenet of Stoicism is that it is in your power to direct whether or not you live a good life, a life worth living. But first you must recognize that what constitutes a good life is not acquisition of those goods found outside yourself that you cannot control. Instead, living the good life depends on cultivating those internal goods that can be made immune to the unfeeling machinations of fate.

According to Stoicism, the one thing we always control is our own will. And it is by our will that we decide how to respond to events in our lives. We have exclusive rule over our inner selves: our mind and emotions. None of us can control whether or not our bodies will remain healthy. However, Zeno assured his students, if we are struck down by an ailment, the way we allow that fate to affect our inner selves is entirely up to us.

Stoics hold the view that nothing that happens to you has the power to make you unhappy unless you choose to let it. Unhappiness comes from wanting what you cannot have. Happiness is achieved by willing yourself to be satisfied with whatever external goods destiny decides to bestow upon you while focusing your energy on improving your inner self so that you can always enjoy those internal goods that no external force can strip away from you, such as your own good character, honor, and integrity.

Stoic philosophy was already an influence in Rome in the last days of the republic, before the rise of Julius Caesar and his nephew Augustus. One of the most prominent early proponents of Stoicism was the influential orator and statesman, Marcus Tullius Cicero. As a man dedicated to public life (he was a successful lawyer who argued many famous cases before the Roman senate, he held the high office of consul of Rome in 63 B.C. and put down an attempted coup d'état, and he served from 51 to 50 B.C. as governor of the Roman province of Cilicia in Asia Minor), Cicero was attracted to the Stoic emphasis on order, duty, and self-discipline. He wrote several essays promoting Stoic ethics, including *On Duties*, *The Boundaries of Good and Evil*, *On Friendship*, *On the Laws*, and *On the State*.

Building on the lessons of the early stoa, Cicero's essays emphasize that the greatest loss anyone can suffer is the loss of character, the lapse of virtue. Since there is no life after death in the Stoic vision, the time that we have on earth is our only opportunity to define ourselves. We can choose to exhibit nobility of character by always doing our moral duty and behaving honorably toward our fellow human beings, or else we can abandon the pursuit of virtue, undercut others to achieve our own selfish ends, and expend our energies on the pursuit of meaningless pleasures and transient goods. Not only is the noble life morally superior, but also it is ultimately more satisfying, since the goals we set for our own character development are within our power to realize, whereas, as Zeno taught, our quests for externally based happiness are likely to be frustrated by twists of fate.

In his essay *How to Make the Right Decisions*, Cicero writes:

> a man who wrongs another for his own benefit either imagines, presumably, that he is not doing anything unnatural, or he does not agree that death, destitution, pain, the loss of children, relations, friends, are less deplorable than doing wrong to another person. But if he sees nothing unnatural in wronging a fellow-being, how can you argue with him?—he is taking away from man all that makes him man. If, however, he concedes that this ought to be avoided, but regards death, destitution, and pain as even more undesirable, he is mistaken in believing that any damage, either to his person or his property, is worse than moral failure.[6]

This passage of Cicero's highlights the demanding nature of Stoic ethics. The dedicated Stoic must be so committed to his moral duty that no physical or emotional distractions will be able to sway him or her from doing what is right. Not even the loss of a loved one can be claimed as justification for the most minor moral infraction.

Cicero himself was criticized by his Stoic friend Servius Rufus for using the untimely death of his beloved daughter Tullia in 45 B.C. as an excuse for withdrawing from public life. A letter from Servius to Cicero has survived the years, providing us a unique insight into practical Stoic thought. In the following passage, Servius attempts to console Cicero for his loss, while reminding him of his Stoic obligations:

> I want to tell you something which brought me no small comfort; perhaps this same thought can lessen your grief. When I was returning from Asia, . . . I began to look at the regions all around me. Behind me was Aegina, in front was Megara, on the right Piraeus, on the left Corinth. These were once flourishing towns, but now they lay lifeless and ruined before my eyes. I began to think to myself: "Ah! Are we little men, whose lives are necessarily too brief, indignant if one of us dies or is killed, when in one place so many corpses of towns lie abandoned? Please pull yourself together, Servius, and remember that you were born a mortal man." Believe me, I was strengthened considerably by this thought. If it seems to you wise, please put this same image before your eyes. Just a short time ago, so many illustrious men perished, so serious a weakening of the power of the Roman state took place, all our provinces were shaken to their very foundations; are you moved by such deep sorrow if we lose the frail little soul of one frail little woman? Even if she had not died at this time, she must nevertheless

have died a few years from now because she was born a mortal. Take your mind and your thoughts away from these things and reflect instead on things which are worthy of the person that you are. Consider, for example, that she lived as long as it was necessary, that is, she lived as long as the republic lived. She saw you, her father, a praetor, then a consul, and an augur, she was married to men from noble families; she enjoyed almost all of life's blessings. And she departed from life when the republic died. How, then, can you or she complain about fate on this account?

Do not, in short, forget that you are Cicero, a man who was accustomed to counsel others and to give advice. Don't act like a bad doctor who professes to have medical knowledge about other people's ailments but is unable to cure himself. Instead, bring to your own attention and place before your mind that advice which you are accustomed to offer to others. There is no grief which the passage of time does not lessen or soften; but it is unworthy of you to wait for the time to pass rather than anticipating this result with your own good sense. . . . [Y]ield to your fatherland so that, if need arises, it can use your service and counsel. . . .

. . . We have, on a number of occasions, seen you sustain good fortune very decorously and thereby gain great glory. Now act in such a way that we may know that you can also sustain bad fortune just as decorously and that it does not seem to you a greater burden than it should be, lest you, who are endowed with all fine qualities, appear to lack this one.[7]

Servius's charge that Cicero must start to practice the Stoicism he has preached now that he is confronted with a personal tragedy may not strike us as especially warm or understanding, coming from a friend. But it is certainly consistent with Stoic teachings. It would be meaningless to claim a commitment to Stoicism and then crumble at the first test of fortitude. As Servius delicately observes in the last paragraph quoted above, to be Stoic in the face of *good* fortune is not enough. The true Stoic should be able to find contentment through virtue, duty, and self-discipline even in the most brutal circumstances.

There were several other well-known Stoics of the Roman era who attempted despite serious personal trials to embody the principles they advocated. Three of the most famous of these were Seneca the Younger, Epictetus, and Emperor Marcus Aurelius. Some have questioned Seneca's successful adherence to his Stoic beliefs, but most historians agree that the lives of Epictetus and Aurelius did in fact do justice to the ideals they embraced.

Seneca the Younger lived from 4 B.C. to 65 A.D. and served as an adviser to two of the Julio-Claudian emperors, Claudius and Nero. In Nero's youth, Seneca also played the role of a tutor, although he apparently failed to indoctrinate the future tyrant with any Stoic principles. Seneca was a prolific writer, producing numerous tragic plays, essays, letters, and epigrams, many of which have been preserved. All of his works, whether fiction or nonfiction, feature Stoic themes.

Seneca paid particular attention in his Stoic writing to the subjects of fate and death. He drew an analogy between a human life in the hands of fate and a dog being walked on a leash. The dog on the leash has two choices. He is going to be taken from point A to point B; that much is unavoidable. But it is up to him whether he fights the leash and forces his trainer to drag him from A to B, protesting painfully all along the way, or whether he chooses instead to cover the distance in a calm and orderly fashion, accepting without question his trainer's view that to go from A to B is the most rational thing for him to do. For humans, fate is the leash; and God, understood as the source of all logic and order in the universe, is the trainer. So Seneca writes in *An Essay about Providence:*

> Good men are not dragged by Fate; they follow it and keep in step. . . .
> Demetrius said: "I am not being forced into anything and I am not putting up with anything against my will. I do not submit to God, I agree with him, and I strongly agree with him because I know that all things happen according to a law which is valid and established for eternity."[8]

Here we clearly see Stoic metaphysics affecting Stoic ethics. As already noted, the Stoics did not accept the idea that their lives were ruled by a pantheon of capricious gods and goddesses who held court up in the heavens. Rather, they believed the universe to be an ordered place, governed by reason: a well-oiled machine set up to run a smooth course. Every individual has a duty to try to understand what part he or she is supposed to play in the grand scheme of things and then to play that part to the best of his or her abilities and without complaint.

Historian Jo-Ann Shelton explains this aspect of Stoic philosophy in *As the Romans Did:* "For the Stoics, . . . the plan in the universe—called Nature, God, Fate, Providence and so on—was rational and was, in fact, Reason (*ratio*) itself. Since man's soul was part of this Reason or plan, he would be truly happy only when he allowed Reason to govern his life. He would then be in harmony with the spirit of the universe (with Nature, God, Fate, etc.)."[9] Her analysis is well supported by further comments about nature, reason, and fate in the *Letters* of Seneca:

> We Stoics maintain that happiness is living in accordance with Nature. . . .
> Only that which is perfectly in accordance with Nature as a whole is truly perfect. And Nature as a whole is rational.[10]

> For the man who is in perfect harmony with Nature, his every plan will coincide with the plan of Nature (Fate or Providence). He will choose of his free will to do what Fate had planned for him to do. He will thus never suffer anxiety or distress.[11]

> The truly wise man does nothing unwillingly. He escapes necessity because he chooses to do, of his free will, whatever necessity would later force him to do.[12]

When Seneca writes about death, he insists that death is not an evil. If there is no life after death, then the state of being dead is simply the state of nonexistence. There is no self left after death to experience anything at all, negative or positive. Suffering requires existence; therefore death is freedom from suffering. Those who fear death, Seneca contends, are deluded by their mistaken belief in an afterlife. These views are clearly expressed in the following epigram by Seneca, translated into English by John Wilmot, earl of Rochester (1647–1680):

Death Is Nothing

After death nothing is, and nothing death:
The utmost limits of a gasp of breath.
Let the ambitious zealot lay aside
His hopes of heaven; whose faith is but his pride.
Let slavish souls lay by their feat,
Nor be concerned which way or where
After this life they shall be hurled:
Dead, we become the lumber of the world,
And to that mass of matter shall be swept
Where things destroyed with things unborn are kept:
Devouring time swallows us whole,
Impartial death confounds body and soul.
For Hell, and the foul Fiend that rules[13]
The everlasting fiery gaols,
Devised by rogues, dreaded by fools,
With his grim grisly dog that keeps the door,
Are senseless stories, idle tales,
Dreams, whimsies, and no more.

Seneca staunchly supported the Stoic belief that taking one's own life is warranted if the only alternative is to fail one's moral duty in some way. Since death is nothing, a true Stoic should never allow the fear of death to drive him or her to act dishonorably. Suicide should always be preferable to forsaking one's commitments, even under duress. In the following two excerpts from his *Letters*, Seneca first explains why a virtuous person should be willing to commit suicide and then provides examples of two suicides undertaken with the proper attitude, reflecting the prioritizing of one's character above one's physical self:

I will not allow any wound to penetrate through the body to the real me. My body is that part of me which can be injured; but within this fragile dwelling-place lives a soul which is free. And never will that flesh drive me to fear, never to a role which is unworthy of a good man. Never will I tell lies for the sake of this silly little body. Whenever it seems the right time, I will end my partnership with the body.[14]

Recently, . . . a German who was destined to be one of the wild animal fighters at a public entertainment was preparing for the morning show. He withdrew from the rest for a moment to relieve himself (he was given no other
opportunity to withdraw without a guard). There, in the toilet area, he
found a wooden stick with a sponge attached to the end (it was used for
wiping away the excrement). He stuffed the whole thing down his throat
and choked to death. . . . Though apparently without any resources, he
devised both a method and a means of death. From his example you, too,
can learn that the only thing which makes us hesitate to die is the lack of
will. . . . Recently, again, when a man was being carted off under close guard
to the morning show, he pretended to nod his head in sleep. Then he lowered his head until he had stuck it between the spokes of the cartwheel, and
remained calmly in his seat until his neck was broken by the turning wheel.
And so, he used the very vehicle which was carrying him to punishment to
escape it.[15]

The examples that he gives are both of men opting to die at their own
hands rather than permit their deaths to become base spectacles for the
entertainment of the Roman masses. The German to whom he refers is no
doubt a prisoner of war from the Roman campaigns against the Germanic tribes. Romans would commonly parade their captured opponents
before their own cheering populations as an act of pro-war propaganda
and then force them to fight wild beasts (or each other) in an arena, surrounded by jeering crowds baying for their blood.

As I hinted earlier, Seneca may not at all times have lived up to the
noble principles he espoused. It is difficult to imagine anyone working
for the corrupt Emperor Nero for so many years without compromising
his integrity to some degree. And there were charges made against
Seneca in the Roman senate that his enormous financial gains while in
Nero's employ were suspicious and suggested unethical dealings. Nero
himself cast aspersions on Seneca's credibility by demanding, "'By what
wisdom, by what philosophical precepts had he made 300 million ses-
terces in four years of friendship with the emperor?'"[16] As historian Colin
Wells notes, "It was a valid, damning and unanswerable question."[17]
However, when he finally fell completely out of favor with Nero, Seneca
reasserted his Stoicism by choosing to commit suicide rather than be
party to the perverse pleasure the emperor might have taken in having
him executed.

Despite his own possible shortcomings, Seneca did an excellent job of
expressing the Stoic tenet that what should matter most to any human
being are those things that can never be taken away. The Stoic wisdom
Seneca presented was the view that nothing or no one can do damage to
your character without your complicity. Fate controls many things, but
not your own possession, or lack, of virtue (virtus). In his Essay about Con-
stancy, Seneca writes:

The wise man cannot suffer injury or loss, because he keeps all his "valu-
ables" within himself and trusts nothing to Fortune. He has "goods" which
are safe and secure because he finds satisfaction in *virtus*, which does not
depend on chance occurrences. . . . Fortune does not snatch away what she
herself has not given; and certainly *virtus* is not a gift of Fortune, so it cannot be taken from us. *Virtus* is free, inviolable, immovable, unshaken, and so
steeled against the blows of chance that it cannot be bent, much less toppled. It looks straight at the instruments of torture and does not flinch; its
expression never changes, whether adversity or prosperity comes into its
view. The wise man therefore will lose nothing which he might perceive as
a loss, for his only possession is *virtus*, and he can never be separated from
it. He treats everything else like someone else's property, and who can be
distressed by the loss of things which are not yours? And so it follows that
if injury can do no harm to the things which truly belong to the wise man,
and if his things are secure because his virtus is secure, then injury cannot
harm the wise man.[18]

Seneca's position is that we are ourselves fully responsible for devel-
oping the excellence of our own characters. This should be the central project of our lives. And he advises in his *Letters* that we take advantage of
the few peaceful moments we are given to prepare for the more demanding ones:

The soul should use times of security to prepare itself for harsh circumstances. It should fortify itself, when enjoying the blessings of Fortune,
against the blows of Fortune. A soldier practices maneuvers during peacetime and constructs defensive ramparts, although no enemy is near, and
wearies himself with nonessential exertion so that he can be ready for necessary exertion. If you don't want someone to panic in a crisis, you must
train him before the crisis. And people who simulate poverty every month
and come close to real need are following the same plan as the soldier, so
that they will never panic at what they have often learned to deal with.[19]

The great Stoic writer Epictetus, who was born about five or ten years
before Seneca's death (historians dispute the date of his birth), actually
appears to have employed all of the demanding precepts of Stoicism in
the direction of his own life, despite (or perhaps because of) the many
challenges he faced. Born the son of a slave mother, Epictetus was himself
enslaved to a freedman by the name of Epaphroditus, who may have been
the emperor Nero's administrative secretary. It was Epaphroditus who
sent Epictetus to be educated by a philosopher named C. Musonius
Rufus, a powerful proponent of the Stoic perspective.[20] Ironically, Epaphroditus then provided the first testing grounds for Epictetus's Stoicism
by punishing and even torturing him for no reason other than his own
sadistic pleasure. According to one story, Epictetus was left with a permanently lame leg after Epaphroditus twisted it with such force that he
destroyed the knee joint.

It is not clear how or why, but Epictetus was eventually set free and became a teacher of Stoic philosophy in Rome. He taught there for many years until he was expelled in 89 A.D. by the emperor Domitian, who viewed Stoicism as subversive. (Epictetus got off lightly; in 93 A.D. Domitian had several "subversive" Stoics executed.) Epictetus then moved to Nicopolis in northwest Greece, where he set up his own school of philosophy and continued to advance Stoic views. He never wrote down any of his teachings, but notes from his lectures taken by one of his students were preserved and are now known as the *Enchiridion*, or handbook, of Epictetus.

Providing a portrait of the philosopher for the *Encyclopedia of Philosophy*, Philip Hallie describes Epictetus as "a man of great sweetness, as well as personal simplicity, who was humble, charitable, and especially loving towards children, but he was also possessed of great moral and religious intensity."[21] The details of Epictetus's life bear out this description:

> In his old age he married in order to bring up a child whose parents, friends of his, were going to expose it. In Rome and in Nicopolis he lived in a house with only a rush mat, a simple pallet, and an earthenware lamp (after the iron one was stolen).
>
> ... Epictetus was a moral activist, insisting on rigorous, continuing moral instruction and effort. Thus, he required daily self-examination, whose ultimate purpose was to learn how to judge one's actions clearly and firmly; he wanted each man to see that he alone was totally responsible for his deeds because he had given his assent to the external circumstances of the deed. . . . Epictetus was one of the great defenders of the prosopon, or proper character and personality of a man. He insisted that each man was free to mold it and had an obligation to the rest of the world to display it once it was molded.[22]

The contents of the *Enchiridion* echo the insights that I have already summarized from the writings of earlier Stoics. In relating Stoic principles, Epictetus places special emphasis on personal responsibility and accountability. The Stoicism he describes requires constant self-vigilance and mental discipline. If you allow anything to disturb you or cause you distress, you have nothing to blame but your own weakness of will. When you become a true Stoic, you will have no more need to blame anyone (including yourself) for anything, because no real harm (that is, nothing that you allow yourself to consider a harm) will ever befall you:

> When . . . we are impeded or disturbed or grieved, let us never blame others, but ourselves, that is, our opinions. It is the act of an ill-instructed man to blame others for his own bad condition; it is the act of one who has begun to be instructed, to lay the blame on himself; and of one whose instruction is completed, neither to blame another, nor himself.[23]

Epictetus urges Stoics-in-training to view everything that happens to

them as an opportunity to strengthen particular virtues within themselves. Nothing that appears bad is really so if seen in the right light: as a
possible step toward self-perfection. Thus he offers the following advice:

> On the occasion of every accident (event) that befalls you, remember to turn
> to yourself and inquire what power you have for turning it to use. If you see
> a fair man or a fair woman, you will find that the power to resist is temper-
> ance (continence). If labor (pain) be presented to you, you will find that it is
> endurance. If it be abusive words, you will find it to be patience. And if you
> have been thus formed to the (proper) habit, the appearances will not carry
> you along with them.[24]

A great deal of the *Enchiridion* also deals with the importance of
detaching yourself from emotional ties that have the power to distract
you from your duties. Epictetus does not advocate the adoption of a her-
mit's life. He expects his pupils to acquire friends, husbands, wives, and
children. But he insists that affection for these persons must never be separated in the mind from the awareness that the enjoyment of their company is necessarily temporary. These excerpts stress the importance of
Stoic detachment:

> In everything which pleases the soul, or supplies a want, or is loved,
> remember to add this to the (description, notion): What is the nature of each
> thing, beginning from the smallest? If you love an earthen vessel, say it is an
> earthen vessel which you love; for when it has been broken, you will not be
> disturbed. If you are kissing your child or wife, say that it is a human being
> whom you are kissing, for when the wife or child dies, you will not be dis-
> turbed.[25]

> As on a voyage when the vessel has reached a port, if you go out to get
> water, it is an amusement by the way to pick up a shellfish or some bulb, but
> your thoughts ought to be directed to the ship, and you ought to be con-
> stantly watching if the captain should call, and then you must throw away
> all those things, that you may not be bound and pitched into the ship like
> sheep: so in life also, if there be given to you instead of a little bulb and a
> shell a wife and a child, there will be nothing to prevent (you from taking
> them). But if the captain should call, run to the ship, and leave all those
> things without regard to them.[26]

> Never say about anything, I have lost it, but say I have restored it. Is your
> child dead? It has been restored. Is your wife dead? She has been restored.
> Has your estate been taken from you? Has not then this also been restored?
> But he who has taken it from me is a bad man. But what is it to you, by
> whose hands the giver demanded it back? So long as he may allow you, take
> care of it as a thing which belongs to another, as travelers do with their inn.[27]

Epictetus is believed to have died in 120 A.D., one year before the birth of the future emperor Marcus Aurelius, whose commitment to Stoicism would be equally sincere. Marcus certainly had many opportunities to apply Epictetus's advice regarding proper Stoic attitudes of emotional detachment. He was orphaned at a young age, plagued by health problems all of his life, and was predeceased not only by his beloved (though by some accounts repeatedly unfaithful) wife but also by four of his five sons. During his reign Marcus had to contend with barbarian invasions along the northeastern and eastern borders of the empire, a devastating plague that swept through the entire empire, and an attempted coup d'état led by Avidius Cassius, commander of the Roman forces in Asia (which was brought to a swift end when Avidius was murdered by his own subordinate officers). Duty required Marcus to be a general to his legions and an administrator of the most complex bureaucracy the world had ever seen, when he would rather have lived a quiet life of contemplation and philosophical reflection. He is described as "by nature a saint and a sage, by profession a ruler and a warrior."[28]

Marcus Aurelius spelled out his understanding of Stoicism in his private *Meditations*. Much of the work was written while Marcus was on military campaign, defending the Roman frontiers. As Barrow explains:

[A]ll unwillingly he [Marcus] shouldered his duty to turn himself from a meditative student into the commander of an army defending the Northern frontier of the Roman Empire. And conscientiously and successfully he did it. But at times he withdrew into himself; and, as he fought with some of his problems in the melancholy places of his mind, he jotted down his musings and wrestlings and resolutions, and by some queer accident his jottings have come down to us.[29]

Some of the emperor's reflections deal expressly with the value of Stoicism for those in the profession of arms, and many of his points are illustrated with martial examples.

It should not be difficult to see why Stoic philosophy appealed to those charged with the training and leadership of Rome's legions. As Maxwell Staniforth notes in the introduction to his translation of Marcus Aurelius's *Meditations*, Stoicism offered the ideal code for the Roman warrior: "A code which was manly, rational, and temperate, a code which insisted on just and virtuous dealing, self-discipline, unflinching fortitude, and complete freedom from the storms of passion was admirably suited to the Roman character."[30] Emperor Aurelius's interpretation of Stoicism is especially practical, as he explains how to apply the "no excuses" ethic in daily life.

Book 7 of his *Meditations* contains some of Marcus's most powerful statements of the Stoic doctrine of self-regulation. The ideal Stoic warrior, according to the emperor, would not allow any disturbance in life to provoke him to act in a way that would taint his personal honor. Again, even the experience of evil cannot supply sufficient warrant for any moral transgression, however slight.

Marcus suggests that the way to make oneself immune to the influence of evil is to see it as both commonplace and impermanent. Encounters with evil should not rattle our composure, because they are an expected feature of our earthly existence. Why should we be thrown if, for example, we find ourselves betrayed? Acts of betrayal are hardly rare in human history. And the effects of that betrayal, whatever they may be, cannot last forever. So Marcus writes:

> What is evil? A thing you have seen times out of number. Likewise with every other sort of occurrence also, be prompt to remind yourself that this, too, you have witnessed many times before. For everywhere, above and below, you will find nothing but the selfsame things; they fill the pages of all history, ancient, modern, and contemporary; and they fill our cities and homes today. There is no such thing as novelty; all is as trite as it is transitory.[31]

When events threaten to disturb our composure, Marcus advises us to employ mental discipline to remind ourselves how we felt before the world conspired to alter our perspective. Then we are, as a sheer act of will, to cause ourselves to return to our former way of viewing matters, as though nothing unpleasant had occurred. To the person who can master this technique, Marcus proclaims, "A new life lies within your grasp. You have only to see things once more in the light of your first and earlier vision, and life begins anew."[32]

Consider how this advice might have played out in the life of a Roman legionnaire. The Roman Empire maintained a fighting force of approximately thirty legions, with 5,400 men in each legion.[33] These men were stationed in all corners of the empire, from Egypt to Gaul, often thousands of miles away from where they were recruited. Their training was intense, and they were committed to serve for at least twenty-five years. They fought in tight formations, where they learned to rely on one another implicitly. The ancient historian Josephus recorded his observations of the Roman army in his *History of the Jewish War*:

> If you study very carefully the organization of the Roman army, you will realize that they possess their great empire as a reward for valor, not as a gift of fortune. For the Romans, the wielding of arms does not begin with the outbreak of war, nor do they sit idly by in peacetime and move their hands only during times of need. Quite the opposite! As if born for the sole purpose of wielding arms, they never take a break from training, never wait for a situation requiring arms. Their practice sessions are no less strenuous than real battles. Each soldier trains every day with all his energy as if in war. And therefore they bear the stress of battle with the greatest ease. No con-

fusion causes them to break from their accustomed formation, no fear causes them to shrink back, no exertion tires them. Certain victory always
attends them since their opponents are never equal to them. And so it
would not be wrong to call their practice sessions bloodless battles and their
battles bloody practice sessions.[34]

Given the harsh conditions of their service and the fact that they were
often torn from the familiar and asked to defend Roman interests in what
must have seemed to them disturbingly alien lands, it is not surprising
that the legionnaires carved out some sense of stability in their lives by
forging close-knit friendships with their comrades-in-arms. Though clearly beneficial, these bonds among the empire's professional soldiers also
left them open to the pain of constant bereavement. The Roman legions
were a superior fighting force, seldom failing to meet their objectives. But
their successes came at a price. The average Roman soldier had less than
a 50 percent chance of surviving until retirement.[35]

The wisdom of Marcus Aurelius and his Stoic predecessors would
have directed the legionaries not to allow the loss of their comrades to
affect their performance in battle or the completion of any of their professional obligations. Seeing your best friend skewered by a Gaulish
spear would be no excuse for falling out of step in an advance or failing
to keep an adequate watch the following day. According to the Stoics, it
is your choice whether or not to let any experience distract you from
your duties. Emotional disturbance is just an indication of weakness of
will.

Marcus provides a useful image for aspiring Stoics to hold in their
minds to keep them focused on maintaining their personal honor and
behaving virtuously (performing their moral duty) no matter what occurs
around or to them and with no regard for the reactions of others: "15.
Whatever the world may say or do, my part is to keep myself good; just
as . . . an emerald . . . insists perpetually, 'Whatever the world may say or
do, my part is to remain and emerald and keep my color true.'"[36]

Nor does the emperor hesitate to spell out the military applications of
this Stoic instruction to remain true in all situations and at all costs.
Always he returns to the theme that to endure physical pain or death is
vastly preferable to suffering the loss of honor that must necessarily
attend any act of cowardice or dereliction of duty. For example, to emphasize the need for the Stoic warrior to set aside any concern for his own
well being when military objects are at stake, he draws on a quote from
the Greek philosopher Plato, whom he holds in high regard for recognizing the moral importance of service to the state:

45. For thus it is, men of Athens, in truth: wherever a man has placed himself thinking it the best place for him, or has been placed by a commander,

there in my opinion he ought to stay and to abide the hazard, taking nothing into the reckoning, either death or anything else, before the baseness of
deserting his post.[37]

Marcus's reflections on the tolerance of pain also imply that he would
expect the Stoic warrior to resist the mental effects of torture if captured
by an enemy. A true Stoic would not permit the threat or actual infliction
of physical agony to compel him to compromise his integrity. Marcus
comments:

33. Of Pain. If it is past bearing, it makes an end of us; if it lasts, it can be
borne. The mind, holding itself aloof from the body, retains its calm, and the
master-reason remains unaffected. As for the parts injured by the pain, let
them, if they can, declare their own grief.[38]

In other words, the emperor's position on pain is that it must fall into
one of two categories: either it kills you (and recall the Stoic view that
death is nothing to fear) or it can, technically, be tolerated. He does not
entertain the possibility that there could be some form of nonlethal but
intolerable pain that no human will could resist. He trusts that strict mental discipline will fortify the Stoic against all assaults on his physical self.
So he advises:

68. Live out your days in untroubled serenity, refusing to be coerced though
the whole world deafen you with its demands, and though wild beasts rend
piecemeal this poor envelope of clay.[39]

Marcus's philosophy certainly is unforgiving toward the Stoic himself,
but it is important to note that another recurring message in his *Meditations* is that the dedicated Stoic should never assume a haughty or superior attitude or find fault with those who are not yet persuaded of the wisdom of pursuing the Stoic lifestyle. Humility is a Stoic virtue, both
because excessive pride can mar the performance of one's duties (remember how hubris led to the downfall of the Homeric heroes) and because
lauding one's achievements over others is a misdirection of energies that
are better turned to more honorable pursuits.

The emperor is at pains to point out that dwelling on the weaknesses
of others and parceling out blame for failures advances no worthwhile
cause. Several of his meditations express the idea that identifying others'
faults is a useless distraction from the project of correcting our own. A
Stoic should only be interested in the subpar performance of others if he
can help to improve it for some greater good. Consider the following
remarks:

17. . . . . All thoughts of blame are out of place. If you can, correct the offender; if not, correct the offence; if that too is impossible, what is the point of recriminations? Nothing is worth doing pointlessly.[40]

20. Leave another's wrongdoing where it lies. [41]

4. If a man makes a slip, admonish him gently and show him his mistake. If you fail to convince him, blame yourself, or else blame nobody.[42]

30. When another's fault offends you, turn to yourself and consider what similar shortcomings are found in you. Do you, too, find your good in riches, pleasure, reputation, or such like? Think of this, and your anger will soon be forgotten in the reflection that he is only acting under pressure; what else could he do? Alternatively, if you are able, contrive his release from that pressure.[43]

Marcus reminds us that Stoics view their lives as opportunities to play out to the best of their abilities the roles that fate has assigned them. It is the actual accomplishment of tasks that matters, not pride or credit or fame. In a sequence of three aphorisms, he addresses the importance of the frank acknowledgment of one's own limitations, the unimportance of reputation, and the practical value of Stoic humility:

5. Is my understanding equal to this task, or not? If it is, I apply it to the work as a tool presented to me by Nature. If not, then either I make way—if my duty permits it—for someone more capable of doing the business, or else I do the best I can with the help of some assistant, who will avail himself of my inspiration to achieve what is timely and serviceable for the community. For everything I do, whether by myself or with another, must have as its sole aim the service and harmony of all.

6. How many whose praise used once to be sung so loudly are now relegated to oblivion; and how many of the singers themselves have long since passed from our sight!

7. Think it no shame to be helped. Your business is to do your appointed duty, like a soldier in the breach. How, then, if you are lame, and unable to scale the battlements yourself, but could do it if you had the aid of a comrade?[44]

Expounding further on the subject of legacy and reputation, the emperor appeals to the fundamental principle that whatever is beyond the Stoic's control should not concern him. Our reputations are formed by the opinions and expressions of others and so are clearly beyond our control. However well we behave, it is always possible for others to think or speak ill of us, either from misapprehension or from malice. And even if we achieve some positive fame while living, we cannot control how future generations will regard us. No one can ever guarantee that his or her complete and accurate life history will be remembered forever.

Beyond the practical consideration that such matters cannot be controlled, Marcus makes the additional argument that it is beneath the dignity of a Stoic to crave praise, reputation, or fame. He asks, "When you have done a good action, and another has had the benefit of it, why crave for yet more in addition applause for your kindness, or some favour in return as the foolish do?"[45] And he comments further on the same subject in books 7 and 8:

> 34. Of Fame. Take a look at the minds of her suitors, their ambitions and their aversions. Furthermore, reflect how speedily in this life the things of today are buried under those of tomorrow, even as one layer of drifting sand is quickly covered by the next.[46]

> 44. Make the best of today. Those who aim instead at tomorrow's plaudits fail to remember that future generations will be nowise different from the contemporaries who so try their patience now, and nowise less mortal. In any case, can it matter to you how the tongues of posterity may wag, or what views of yourself it may entertain?[47]

In considering what benefits Stoicism has to offer prospective followers, certainly one answer is not immortality of any kind. The Stoic was not meant to look toward a life after death, either in the literal sense or in terms of some lasting legacy. The Stoic focus is always on the present moment, on making the best of the here and now.

But if there is no final reward for virtuous Stoics—no Heaven or Valhalla or even earthbound celebrity—then how are they motivated to maintain their Stoic discipline? How do they find any meaning in their efforts if everything in life is just fleeting experience with no ties to the eternal? Why should they struggle to uphold high moral standards when the only inescapable judgment they must face is the one that they pass on themselves?

The Stoic emperor embraces the conclusion that if life on earth, from birth to death, is all that there is, then the only possible way to make that life worth living is to pursue virtue. Exposing his own humanity, he explains that this conclusion was not self-evident to him from the start. Rather, he found empirical support for the superiority of the Stoic path by exploring its weaker alternatives firsthand. In the first meditation of book 8, Marcus admits that he was not always such a committed Stoic. As if to reinforce his own decision to adopt the Stoic perspective, he reminds himself,

> Up to now, all your wanderings in search of the good life have been unsuccessful; it was not to be found in the casuistries of logic, nor in wealth, celebrity, worldly pleasures, or anything else. Where, then, lies the secret? In doing what man's nature seeks. How so? By adopting strict principles for

the regulation of impulse and action. Such as? Principles regarding what is good or bad for us: thus, for example, that nothing can be good for a man unless it helps to make him just, self-disciplined, courageous, and independent; and nothing bad unless it has the contrary effect.[48]

Marcus's motivation to be a Stoic springs from his conviction that no other style of life can ultimately offer any peace or satisfaction. The good life must include a sense of purpose. The pursuit of pleasure may seem appealing, especially when it carries no threat of postmortem punishment, but its lure loses force over time as the law of diminishing returns ensures that pinnacles of delight will become harder and harder to achieve or sustain. Costs will accrue for which no commensurate benefits are received. At the end of the day, Marcus reflects, those who live for pleasure alone will be left with nothing but regrets, whereas those who chose a more disciplined path can make even a brief life count.

> 10. Repentance is remorse for the loss of some helpful opportunity. Now, what is good is always helpful, and must be the concern of every good man; but an opportunity of pleasure is something no good man would ever repent of having let pass. It follows, therefore, that pleasure is neither good nor helpful.[49]

Following the Stoic perception that individual human lives pass quickly, end completely, and are then forgotten, the emperor argues that the only fulfilling life must be one that aims at the good for humanity as a whole. Even with no expectation of life after death, a Stoic can find meaning in life by making a positive contribution to his society, by being part of something larger than himself. In book 8, Marcus asks, "For what task, then, were you created? For pleasure? Can such a thought be tolerated?"[50] And in books 11 and 12, he spells out the direction that a meaningful life should take:

> 21. If a man's life has no consistent and uniform aim, it cannot itself remain consistent or uniform. Yet that statement does not go far enough unless you can also add something of what the aim should be. Now, it is not upon the whole range of things which are generally assumed to be good that we find uniformity of opinion to exist, but only upon things of a certain kind: namely, those which affect the welfare of society. Accordingly, the aim we should propose to ourselves must be the benefit of our fellows and the community. Whoso directs his every effort to this will be imparting a uniformity to all his actions, and so will achieve consistency with himself.[51]

> 20. Firstly, avoid all actions that are haphazard or purposeless; and secondly, let every action aim solely at the common good.[52]

A Stoic legionnaire facing likely death in battle could not find consolation in dreams of lasting glory or eternity in the Elysian fields. But he could take solace instead in the thought that his life will serve some useful purpose. If death finds him, he will fall fighting beside his comrades, in the service of his state.

The final goal of Stoic dedication is to become a "sage"—the perfect embodiment of Stoic ideals. In *The Romans*, Barrow paints a vivid picture for us of the Stoic sage:

> Neither trouble nor tribulation distresses the sage. He is superior to riches and poverty, to opinion critical and friendly; he does all for conscience's sake. He is kind to friends and to enemies merciful, and his forgiveness outstrips requests for it. His neighbours, whether in city or state or the world, he respects, and he does nothing to reduce their liberty. He will depart this world with the consciousness that in independence of spirit he has borne alike its joys and its sorrows and that death holds no terrors.[53]

We may wonder if Rome would ever have fallen if every soldier in her legions had been a sage and if her senators, citizens, and emperors had all faithfully adhered to a Stoic code as well. However, such uniformity of moral conviction has never existed across so large a population. And no accurate account of life in Roman times could leave the listener persuaded that Stoicism was the overriding philosophy of the day.

Barrow explains:

> As an answer to the urgent moral and religious hunger of the times Stoicism failed. It offered no grounds of belief and attempted to tread a hazardous tight-rope of suspended judgment. It offered a noble ideal, but no reason for enthusiasm, no motive of affection or sympathy. It demanded that a man should save himself by his own resources, in calm detachment, ignoring the desperate cries of a world protesting that salvation was not contained within it. To the sage all was easy; but how to become a sage? And no clue was forthcoming. A few might achieve an ethical integrity based upon no sanctions and find satisfaction in their sad and melancholy resignation; there was nothing for people of vigorously pulsing life, with a measureless capacity for good and evil, and with energy and strong hate and love, anxiously seeking help wherever they thought they could find it—in astrology and magic, in the ritual and lustrations and promises of alien cults, in popular nostrums and secret superstitions. And so the multitude despised the Stoic philosopher for his barren gospel.[54]

As I indicated earlier, Stoicism had a sharply contrasting rival in the form of hedonism. To fully understand the Roman world we have to take a look at this alternative, the other face of Janus. The roots of Roman hedonism may be found in the philosophy of a fourth-century B.C. Athenian by the name of Epicurus (341–271 B.C.). But the sentiments and insights of

Epicurus were far too tame to support the actual practice of hedonism that came to flourish across the Roman Empire.

In his youth, Epicurus served two years in the Athenian military. Then, at the age of twenty, he moved to Colophon on the Asiatic coast, where he studied philosophy for ten years. He then made two attempts to establish his own school of philosophy, first in Mytilene, on the island of Lesbos, and next in Lampsacus, a city in Asia Minor. Finally, in 306 B.C., he opened a school in Athens that became his home until his death.

Epicurus's Athenian school was known as "the Garden," and his students included slaves as well as free citizens, women as well as men. From our present-day perspective we might view the Garden as a kind of cult or commune. Eugene O'Connor comments on the unique nature of the school in his introduction to *The Essential Epicurus:*

> Epicureanism became not only a philosophy but a way of life. Its adherents were bound by ties of amity, they addressed each other as "friends" and "intimates." The wealthier friends of the school were called upon to give financial support to the others, including Epicurus himself.... The students of the school were devoted to their master; together they pledged themselves to a life of simple community, withdrawal from politics, and quiet study of the master's world-system.[55]

Like the Stoics, the Epicureans scorned the belief in life after death. A strict materialist, Epicurus also argued that there was no empirical evidence to support a belief in gods who took any interest in human affairs. Epicurus went further with his skepticism than the Stoics, rejecting as well the idea that human lives are bound by destiny or guided by fate. According to Epicurus, everything we experience is relational and contingent. Our own unique perception of our lives, our interactions with others, together with random elements of chance, help to shape our existence. There is no overriding order to the universe.

The philosophy of the Garden was to embrace pleasure and avoid pain. The followers of Epicurus tried to sidestep every occasion for suffering by keeping their lives as simple as possible. They desired an existence that was peaceful, calm, and away from public view.

Epicurus does not define virtue with reference to duty and honor. Rather, he equates virtue with freedom from fear. Most people, he argues, allow fear to fully govern their lives. Their fear of the gods makes them obey moral laws. Their fear of poverty and deprivation leads them to struggle to accumulate wealth and property. Their fear of being forgotten drives them into public life to court fame.

Making a move similar to that found in Stoic arguments, Epicurus reasons that these fears can be conquered by limiting what you desire to that which you can guarantee for yourself. But where the Stoic finds this anchor in his duty to the common good, Epicurus finds contentment in his own experience of simple, easily procured pleasures. Virtue comes from recognizing that one needs very little to live a contented life. And the less one requires, the less one has to fear:

> Man's goal is happiness—not over-indulgence in pleasure, for this may bring pain; calm of body and of mind is the aim. Above all, get rid of fears, fear of death and the displeasure of the gods; death is unconsciousness; the displeasure of the gods is a myth.[56]

Epicurus clarifies the central tenets of his philosophy in a letter to a man named Menoeceus:

> We regard self-sufficiency as a great good, not that we may always have the enjoyment of but a few things, but that if we do not have many, we may have but few enjoyments in the genuine conviction that they take the sweetest pleasure in luxury who have least need of it, and that everything easy to procure is natural while everything difficult to obtain is superfluous. Plain dishes offer the same pleasure as a luxurious table, when the pain that comes from want is taken away. Bread and water offer the greatest pleasure when someone in need partakes of them. Becoming accustomed, therefore, to simple and not luxurious fare is productive of health and makes humankind resolved to perform the necessary business of life. When we approach luxuries after long intervals, it makes us better disposed toward them and renders us fearless of fortune.[57]

In the same letter Epicurus further explains that to become truly "fearless of fortune" requires prudence. He and his followers desire a pleasant life as free from discomfort as possible. Therefore they do not pursue pleasure blindly, as the thoughtless pursuit of pleasure can lead to misfortune. They employ practical reasoning to temper their actions, acknowledging that excessive or extravagant pleasures are more trouble than they are worth:

> When we say that pleasure is the goal, we are not talking about the pleasure of profligates or that which lies in sensuality, as some ignorant persons think, or else those who do not agree with us or have followed our argument badly; rather, it is freedom from bodily pain and mental anguish. For it is not continuous drinking and revels, nor the enjoyment of women and young boys, nor of fish and other viands that a luxurious table holds, which make for a pleasant life, but sober reasoning, which examines the motives for every choice and avoidance, and which drives away those opinions resulting in the greatest disturbance to the soul.[58]

And in the Principal Doctrines, Epicurus presents a more detailed account of the nature of pleasure and the rationale that ought to govern its pursuit. Consider the following aphorisms:

impossible to live pleasantly without living prudently, well, and just-
nor is it possible to live prudently, well, and justly without living pleasantly. . . .

8. No pleasure is an evil in itself; but the means of obtaining some pleasures bring in their wake troubles many times greater than the pleasures. ...

18. The pleasure in the flesh will not be increased when once the pain
resulting from want is taken away, but only varied. The limit of understanding as regards pleasure is obtained by a reflection on these same pleasures and the sensations akin to them, which used to furnish the mind with
its greatest fears. . . .

26. Those desires that do not lead to pain, if they are not fulfilled, are not
necessary. They involve a longing that is easily dispelled, whenever it is difficult to fulfill the desires or they appear likely to lead to harm.[59]

If they allowed their actions to be guided by these reflections, the
denizens of the Garden may not have made any positive contribution to
the common good, but they likely were not a hindrance to it either. They
probably lived comfortably and quietly, causing harm to no one. But, as
Eugene O'Connor observes, their reputation was otherwise:

Because his school admitted students of both sexes and practiced a life of
retirement, the Garden was accused of sponsoring secret orgies. Epicurus
himself was maligned as a casuist and a debauchee as well as a charlatan
profoundly ignorant of philosophy, whose works were shameless plagia-
risms of other authors. Epicurus' ethical theory, which gave prominence to
the role of the feelings and the pursuit of pleasure (largely meaning the
avoidance of pain) was misconstrued as merely an open invitation to
license.[60]

Despite this harsh criticism, the teachings of Epicurus endured as an
influence in the ancient world long past the death of the "master" in 271
B.C. In Rome, the cause of Epicureanism was championed by several
prominent figures, such as the poet Lucretius (100–55 B.C.) and the statesman Cicero (106–43 B.C.), the latter being the same Cicero noted earlier as
an early proponent of Stoicism (providing further evidence of the eclectic
taste of Roman ethicists). Even the devoted Stoic Marcus Aurelius
expressed approval for some of Epicurus's insights regarding the value of
the simple life.

Unfortunately, the average citizens of Rome, along with some of their
most powerful civilian leaders, were not all interested in exploring the
subtleties of Epicurean advice. Instead, many latched onto the crude idea
that had so horrified the Garden's critics, neatly summed up in the familiar phrase "Eat, drink, and be merry!" This led to a corruption of Epicureanism: hedonism, the mindless obsession with pleasure and novelty.

As the legions of Rome conquered more territory and the empire
expanded, the aristocratic class of Romans, known as the patricians,

acquired great material wealth. They used their money to improve their living conditions, building luxurious homes complete with running water.

These palaces of Rome required a great deal of maintenance, but wealth again provided the solution: slave labor. At the height of the empire, slaves in Rome outnumbered citizens by at least ten to one. Their uncompensated labor afforded patrician leaders the leisure to indulge their hedonistic appetites.

Patrician excesses in the imperial era are legendary. It may be that some of the tales of massive orgies, lavish and exotic banquets, and vomitoriums (special rooms set aside for banquet guests to purge overindulgences of rich food and wine) are hyperbolic. But even ancient commentators were appalled by the decadence of the upper classes and ruling families of Rome. For example, the Roman historian Tacitus complained bitterly about the decline in commitment to traditional Roman values that he witnessed at the close of the Julio-Claudian era:

> [L]ittle by little, our traditional moral values weakened and then were completely subverted by an imported licentiousness, so that we began to see here in our city everything that could corrupt or be corrupted: our young men were ruined by their eagerness for foreign ways, their enthusiasm for gymnasia, for idleness, for perverted sex, and all with the approval of the emperor and the Senate, who not only granted permission for such offensive behavior but even applied pressure on Roman noblemen to disgrace themselves![61]

Nor was the common, or plebeian, class free of unwholesome habits. A famous cynical observation by the Roman satirist Juvenal states that all a politician must do to maintain popularity with the Roman people is to keep them constantly fed and entertained:

> Long since, because we [politicians] can sell our votes to no one,
> We have thrown off our cares; those who once bestowed
> Rule, the fasces, legions, everything, now refrain,
> And [the people] hunger for only two things:
> Bread and circuses![62]

The circuses for which the Roman citizens longed were not of the Ringling Brothers and Barnum and Bailey variety. Roman taste in entertainment ran to the bloody, the brutal, and the bizarre. The term "circus" actually referred to the oval tracks where highly competitive (and often deadly) chariot races were run. But the primary venue for the Roman spectator was the amphitheater: a "theater of terror"[63] in which enslaved gladiators were forced to fight one another to the death, wild animals were slaughtered by the hundreds, criminals were tortured, and Christians were martyred.

Colin Wells comments extensively in *The Roman Empire.* on the role of the amphitheater in Roman life. First, he points out that although the largest and most famous amphitheater, the Colosseum, was in the city of Rome itself, the phenomenon of state-sanctioned displays of violence for the amusement of the masses ranged all across the empire:

> Moderns find it hard to reconcile the positive aspects of Roman civilization with the gladiators, the wild beasts, and the savage executions. These were not however a mere aberration. They were fundamental to the culture and to the social system. The Flavian Amphitheater (Colosseum) at Rome seated some 50,000 spectators. The very largest amphitheaters included in addition those at Capua, Verona and Milan in Italy, Pola in Yugoslavia, Augustoduumum (Autun) in Gaul, Carthage and Thysdrus (El Djem) in Africa. None of these can have held less than 30,000 people. . . . Even small towns in the western provinces had their own, often quite small.[64]

Wells notes that great outlays of public, and in some cases private, patrician and imperial funds were expended in order to sustain the amphitheater shows, implying that the ruling class of Romans recognized some great value in providing that particular form of entertainment to the people:

> 'Where your treasure is, there will your heart be also,' said Christ, and the converse is also true: by how a society invests its resources you can tell where its real priorities are. In most towns and cities, the amphitheater was the biggest building (its only rival would normally be the circus, if there was one, or the public baths). . . . Public slaughter was clearly for the Romans a fundamental institution, a social, if not a religious, ritual which had to be properly housed and to which society was prepared to devote extensive resources. . . .
>
> Bulls and bears were among the less exotic fauna on display. Pliny records the appearance of tigers, crocodiles . . . , giraffes, lynxes, rhinoceroses, ostriches, hippopotami (*Natural History* viii.65). Lions were commonplace—six hundred in a single show. . . . Elephants were also seen, and slaughtered. . . . The scale of operations, from the capture of such beasts to their transport, their nourishment in captivity, and their eventual delivery to the arena, was enormous. . . . It is hard to imagine any activity less productive than the capture and shipment of wild animals for mass slaughter, and the resources devoted to it demonstrate not only the importance attached to the amphitheater, but also the sheer wealth of the Empire, and the extent to which this wealth might be unproductively squandered.[65]

Wells suggests that the perceived benefits of the shows may have extended beyond the notion of giving the people what they want (simply catering to base appetites) to discouraging discontent with the social order. The callous disregard for the suffering of those not viewed as having rights under Roman law, the casual exercise of power over life and death by emperors and other figures of authority, even the class-based seating arrangements all may have served as none-too-subtle threats and reminders to reinforce the existing hierarchy and keep potential reformers in their place:

> The amphitheater was part of . . . [the] theater of terror. It was a lesson in pain and death, in the uncertainty of life, in the stratification of society and the arbitrariness of power. . . . Those who died in the arena died for the established social order. It was not just entertainment to keep people quiet, though it was that as well. . . . More importantly, it was a terrifying demonstration of what could happen to those who failed to please their masters, who failed to conform to the established order: slaves, criminals, Christians, and not these alone. A spectator who was witty at [the emperor] Domitian's expense was dragged out and thrown to the dogs in the arena (Suetonius, *Domitian* 10).[66]

But however much *more* than mere entertainment the amphitheater events may have been, they were, as Wells concedes, "that as well." Roman spectators were not forced to turn out for the bloody exhibits, but the arena seats were always filled. And it was the crowd's constant demands for something new, something extreme, something never before seen that fueled the frantic import of unusual animals, the training of tougher and tougher fighters, the invention of novel ways to inflict agony. The Stoic Seneca expressed his disgust for the spectacles of the amphitheater in his *Letters:*

> There is nothing more harmful to one's character than attendance at some spectacle, because vices more easily creep into your soul while you are being entertained. When I return from some spectacle, I am greedier, more aggressive, and more addicted to pleasurable sensations; I am more cruel and inhumane—all because I have been with other humans! Recently I happened to stop at a noon-hour entertainment, expecting humor, wit, and some relaxing intermission when men's eyes could rest from watching men's blood. But it was quite the opposite. The morning matches had been merciful in comparison. Now all niceties were put aside, and it was pure and simple murder. The combatants have absolutely no protection. Their whole bodies are exposed to one another's blows, and thus each never fails to injure his opponent. Most people in the audience prefer this type of match to the regular gladiators or the request bouts. And why not! There are no helmets or shields to deflect the swords. Who needs armor anyway? Who needs skill? These are all just ways to delay death. In the morning, men are thrown to the lions and the bears; at noon, they are thrown to the spectators. The spectators demand that combatants who have killed their opponents be thrown to combatants who will in turn kill them, and they make a victor stay for another slaughter. For every combatant, therefore, the outcome is certain death. They fight with swords and with fire. . . . "Kill him, whip him, burn him! Why does he approach combat so timidly? Why does

he kill so reluctantly? Why does he die so unwillingly? Why must he be driven with whiplashes to face sword wounds? Let them expose their naked chests to one another's weapons. This is the intermission for the gladiators. So let's have some men murdered. Don't just stop the entertainment!"[67]

It is impossible to deny the hedonistic excesses of Roman society. But what of her warrior class? We know that the face of Stoicism was displayed in her disciplined legions, but was the face of hedonism seen there, as well?

The soldiers of the Roman army, it has been noted, were not all Stoic sages, nor were they immune to vice. Drinking and gambling were popular ways to pass precious leisure hours (which were few and far between), and legionary encampments attracted the typical camp followers, including prostitutes. From the time of Augustus, legionnaires were not allowed to marry legally, but they nevertheless frequently found temporary mates among the locals of whatever territory they were sent to guard. As Wells notes, this fact was actually advantageous for army recruitment, since the illegitimate (male) children of soldiers would frequently enlist in the army themselves in order to win Roman citizenship.[68]

The life of a soldier did not provide the same opportunities for hedonistic indulgence as the life of a wealthy patrician. But practical constraints, rather than moral convictions, may have been all that held some legionnaires back from imitating the dissolute behavior of their civilian counterparts. Yet regardless of how many members of the legions might have strayed far from the ideals of Zeno, Cicero, Seneca, Epictetus, and Marcus Aurelius, the image of the Roman army that has survived to inspire soldiers through the centuries is clearly its Stoic face.

Hedonism is hardly unique to the Roman Empire. But Stoicism, though originating in Greece, was stamped indelibly with Roman features. As Barrow comments, "In the Greco-Roman civilization of the Empire there were many other philosophies which a man could adopt. But . . . we are considering the Romans, and the specifically Roman philosophy was Stoicism."[69]

The lasting impression that history holds of the Roman legionnaire is that of an efficient and committed professional warrior, unwavering in his focus as he marches with his comrades in perfect formation, winning battle after battle. It does not matter that sometimes the Romans were defeated by foes they considered mere barbarians, that discipline was often maintained only by the fear of draconian punishments, or even that violent mutinies were not unheard of in the Roman legions. What is remembered is the strength of the Stoic face of Rome and the awe that it evoked in others. Consider these further observations by the Jewish historian Josephus, describing the Roman army in the reign of the emperor Vespasian:

All their duties are performed with the same discipline, the same safety precautions: gathering wood, securing food if supplies are low, hauling water—all these are done in turn by each unit. Nor does each man eat breakfast or dinner whenever he feels like it; they all eat together. Trumpets signal the hours for sleep, guard duty, and waking. Nothing is done except by command. . . . Absolute obedience to the officers creates an army which is well behaved in peacetime and which moves as a single body when in battle—so cohesive are the ranks, so correct are the turns, so quick are the soldiers' ears for orders, eyes for signals, and hands for action. . . . One might rightfully say that the people who created the Roman Empire are greater than the Empire itself.[70]

NOTES

1. The republic was already on its deathbed years earlier when, in 46 B.C., Julius Caesar was appointed dictator for life by the Roman senate. But the transition from republic to empire was not considered complete until Julius's nephew, Augustus (then called Octavian), ended the civil wars with his defeat of Marc Antony and Queen Cleopatra of Egypt at the battle of Actium in 31 B.C. Augustus Caesar was certainly hailed as emperor of Rome from 27 B.C. until his death in A.D. 14.

2. R. H. Barrow, *The Romans* (1949; reprint, New York: Penguin, 1986), 151.

3. Barrow, *The Romans*, 152.

4. Barrow, *The Romans*, 22–23.

5. Philip P. Hallie, "Epictetus," in *The Encyclopedia of Philosophy* (New York: Macmillan, 1967), 3: 1.

6. Michael Grant, *Latin Literature: An Anthology* (New York: Penguin, 1958), 35.

7. Jo-Ann Shelton, *As the Romans Did: A Source Book in Roman Social History* (New York: Oxford University Press, 1988), 95–96.

8. Shelton, *As the Romans Did*, 433.

9. Shelton, *As the Romans Did*, 432.

10. Seneca, quoted in Shelton, *As the Romans Did*, 432.

11. Shelton, *As the Romans Did*, 433.

12. Shelton, *As the Romans Did*, 89.

13. Wilmot's translation uses some anachronistic Christian imagery here. In the original Latin, Seneca would have referred to Hades/Pluto. Therefore the "grim grisly dog" three lines down would be the mythical three-headed hound of Hades, Cerberus. *The Complete Poems of John Wilmot, Earl of Rochester,* ed. David M. Vieth (New Haven: Yale University Press, 1968), 150–51.

14. Shelton, *As the Romans Did*, 435.

15. Shelton, *As the Romans Did*, 350.

16. Tacitus, *Annals* 13.42, translated in Colin Wells, *The Roman Empire* (Stanford: Stanford University Press, 1984), 127.

17. Wells, *The Roman Empire*, 127.

18. Shelton, *As the Romans Did*, 434.

19. Shelton, *As the Romans Did*, 424.

20. Hallie, "Epictetus," 3: 1.

21. Hallie, "Epictetus," 3: 1.

22. Hallie, "Epictetus," 3: 1.

23. Epictetus, *Enchiridion*, , trans. George Long (New York: Prometheus Books, 1991), aphorism 5.

24. Epictetus, *Enchiridion*, aphorism 10.

25. Epictetus, *Enchiridion*, aphorism 3.

26. Epictetus, *Enchiridion*, aphorism 7.

27. Epictetus, *Enchiridion*, aphorism 11.

28. Marcus Aurelius, *Meditations*, trans. Maxwell Staniforth (New York: Penguin, 1964), 22. All references are to this translation.

29. Barrow, *The Romans*, 156.

30. Barrow, *The Romans*, 10.

31. Marcus Aurelius, *Meditations*, bk. 7.

32. Marcus Aurelius, *Meditations*, bk. 7.

33. There were twenty-eight legions under the emperor Augustus. After Varus's defeat by the German "barbarians," the number of legions fell to twenty-five, rising to thirty-three for a brief time under the emperor Septimus Severus. In the reign of Marcus Aurelius, there were thirty legions. (For a very clear account of the fluctuation of legion numbers, see Colin Wells, *The Roman Empire*, chap. 6, "The Army and the Provinces in the First Century AD.")

34. Josephus, *A History of the Jewish War*, 3.71–97, cited in Shelton, *As the Romans Did*, 260.

35. Those who did make it to retirement, however, were given a fairly generous pension, their own parcel of land on which to live and farm, and of course all the benefits of Roman citizenship. See Wells, *The Roman Empire*, 136–40.

36. Marcus Aurelius, *Meditations*, bk. 7.

37. Marcus Aurelius, *Meditations*, in *Ancient Philosophy*, ed. Walter Kaufman and Forrest E. Baird (Englewood Cliffs, N.J.: Prentice Hall, 1994), 450.

38. Marcus Aurelius, *Meditations*, bk. 7.

39. Marcus Aurelius, *Meditations*, bk. 7.

40. Marcus Aurelius, *Meditations*, bk. 8.

41. Marcus Aurelius, *Meditations*, bk. 9.

42. Marcus Aurelius, *Meditations*, bk. 10.

43. Marcus Aurelius, *Meditations*, bk. 10.

44. Marcus Aurelius, *Meditations*, bk. 7.

45 Marcus Aurelius, *Meditations*, bk. 7, aphorism 73.

46. Marcus Aurelius, *Meditations*, bk. 7.

47. Marcus Aurelius, *Meditations*, bk. 8.

48. Marcus Aurelius, *Meditations*, bk. 8.

49 Marcus Aurelius, *Meditations*, bk. 8.

50. Marcus Aurelius, *Meditations*, bk. 8, aphorism 19.

51. Marcus Aurelius, *Meditations*, bk. 11.

52. Marcus Aurelius, *Meditations*, bk. 12.

53. Barrow, *The Romans*, 159.

54. Barrow, *The Romans*, 160.

55. Eugene O'Connor, *The Essential Epicurus* (Buffalo, N.Y.: Prometheus Books, 1993), 10.

56. Barrow, *The Romans*, 149.

57. O'Connor, *The Essential Epicurus*, 66.

58. O'Connor, *The Essential Epicurus*, 66.

59. O'Connor, *The Essential Epicurus*, 70–73.

60. O'Connor, *The Essential Epicurus*, 12–13.

61. Tacitus, *Annals* 14.20, cited in Shelton, *As the Romans Did*, 339.

62. Juvenal, "Tenth Satire," 51. 78–82, in *Nota Bene*, ed. Robin Langley Sommer (Oxford: Past Times Press, 1996), 23.

63. Wells, *The Roman Empire*, 277.

64. Wells, *The Roman Empire*, 272.

65. Wells, *The Roman Empire*, 273, 275–76.

66. Wells, *The Roman Empire*, 277.

67. Seneca, *Letters* 7.2–5, cited in Shelton, *As the Romans Did*, 348–49.

68. Wells, *The Roman Empire*, 137.

69. Barrow, *The Romans*, 162.

70. Josephus, *History of the Jewish War*, 3.71–97, 104, 105, 107, 108, cited in Shelton, *As the Romans Did*, 260–61.

4

Vikings: Vengeance, Valkyries, and Valhalla

When most people think about Vikings, the first words that come to mind are probably *not* "honor," "restraint," and "ethics." Reflections on Viking behavior are likely to include images of rape, pillage, and plunder, or perhaps the vicious slaughter of helpless Irish monks. However, if we search the pages of ancient Scandinavian poetry and literature and consider the elements of Norse mythology, we can tease out a warrior ideal that is far removed from piracy, greed, and blood lust. The code of the Vikings is never spelled out as such in any work that I have found. Nor am I qualified to answer the question of whether any actual Viking ever lived up to the standards set for fictional Norse heroes. Worse yet, the term "Viking" does not have a clear reference but has been applied to a variety of people, including but not limited to Norwegians, Finns, Danes, and Swedes, from different regions and cultures in northern Europe who explored by sea and conducted coastal raids. However, even if actual embodiments of a Vikings' code never existed, understanding how those who have romanticized the great barbarian warriors of the north have characterized their warrior ethos may yet prove valuable to the modern warrior as a source of inspiration.

In addition to Viking sources, this chapter includes some material concerning the Celtic warrior tradition. Although the Celts are most directly associated with Ireland, Celtic influence once extended throughout Europe from Britain to northern Italy. It is not my intention to shortchange or dismiss the Celts by lumping them in with their northern brethren. (I certainly do not want to set my own Irish ancestors spinning in their graves.) Rather, I am placing them in this context to highlight the significant similarities among these ancient Western pagan tribal cultures. Nordic, Celtic, Gaulish, and Germanic tribes all fall into the larger category of Western "barbarian" societies that dominated Europe until the end of the first millennium, when they began to gradually convert into more stable and "civilized" feudal communities that ultimately abandoned their nature-based, pagan, polytheistic beliefs in favor of Christianity. There was a great deal of interaction among these tribal societies, both peaceful and otherwise, which left its mark in the form of a cross-pollination of religious and secular values, including similar concepts of honor and justice.

The beginning of the Viking era is often set at approximately 1000 B.C., which is when the tribes of Scandinavia can be identified as sharing a common language and customs. Historians from the ancient world give us the most information about Viking culture. Many of these historians are Greek or Roman, and their writing covers the period from about the fifth century B.C. (the time of the Golden Age of Greece, the height of Athenian power and influence) forward to the Christian era, and up to A.D. 1066, which is generally considered the end of the Viking age (1066 is the year in which the Viking king Harald the Ruthless was defeated by the English king Harold Godwinsson, just before Harold, in turn, was himself defeated by William the Conqueror, bringing the Norman invasion to Britain).[1] But the richest insights into a possible Viking warrior ethos can be derived not from historical texts but from that treasure hoard of Viking literature that is the Icelandic sagas.

The respected nineteenth-century translator of Icelandic sagas, Sir George Dasent, explained the critical role of the sagas for understanding Viking culture in the original preface to his version of *The Saga of Burnt Njal*:

> What is a Saga? A Saga is a story, or telling in prose, sometimes mixed with verse. There are many kinds of Sagas, of all degrees of truth. There are the mythical Sagas, in which the wondrous deeds of heroes of old time, half-gods and half-men, as Sigurd and Ragnar, are told as they were handed down from father to son in the traditions of the Northern race. Then there are Sagas recounting the history of the kings of Norway and other countries, of the great line of Orkney Jarls, and of the chiefs who ruled in Faroe. These are all more or less trustworthy, and, in general, far worthier of belief than much that passes for the early history of other races. Again, there are Sagas relating to Iceland, narrating the lives and feuds, the ends of mighty chiefs, the heads of the great families which dwelt in this or that district of the island. These were told by men who lived on the very spot, and told with a minuteness and exactness as to time and place that will bear the strictest examination. [These Sagas were] handed down by word of mouth told from Althing to Althing, at Spring Thing, and Autumn Leet, at all great gatherings of the people, and over many a fireside, on sea strand or river bank, or up among the dales and hills.[2]

I have chosen to focus mainly on *The Saga of the Volsungs* and *The Saga*

of Burnt Njal. Dasent praises the latter as "compared with all similar compositions, as gold as to brass."[3] The former is one of the "mythical Sagas"
referenced by Dasent in the above passage. It contains the legend of Sigurd the Dragon-Slayer and his ill-fated romance with Brynhild the Shield-
Maiden and was the basis of Richard Wagner's operatic *Ring* cycle (as
well as a strong influence on the work of renowned Oxford scholar and
fantasy scribe J. R. R. Tolkien, author of *The Hobbit* and *The Lord of the
Rings*). *The Saga of Burnt Njal* contains fewer familiar elements but presents marvelous details about early Scandinavian systems of justice and
rules for vengeance. As Dasent notes, all of the sagas that have survived
to the present day were, like the Homeric epics, originally derived from
ancient oral compositions. Unknown authors finally wrote down the
established, Icelandic versions of *The Saga of the Volsungs* and *The Saga of
Burnt Njal* at the beginning of the thirteenth century A.D.

    The Saga of the Volsungs chronicles the history of the Volsung family, a
great clan of Viking warriors. In the opening chapters of the saga, we meet
King Volsung, a direct descendent of Odin, the one-eyed Norse god of
war, wisdom, heroic poetry, and death. The saga relates that even as a
teenager, Volsung was "big, strong, and daring in what were thought to
be tests of manhood and prowess. He became the greatest of warriors and
was victorious in the battles he fought on his expeditions."[4] When he
reached adulthood he married Hljod, the daughter of giant who was herself a magical creature known as a "wish-maiden." Wish-maidens were
capable of changing their shape to undertake missions for the gods when
the gods chose to offer assistance to mortals. The fact that Volsung was
given a wish-maiden to be his bride indicates that the gods favored him.

    Volsung and Hljod proceeded to have eleven children. The eldest two
were twins, a boy and a girl, named Sigmund and Signy, and the other
nine were all sons. The saga describes the Volsung brood:

> [I]n all things [the twins] were the foremost and the finest-looking of the
> children of King Volsung, though all of the other sons were imposing. It has
> long been remembered and highly spoken of that the descendants of Vol-
> sung were exceptionally ambitious. They surpassed most men named in old
> sagas in both knowledge and accomplishments and in the desire to win.[5]

This description of the younger Volsungs exposes several key Viking
values. First of all, it is not incidental that the saga gives the Volsung line
a divine origin and then tightens their connection to the supernatural
realm even further by having King Volsung marry a wish-maiden. Viking
society was highly stratified, and nobility of character was thought to be
the product of parentage and breeding. In addition to slaves captured
from other cultures or conquered in raids, the Vikings enslaved a portion
of their own population on the grounds of their perceived natural inferi-
ority. Vikings believed that their slaves, or "thralls," were born for a

servile existence because they were not thought to possess the same level of innate intelligence, beauty, ability, and physical potential as the children of the ruling class. Thralls were even given mocking names that stressed their imperfections, such as those that in English could be rendered as "Blob-nose" or "Fat-thighs."[6]

Like slave owners in other cultures, the Vikings clung to their rationalizations in the face of obvious evidence contradicting their bigoted beliefs. Their literature betrays their inconsistencies. For example, in *The Saga of Burnt Njal* a thrall named Thiostolf manages to overcome Thorwald, a Viking warrior from one of the ruling families, in single combat. Thiostolf's success should not have been possible for a naturally inferior being.[7] Seen as a dangerous upstart, Thiostolf is punished for his deed. He certainly is not elevated to a higher status as a reward for his martial merit.

In order to be a respected warrior among the Northmen, you had to belong to a respected family (or clan) within the ruling class. Before engaging combat, Viking warriors declared their worthiness to friends and enemies alike by invoking the names of their parents and the name of their clan. All of their achievements would then be judged in the light of that heritage. They had the potential to rise in rank within their own social stratum by acquiring wealth and property. This could be done by serving their superiors well, as clan chieftains tended to use generosity to secure the loyalty of their warriors. A man who showed unusual courage or was an especially valuable member of a raiding party could expect material rewards such as gold, cattle, property, or perhaps even the hand of a higher-ranking warrior's daughter. Nevertheless, in the end, the single most important factor in determining a warrior's status was the status of the family he represented.

In addition to having the "correct" bloodlines, it is clear from the description of the brood of Volsungs that ideal Viking youths were expected to be well trained and well educated by their families. The Volsung children are praised for their "knowledge and accomplishments." Indeed, the stereotypical conception of Vikings as mindless brutes is not borne out by an examination of Nordic culture. In *The Saga of Burn Njal* both the title character, Njal, and the saga's other central figure, Gunnar, are held in high regard by their peers because of their good sense, excellence of address, talent for persuasive speech, and impressive command of the complexity of Viking law and customs. Njal, in particular, is not distinguished for his martial skills compared to the other Vikings, but still he maintains status among his peers because of his talent for adjudicating disputes and dispensing sound legal advice.[8]

In a similar vein, descriptions of the legendary Irish hero, Cúchulainn, found in the powerful Celtic epic, the *Táin Bó Cuailnge*, also emphasize that his superiority is founded on more than just his outstanding martial prowess. While Cúchulainn is still a boy, his potential for greatness is recognized by senior members of the Celtic warrior community, who then decide how his education should proceed:

> "He should be given to Conchobar, for he is Finnchaem's kin. Sencha can teach him eloquence and oratory, Blai Briuga can provide for him, Fergus can take him on his knee, Amargin can be his teacher, with Conall Cernach as foster-brother. . . . In this manner he will be formed by all—chariot-fighter, prince, and sage. He will be cherished by many, this boy, and he will settle your trials of honour and win your ford-fights and all your battles."[9]

Back in *The Saga of the Volsungs,* the Volsung children are also given credit for being "exceptionally ambitious" and for possessing "the desire to win." The heroes and heroines of Viking lore are nothing if not completely committed to the accomplishment of their goals. Their "get it done or die in the attempt" dogged determination is an inescapable theme that runs through both sagas. This is hardly surprising, given that the culture they celebrate belonged to men and women with the grit to survive harsh Scandinavian winters and the courage to journey across vast, uncharted seas.

"Death before dishonor" would be an appropriate motto for the Volsung clan. The best illustration of the demanding Volsung honor concept can be found in the portion of the saga that deals with the death of King Volsung at the hands of his conniving son-in-law, King Siggeir, and the subsequent revenge that the Volsung twins, Sigmund and Signy, orchestrate against the traitorous Siggeir. Siggeir's betrayal of his in-laws is motivated both by greed (he hopes to get his hands on the Volsung family treasure) and by hatred of the youth Sigmund, fueled by envy. Earlier in the saga, at Signy and Siggeir's wedding feast, Sigmund embarrassed and angered Siggeir by drawing a magical sword from a fantastic tree called Barnstock that grew right in the middle of the dining hall and then refusing to give the sword to Siggeir as a wedding gift.

The tale may call to mind the legend of King Arthur and the sword in the stone. The god Odin, disguised as an old man with a patch over one eye, thrusts the sword into the tree, saying, "He who draws this sword out of the trunk shall receive it from me as a gift, and he himself shall prove that he has never carried a better sword than this one."[10] Odin then departs, and all the warriors in the hall attempt to draw the sword from the tree, including King Siggeir. Only the untried son of King Volsung, Sigmund, is left to take the challenge. When he places his hands on the sword's hilt, it slides easily free from Barnstock. He holds it up before the assembled warriors. Siggeir immediately offers Sigmund triple its weight in gold for the sword, but Sigmund refuses to relinquish his prize for any price. Siggeir takes offense and returns to his own land, Gautland, the next day with his bride. Before leaving her family, Signy confides in her father that she does not trust her new husband and foresees a miserable future with him. But Volsung replies, "It would be shameful both for him and for us to break our agreement without cause. And if it is broken we could neither have his trust nor bind him in a friendly alliance. He would repay us with as much ill as he could. The one honorable thing is to hold to our side of the bargain."[11] Such oath keeping and holding to bargains is a recurring theme in the Icelandic sagas. In Norse mythology, the powerful warrior god Thor was a symbol of courage and brute strength. He also was unfailingly honest, literally incapable of using deception. Thus it was by Thor that most oaths were sworn, in the hope that the divine warrior would guarantee their lasting strength.

It was traditional for the bride's family to make a visit to her new home early in her marriage to check on the couple's welfare. Unaware of King Siggeir's hatred for them, King Volsung and his ten sons sail right into the trap:

> Now is the time to tell that King Volsung and his sons journeyed to Gautland at the appointed time, according to the invitation of their in-law, King Siggeir. They set off in three ships, all well manned, and the voyage went well. When they arrived off Gautland in their ships it was already late evening. That same evening Signy, the daughter of King Volsung, came and called her father and brothers together for a private talk. She told them of King Siggeir's plans: that Siggeir had gathered an unbeatable army, "and he plans to betray you. Now I ask you," she said, "to return at once to your own kingdom and gather the largest force you can; then come back here and avenge yourselves. But do not put yourselves in this trap, for you will not escape his treachery if you do not do as I advise."
>
> King Volsung then spoke: "All peoples will bear witness that unborn I spoke one word and made the vow that I would flee neither fire nor iron from fear, and so I have done until now. Why should I not fulfill that vow in my old age? Maidens will not taunt my sons during games by saying that they feared their deaths, for each man must at one time die. No one may escape dying that once, and it is my counsel that we not flee, but for our own part act the bravest. I have fought a hundred times, sometimes with a larger army and sometimes with a lesser one. Both ways I have had the victory, and it will not be reported that I either fled or asked for peace."[12]

It is important to notice that King Volsung's sense of honor requires that he not leave Gautland after Signy warns him of her husband's intended treachery. Perhaps he could have been persuaded to depart had Signy presented some deceptive reason as to why he should not remain in his host's home. But he could not depart merely because remaining where he was would clearly endanger his life (and the lives of the other Volsungs). Volsungs face threats, they do not flee them. By making her father aware of his peril, Signy left him no honorable alternative but to stay and fight.

King Siggeir's men overwhelm the Volsungs, and King Volsung is killed in the fray. His ten sons are taken prisoner, soon to face execution. Signy, in what seems at first a curious move, begs her husband to give her brothers a slow death. We soon learn that this is a maneuver to buy time. The brothers are placed in stocks in the middle of a nearby forest and left to die. To make matters worse, each night they are visited by a hungry she-wolf who devours one of them for her dinner. The wolf turns out to be none other than Signy's mother-in-law, who is apparently a female werewolf. Wolves are symbolic of evil in Norse mythology and are associated with the devilish god Loki. That Siggeir's mother is a part-time wolf simply underlines the point that his bloodline is ignoble (especially when compared to that of the Volsungs).

Finally, when it is almost too late (there is only one brother left, Signy's twin, Sigmund), Signy comes up with a rescue plan. She sends a servant to the woods to smear Sigmund's face and mouth with honey. When the she-wolf comes for her final entrée, she is tickled to find it honey-coated. She begins to lick the honey off her victim. As the wolf's tongue slips into his mouth, Sigmund grabs it with his teeth and rips it out by the roots, causing the wolf to die in a spasm of agony that conveniently shatters his stocks, freeing him. He escapes deeper into the woods, where he perfects his skills as a warrior and waits for the opportunity to destroy Siggeir. It does not even occur to Sigmund to return to his homeland, where he would now be the rightful king. There is no life for him without vengeance.

Years pass, and Signy has children by Siggeir. When they are only infants, she tries to ascertain the toughness of her two sons by sewing their baby clothes onto their skin, then ripping the stitches out. She is disappointed when this brutal procedure makes the babies cry. As soon as her sons are old enough to walk and talk, she sends them to their uncle in the woods to train to become participants in the plot against their father. Like Signy, Sigmund decides to test the boys' mettle. He asks them to knead dough in which he has hidden poisonous snakes. When the boys refuse, he sends word to their mother, expressing his disgust at their weakness. Signy calmly writes back that since the boys are of no use, Sigmund should simply kill them. Sigmund, respecting his sister's resolve, immediately murders his hapless nephews.

Signy decides that the only way she will be able to produce a son worthy to fight alongside her brother is if the boy's father is of a better bloodline than the corrupt Siggeir. And in her estimation, the best bloodline around is her own. Therefore she uses magical arts to disguise herself and visits her brother in the forest. They make love, and the resulting child is a full-blood Volsung boy named Sinfjotli.

When Sinfjotli is sent to his uncle (and unwitting father), he surpasses Sigmund's expectations. The two spend years together in the woods, and Sinfjotli grows into an imposing young warrior. After various adventures, Sigmund deems them ready to pursue their quest against Siggeir.

Unfortunately, when they first try to slip into Siggeir's castle under cover of darkness, they are given away by the fearful cries of the youngest surviving children of Signy and Siggeir. As before, Signy directs her brother to slay the offending children. This time, however, Sigmund seems reluctant. Sinfjotli, however, has no qualms. He neatly dispatches his half-siblings, perhaps to prove that he is tougher—even more Volsung—than his father/uncle. Still, the damage has been done, the children's cries alert Siggeir to his danger, and Sigmund and Sinfjotli are captured and buried alive.

Once again Signy helps her brother to freedom, along with Sinfjotli. Together, the Volsung men set fire to Siggeir's main hall, trapping the schemer along with his warriors. Siggeir and his men are all burned alive. Watching the flames with his son/nephew, Sigmund calls his sister to him to "receive from him esteem and great honor." Signy replies:

> "Now you shall know whether I remember the slaying of King Volsung by King Siggeir. I had our children killed when I thought them too slow in avenging our father, and I came to you in the forest in the shape of a sorceress, and Sinfjotli is our son. Because of this he has so much zeal; he is a child of both a son and a daughter of King Volsung. In everything I have worked toward the killing of King Siggeir, although I married him reluctantly."[13]

Then Signy kisses her son and brother good-bye and walks into the fire to die alongside her husband.

Signy's loyalty to her father and brothers is profound. It is she, more than anyone else, who ensures that the final vengeance for her father's death is achieved. What is perhaps most striking to our non-Viking sensibilities is her remarkable willingness to sacrifice her own children to the cause of vengeance.

All of Signy's actions are directed towards the goal of restoring the honor of the Volsungs. The family was under a dark cloud of shame until Siggeir's shameful treatment of her father could be fully avenged. With the honor of the Volsung clan as her supreme goal, Signy judged all of her offspring only in terms of their potential to assist in reaching that goal. If they could not help restore the honor of the Volsungs, then they themselves were a further blot on the family's honor—a blot that could be wiped out only by their deaths. Nor did she hold herself to any lower standard.

Signy's end is her final attempt to secure her family's good name. By her reasoning, everything she did was necessary to bring about her husband's death, demanded by her sense of justice. All her actions were, in that light, honorable. Signy was, from the start, a very reluctant wife to Siggeir, yet despite what he did to her family and her lack of any emotional attachment to him, she recognized that by Viking tradition she was bound by honor to her husband and so should not have plotted against him. Her own father had told her that her place was with her husband when she had asked to stay and fight beside the other Volsungs.

In betraying her husband to avenge her father, Signy acted dishonorably to achieve an honorable end. Her final sacrifice (walking into the fire to die with her husband) was a statement of her conviction that no dishonorable act can be canceled out by an honorable one and that her behavior could not be made noble by a noble motive. She ultimately saw herself as the last blemish on the Volsung tradition and so condemned herself to the same fate as her half-Volsung children. Her actions, although disturbingly extreme, were at least consistent. Both her life and her death were dedicated to restoring her family's honor.

It is the obsession with perfect bloodlines that ultimately leads Signy to have an incestuous encounter with her brother, Sigmund, thereby ensuring that the resulting child of their union, Sigmund's son/nephew, Sinfjotli, would be a pure Volsung and thus up to the task of avenging his grandfather's death. Sadly, this twisted concept of eugenics survived through the centuries, embedded in Nordic and Germanic myth, and was revived in the twentieth century by German nationalists. Certainly the Nazi party did not advocate incest, but Nazi hatemongers did try to invoke the spirit of the legendary Viking warriors in their propaganda that called for the creation of a racially pure Germany. The suggestion made to the German people was that if they wanted to breed a superior race of Aryan heroes, cast in the mold of the Volsungs themselves, they would have to purge their nation of all "undesirable" bloodlines.

In his book *The Day the Universe Changed*, the brilliant spotter of *Connections*, James Burke, describes how the nineteenth-century German scholar and doctor Ernst Haeckel twisted the work of Charles Darwin on evolution and the survival of the fittest into a form of social Darwinism that urged the improvement of the German people through selective breeding:

> Freedom, for Haeckel, meant submission to the authority of the group, which would enhance the opportunities for survival. In this condition moral law was subject to biology. . . . The life of the individual was unimportant. There could be no appeal to an absolute set of ethics higher than those relating to the interest of the community as a whole.
>
> Haeckel's use of Darwin's theories was decisive in the intellectual history of his time. It united trends already developing in Germany of racism, imperialism, romanticism, nationalism, and anti-Semitism. The unity with the group which Haeckel so strongly advocated found favour among the Volkists, a group who believed in the "blood and purity" of the German race above all others.[14]

One of the horrific results of this perverted reasoning was the Holocaust, in which millions of innocent people were slaughtered. Thankfully, modern Ireland did not derive the same dark legacy from the references to bloodlines in the Celtic saga, the *Táin*.

After Signy's death, the main focus of *The Saga of the Volsungs* soon becomes Sigurd, one of Sigmund's sons by his wife, Hjordis:

> Sigurd's hair was brown and splendid to see. It fell in long locks. His beard, of the same color, was thick and short. His nose was high and he had a broad, chiseled face. His eyes flashed so piercingly that few dared look beneath his brow. His shoulders were as broad as if one were looking at two men. His body was well proportioned in height and size and in all respects most becoming. It is a mark of his great height that when he girded himself with the sword Gram, which was seven spans long, and waded through a field of full-grown rye, the tip of the sword's sheath grazed the top of the standing grain. And his strength exceeded his stature.
>
> He well knew how to handle a sword, hurl a spear, cast a javelin, hold a shield, bend a bow, and ride a horse. Sigurd had also learned many courtesies in his youth. He was a wise man, knowing events before they happened, and he understood the language of birds. Because of these abilities, little took him by surprise. He could speak at length, and with such eloquence, that when he took it upon himself to press a matter, everybody agreed even before he was finished speaking that no course other than the one he advocated was possible. It was his pleasure to support his men, to test himself in great deeds, and to take booty from his enemies and give it to his friends. He did not lack in courage and he never knew fear.[15]

Displaying that ambitious nature prized in the earlier batch of Volsungs, Sigurd wins great glory by seeking out and destroying the dragon Fafnir and seizing the serpent's hoard of gold for his own treasure trove. Soon after, he encounters Brynhild, a semidivine female warrior, or Valkyrie.[16] Those chapters of the saga that deal with Sigurd and Brynhild's romance are very revealing of the virtues valued among the Viking warrior elite.

In a fairy-tale-like episode, Sigurd first meets Brynhild and wakes her from an enchanted sleep. Brynhild is a fierce warrior in her own right who angered the god Odin by refusing to throw a battle in favor of one of Odin's chosen champions. Instead, she killed the man, and Odin punished her by putting her in a magical slumber from which she can only be awakened by her true love. Brynhild herself negotiates a caveat: the man she is to love must be none other than the greatest living warrior. Odin agrees, and places a ring of fire around her bed that can only be breached by a man who knows no fear. Precisely fitting that description, Sigurd rides through the fire with ease and finds Brynhild lying like a corpse in rich chain-mail armor.

Removing her helmet and slicing through her mail, Sigurd is shocked to find not a dead male hero but a living, stunning young woman. He correctly guesses that she is Brynhild the Valkyrie, famous for her beauty, martial skills, and oracular powers. He brings her out of her sleep to hear her prophetic insights regarding his future as a Viking warrior as well as to receive her advice on how best to behave in order to maintain his honor and status.

Brynhild's sage advice to Sigurd is uniquely Viking:

"Do well by your kinsmen and take little revenge for their wrongdoings. Endure with patience and you will win long-lasting praise. Beware of ill dealings, both of a maid's love and a man's wife; ill often arises from these. Control your temper with foolish men at crowded gatherings, for they frequently speak worse than they know. When you are called a coward, people may think that you are rightfully named so. Kill the man another day, rewarding him for his malicious words.

"If you travel by a road where evil creatures dwell, be wary. Although caught by nightfall, do not take shelter near the road, for foul beings who bewilder men often live there.

"Even if you see beautiful women at a feast, do not let them entice you so that they interfere with your sleep or distress your mind. Do not allure them with kisses and other tenderness. And if you hear foolish words from drunken men, do not dispute with those who are drunk on wine and have lost their wits. To many men such things bring much grief or even death.

"It is better to fight with your enemies than to be burned at home. And do not swear a false oath, because hard vengeance follows the breaking of truce. Do the right thing by dead men, be they dead from disease, by drowning, or by a weapon. Prepare their bodies with care. And do not trust any man, even though he is young, whose father or brother or close kinsman has been killed by you; often a wolf lies in a young son. Beware of the wiles of friends. I see only a little of your future life, yet it would be better if the hate of your in-laws did not descend upon you."[17]

Sigurd and Brynhild then pledge their love for one another, but their romance is thrown tragically off course by the schemes of Grimhild, a powerful sorceress, who decides that Sigurd should marry Gudrun, the daughter of her husband, King Gjuki, instead of Brynhild. Grimhild drugs Sigurd's ale with a magical potion that causes him to forget ever falling in love with Brynhild and to pledge his faith to Gudrun instead. While still under the effects of this spell, Sigurd not only marries Gudrun but also helps his best friend, Gunnar, deceive Brynhild into believing that Sigurd is dead and that the gods require her to marry Gunnar. When Gunnar brings Brynhild, his reluctant bride, to a feast with Sigurd and Gudrun, Sigurd's memory returns and he finally recognizes how he has betrayed Brynhild, his true love. The lovers reunite, but there is no future for them:

"I should like us both to enter one bed," said Sigurd, "and you to be my wife."

Brynhild answered: "Such things are not to be said. I will not have two kings in one hall. And sooner would I die before I would deceive King Gunnar." Now she recalled their meeting on the mountain and sworn oaths— "but now everything has changed and I do not want to live." "I could not remember your name," said Sigurd. "I did not recognize you until you were married. And that is my deepest sorrow."

Then Brynhild spoke: "I swore an oath to marry that man who would ride though my wavering flames, and that oath I would hold to or else die." "Rather than have you die, I will forsake Gudrun and marry you," said Sigurd. And his sides swelled so that the links of his mail burst. "I do not want you," said Brynhild, "or anyone else." Sigurd went away.[18]

Brynhild still loves Sigurd, but she cannot forgive him for forgetting her—magic ale or no—or for the part he played in marrying her to Gunnar. She demands vengeance and enlists her besotted husband to kill Sigurd. Gunnar refuses to do the deed himself, but he and his middle brother, Hogni, persuade their youngest brother, Guttorm, to attempt the task:

Now the two brothers talked together. Gunnar said it is a valid felony punishable by death for having taken Brynhild's maidenhead, "and let us urge Guttorm on to this deed." They called him to them and offered him gold and great power to perform the act. They took a snake and the flesh of a wolf and cooked them and gave this to him to eat, as the skald says:
Some took wood-fish,
Some sliced a wolf's carrion,
Some gave to Guttorm
The Wolf's flesh
Mixed with ale.
They used these and many other kinds of witchcraft. And with this nourishment and Grimhild's persuasions and everything else, Guttorm became so violent and fierce that he promised to do the deed. They promised him great honor in return.[19]

The methods that the brothers use to prep Guttorm for his encounter with Sigurd suggest a style of fighting commonly used by real "barbarian" shock troops. It was known in the Nordic cultures as "going berserk" and to the Celts as "having a warp-spasm." In either case, warriors would psych themselves into a frenzy before battle, sometimes with the aid of specially prepared herbal and/or alcoholic beverages. They would then lead a mad charge against the enemy, screaming wildly, seemingly impervious to any wounds except those that were immediately fatal. The Viking berserks often wore uncured wolf- or bearskins into battle to enhance their otherworldly appearance, while some Celtic warp-spasmers increased their intimidation factor by fighting in the nude, covered in a blue paint called wode (which may have had helpful coagulating properties), with their hair stuck up in spikes.

Unlike real berserks, who always fought conspicuously out in the open, Guttorm shamefully decides to assault Sigurd in his sleep. He delivers a fatal wound to the sleeping warrior, but Sigurd nevertheless manages to hurl his powerful sword, Gram, at Guttorm, cutting his assailant in half:

> Guttorm went into Sigurd's room the next morning, while he was resting in his bed. But when he looked at him, Guttorm did not dare attack and turned back to leave the room. And so it happened a second time. Sigurd's eyes flashed so sharply that few dared meet their gaze. But the third time he went in, Sigurd was asleep. Guttorm drew his sword and struck at Sigurd so that the blade stuck in the bed beneath him. Sigurd woke up form the wound, as Guttorm was leaving by the door. Sigurd then took the sword Gram and cast it after Guttorm. It struck him in the back and cut him into two at the waist. His lower body fell one way and his head and arms fell back into the room.[20]

After Sigurd's death, Brynhild laments her cruel fate and the role she had in the destruction of Sigurd, the greatest warrior of the age. Unable to live without him, Brynhild stabs herself to death, and her body is burned together with Sigurd's on a massive funeral pyre.

> Brynhild continued: "Now, Gunnar, I ask a final request of you: let one huge funeral pyre be raised on the level field for all of us: for me and Sigurd and for those who were killed with him. Let there be tents reddened with the blood of men. Burn the Hunnish king there at my side, and at his other side my men, two at his head, two at his feet, and two hawks. Thus it will be equally divided. Lay there between us a drawn sword, as before, when we entered into one bed and vowed to become man and wife. The door will not close on his heels if I follow him, and our funerary procession will not be unworthy if, following him, are five bondwomen and eight attendants given me by my father. And those who were killed with Sigurd will also burn there. I would speak further if I were not wounded, but now the gash hisses and the wound is opening. But I have told the truth."
>
> Sigurd's body was then prepared according to the ancient custom and a tall pyre was built. When it was fully kindled, the body of Sigurd, the bane of Fafnir, was laid on top of it, along with his three-year-old son, whom Brynhild had ordered killed, and the body of Guttorm. When the pyre was all ablaze, Brynhild went out upon it and told her chambermaids to take the gold that she wanted them to have. Then Brynhild died and her body burned there with Sigurd. Thus their lives ended.[21]

The description of Sigurd the Dragon-Slayer holds all the elements of the ideal Viking hero. Sigurd comes from a noble bloodline, he is handsome and physically superior to other men, and he is a formidable and accomplished fighter. But beyond these somewhat more superficial points, he is identified as a wise and eloquent man with the gift of foresight and

...ural intuition. As a leader, he is highly regarded for looking after the interests of his troops. He is heralded for his generosity in sharing the plunder of his victories with those who helped him win them, and he is singled out for his unflappable courage.

The virtues valued in Sigurd are also attributed to other prominent characters in Viking and Celtic warrior literature, reinforcing the notion that these were part of the ancient Western pagan conception of warrior perfection. In *The Saga of Burnt Njal,* for example, the description of the warrior Gunnar (who is not the same Gunnar who appears as Brynhild's husband in *The Saga of the Volsungs*) is strikingly similar to that of Sigurd:

There was a man whose name was Gunnar. He was one of Unna's kinsmen, and his mother's name was Rannveig. Gunnar's father was named Hamond. Gunnar Hamond's son dwelt at Lithend, in the Fleetlithe. He was a tall man in growth, and a strong man—best skilled in arms of all men. He could cut or thrust or shoot if he chose as well with his left as with his right hand, and he smote so swiftly with his sword, that three seemed to flash through the air at once. He was the best shot with the bow of all men, and never missed his mark. He could leap more than his own height, with all his war gear, and as far backwards as forwards. He could swim like a seal, and there was no game in which it was any good for anyone to strive with him, and so it has been said that no man was his match. He was handsome of feature, and fair skinned. His nose was straight, and a little turned up at the end. He was blue-eyed and bright-eyed, and ruddy-cheeked. His hair was thick, and of good hue, and hanging down in comely curls. The most courteous of men was he, of sturdy frame and strong will, bountiful and gentle, a fast friend, but hard to please when making them.[22]

And, in the same vein, we have the description of Cúchulainn, Celtic hero of the *Táin* epic:

You'll find no harder warrior against you—no point more sharp, more swift, more slashing; no raven more flesh-ravenous, no hand more deft, no fighter more fierce, no one of his own age one third as good, no lion more ferocious, no barrier in battle, no hard hammer, no gate of battle, no soldiers' doom, no hinderer of hosts, more fine. You will find no one there to measure against him—for youth or vigour; for apparel, horror or eloquence; for splendour, fame or form; for voice or strength or sternness; for cleverness, courage or blows in battle; for fire or fury, victory, doom or turmoil; for stalking, scheming or slaughter in the hunt; for swiftness, alertness or wildness; and no one with the battle-feat 'nine men on each point'—none like Cúchulainn.[23]

The position of women in the warrior cultures found in Viking and Celtic literature is worthy of our attention. You will recall from chapter 2 that among the Homeric warriors women were often awarded as "prizes" or status symbols. The best fighters had their pick of desirable mates, and women were treated more or less like property, first by their fathers and then by their husbands. Even the much-sought-after Helen of Troy was allowed no active role in her own affairs. She was simply given first to Menelaus by her father Tyndarius and then to Paris by the goddess Aphrodite.[24]

Most of the Viking and Celtic heroines play an active part in their own mate selection. Rather than waiting to be handed over by their male guardians as a reward to recognize some man's success on the battlefield, these women insist on setting tests for their suitors so that they can judge their worthiness for themselves. Brynhild, for example, would rather suffer an enchanted sleep within a ring of fire than be bound to any but the greatest warrior of the Vikings. Her pride in her own high status as a Valkyrie would not permit her to offer her affections to a lesser man.

Similarly, the Irish princess Emer from the *Táin Bó Cuailnge* requires that the hero, Cúchulainn, make his case directly to her that he is sufficiently superior to other men to deserve her hand in marriage, even though he is already recognized by his male colleagues as the greatest living warrior. The following excerpt from the Táin details what Cúchulainn had to do to win Emer's heart:

> Cuchulainn caught sight of the girl's breasts over the top of her dress.
> "I see a sweet country," he said. "I could rest my weapon there."
> Emer answered him by saying:
> "No man will travel this country until he has killed a hundred men at every ford from Scenmenn ford on the rive Ailbine, to Banchuing. . . ."
> "In that sweet country I'll rest my weapon," Cuchulainn said.
> "No man will travel this country," she said, "until he has done the feat of the salmon-leap carrying twice his weight in gold, and struck down three groups of nine men with a single stroke, leaving the middle man of each nine unharmed."
> "In that sweet country I'll rest my weapon," Cuchulainn said.
> "No man will travel this country," she said, "who hasn't gone sleepless from Samain, when the summer goes to its rest, until Imbolc to Beltine at the summer's beginning and from Beltine to Bron Trogain, earth's sorrowing autumn."
> "It is said and done," Cuchulainn said.[25]

Both *The Saga of the Volsungs* and *The Saga of Burnt Njal* give several examples of Viking women taking matters into their own hands if they are not sufficiently persuaded that their husbands embody the requisite number of warrior virtues. The Volsung princess Signy, as we have seen, helps to wreak a terrible vengeance on her treacherous husband, Siggeir. Brynhild refuses to return to the bed of her husband, Gunnar, after she discovers that it was not he but a disguised Sigurd who had ridden through the flames to claim her.

In *The Saga of Burnt Njal*, the beautiful but bad-tempered Hallgerda

incites her devoted thrall, Thiostolf, to murder her first husband, Thorwald, whom she considers beneath her (and to whom she was betrothed
without her consent). When another suitor, Glum, expresses interest in the
widow's hand, Hallgerda's father is careful to let her have the final say
about the match:

> Glum said—"There has been some talk between thy father and my brother
> Thorarin and myself about a bargain. It was that I might get thee, Hallger-
> da, if it be thy will, as it is theirs; and now, if thou art a brave woman, thou
> wilt say right out whether the match is at all to thy mind; but if thou hast
> anything in thy heart against this bargain with us, then we will not say any-
> thing more about it." Hallgerda said—"I know well that you are men of
> worth and might, ye brothers. I know too that now I shall be much better
> wedded than I was before; but what I want to know is, what you have said
> already about the match, and how far you have given your words in the
> matter. But so far as I now see of thee, I think I might love thee well if we
> can but hit it off as to temper."[26]

With Hallgerda's full participation, the final bargain is struck. Unfortunately, this more promising match is also cut short by the besotted thrall
Thiostolf, who picks a fight with Glum not long after his wedding to Hallgerda and kills him with an ax. Thiostolf is finally punished after this, and
Hallgerda selects for her third husband none other than the hero Gunnar,
whose description we have already reviewed. Even the proud Hallgerda
cannot object to such a match, but as Gunnar's wife, she continues to
demand that he live up to his warrior reputation and not bring her any
shame.[27]

In addition to encouraging their men to embrace and uphold warrior
values, women in the Viking and Celtic sagas also have the option of
becoming warriors themselves. In *The Saga of the Volsungs,* both Signy and
Brynhild may be viewed as warrior women. Hallgerda and Bergthora, the
wives of Gunnar and Njal, carry out their own bloody feud in *The Saga of
Burnt Njal.* And in the Táin, the male hero, Cúchulainn, is trained for combat by a woman warrior named Scathach and subsequently fights against
several women, including the powerful warrior queens Aife and Medb.

In the introduction to her book *Battle Cries and Lullabies: Women in War
from Prehistory to the Present,* historian Linda Grant DePauw asserts that
"women as a group and as individuals have always had roles in war. If
there is anything fine and ennobling in war, women share the glory. If war
is atrocity, women share the guilt."[28]

Examples of women warriors and female war leaders can be found
throughout history. Even when women have been excluded from the
actual fighting, some have shown up as pro-war players, helping to
encourage men to fight and filling support positions to free men for combat. With or without their compliance, women have also been fought over
in bloody competitions among males since the earliest tribal clashes.

Along with including women in their warrior tradition, the legendary Viking and Celtic heroes also differ sharply from their Homeric Greek counterparts in their intense commitment to family. In the *Iliad*, only Hector seems to have his martial activities partially motivated by his love for his family. And even he acts directly against the wishes of his father, mother, and wife when he leaves the walls of Troy to face Achilles. In contrast, the majority of the Viking and Celtic warriors portrayed in the sagas are driven into battle by their loyalty to kinship ties. It is also a recurring theme that the members of the great Viking clans stand by one another through strife and slaughter.

As already noted in *The Saga of the Volsungs*, Signy sacrifices everything, including her own life and the lives of all her children by King Siggeir, to restore her family's honor. Sigmund and Sinfjotli, too, are Volsungs first, individuals second. Later in the saga, we see Guttorm agreeing to murder Sigurd on behalf of his brother Gunnar, and in the final chapters of the saga, Gudrun (now married to King Atli) berates her sons into action to avenge the unjust death of their sister, Svanhild:

> Gudrun heard of Svanhild's violent death and she spoke to her sons: "How can you sit there so peacefully or speak with cheerful words, when Jormunrek has had your sister shamefully trampled to death under the hooves of horses? You do not have the spirit of Gunnar and Hogni. They would avenge their kinswoman."[29]

Her taunts are effective, and the brothers, to avoid further shame, ride off against Jormunrek, answering their filial commitments. The theme of close ties continues in *The Saga of Burnt Njal*. As the saga's title predicts, Njal is ultimately burnt to death in his home, but not before it is defended by many of his kinfolk, and his final fate is shared by his wife, Bergthora, grandson, Thord, and sons, Skarphedinn and Grim. Only Njal's son-in-law, Kari, manages to survive the blaze by jumping off the burning roof at the last possible moment, and he then dedicates the rest of his life to a vengeance quest for the destruction of Njal's enemies.

Friendship between warriors is another theme that receives considerable attention in *The Saga of Burnt Njal*. Njal, the lawyer, and Gunnar, the warrior, remain fast friends throughout all of their lives, despite events that might have thrust wedges between them. Gunnar's difficult wife, Hallgerda, despises Njal's wife, Bergthora, and attempts to strike at her through her servants. Hallgerda arranges for one of her thralls to kill one of Bergthora's thralls. Bergthora retaliates in kind. Soon, thralls on both sides are dropping like flies.

Rather than be drawn into their wives' conflict, Gunnar and Njal decide to settle their interest in the dispute publicly by paying one another gold (a blood price) as compensation for dead thralls. At every gathering of the Viking clans (or Thing), they meet still as friends and, in one of the saga's more humorous touches, pass the same bag of gold back and forth, leaving it temporarily with whichever of them lost the last thrall. Neither man allows his wife's fury to egg him on to any argument with his friend:

> Njal took the purse of money and handed it to Gunnar. Gunnar knew the money, and saw it was the same that he had paid Njal. Njal went away to his booth, and they were just as good friends as before. When Njal came home he blamed Bergthora; but she said she would never give way to Hallgerda. Hallgerda was very cross with Gunnar, because he had made peace for Kol's slaying. Gunnar told her he would never break with Njal or his sons, and she flew into a great rage; but Gunnar took no heed of that.[30]

When Gunnar is trapped in his home and killed in a fierce battle with his longtime enemy, Mord, Njal is devastated. He commits himself and his sons to a vengeance quest on Gunnar's behalf. They destroy many of Mord's followers, but Mord himself survives. And it is Mord who is later responsible for Njal's own fiery death.

It is difficult to overlook the fact that the tales of Viking heroes never end with their principal figures riding happily off into the sunset. Vikings tend not to fade away; rather, they perish violently. Signy walks into her husband's burning palace; Sigmund falls in battle; Sigurd is murdered by Guttorm; Brynhild shares Sigurd's funeral pyre; Gunnar is ambushed and slain (betrayed in his final moments by his wife, Hallgerda, who refuses to give him a string for his bow because he once slapped her in the face); and Njal is burnt alive in his own house. One reason for all these unhappy endings can be found in pagan Viking religious belief.

According to Norse mythology, the universe is divided into nine worlds: Asgard, Alfheim, Vanaheim, Jotunheim, Midgard, Svartalfheim, Nidavellir, Muspell, and Niflheim. These worlds are arranged on three levels, supported by the powerful roots of Yggdrasil, the Tree of Life. The highest level contains Asgard, home to the Viking gods and goddesses and ruled by the god Odin, the one-eyed All-Father, who, as noted earlier, is associated with war, wisdom, poetry, and death. The middle level holds Midgard, where the mortal heroes stage their struggles, and is surrounded by a mighty ocean that is guarded by Jormungand, a fearsome serpent who, like the Greek Uroborus, eats his own tail. The lowest level boasts two uncomfortable extremes: Niflheim, a frozen wasteland, and Muspell, a lake of fire. Hel, the Viking underworld, is located in the coldest region of Niflheim.[31] The deities that inhabit Asgard are nearly all related in some way to the support of the Viking warrior ethos. Here is a partial list of the Norse gods and goddesses, along with a very brief statement of their defining attributes:

- *Odin:* Known as the All-Father or One-Eyed; the king of the dogs;

sacrifices an eye to learn the mysteries of life and is hung from Yggdrasil for nine days to learn the mysteries of death; a powerful but capricious battle god who demands great sacrifice and sometimes forsakes his faithful worshippers; god of war and destruction; god of wisdom; god of death; associated with spears, hanging, mead, and inspired poetry (especially war ballads).

- *Frigg:* Odin's wife; queen of the gods; the mother goddess; sees every mortal's fate; sympathetic to human beings; very beautiful (and often pursued for her beauty) but always faithful to Odin.

- *Thor:* Odin's eldest son; a god of battle; associated with brute strength (not cleverness, tricks, or magic); god of thunder; causes storms on land and sea with his mighty hammer, Mjollnir; quick to anger but also quick to forgive; not very intelligent; god of law and order (symbolically presides over the Althing, a gathering of the Viking clans at which disputes are settled and blood feuds may sometimes be ended by the payment of a blood price to the family of a victim of an unjust slaying); called "the Keeper of Oaths" and "Thor the Protector"; prayed to by sailors.

- *Sif:* Thor's wife; goddess of the seasons and the harvest; the god Loki cuts off Sif's long, golden, flowing hair and winter covers the earth until it grows back again.

- *Balder:* Son of Odin and Frigg; a kind and gentle god; god of joy and harmony; god of purity and beauty; his death, engineered by the god Loki, is one of the signs of the end of the world.

- *Tyr:* Another battle god; is associated with courage and sacrifice for the common good; when the gods try to bind the monstrous wolf Fenrir in magic cords so that he cannot swallow the sun (Fenrir swallowing the sun is another harbinger of the end of the world), Tyr places his hand in Fenrir's mouth as a gesture of good faith; also known as Tyr the one-handed; god of honor; guarantor of contracts, promises, and pledges.

- *Loki:* The evil god;[32] a son of the Fire Giants of Muspell; Loki is cunning and deceitful and has the power to change shape at will; an extremely unstable god, he is spiteful and envious of the other gods; he and his vile offspring (Fenrir, Jormungand, and Hel) help to bring about the end of the world.

- *Aegir:* A sea god; along with his wife, Ran, Aegir collects mortals who drown at sea and entertains them in their underwater palace until their souls are collected and taken off to Hel.

- *Freya:* Goddess of love and beauty; also a goddess of death; Freya

drives a glorious chariot over fields of battle and selects brave warriors to live in her hall in Asgard after their deaths and be her champions; goddess of witchcraft and visions of the future (patroness of
female prophets).

- *Freyr:* Freyoa's brother; god of peace and prosperity; land dedicated
  to Freyr was sanctuary land (a "safe zone," so to speak) on which no
  blood could be shed; warriors often wore his symbol for protection;
  he is also identified with a magical unbreakable sword and a magic
  ship named Skidbladnir.

- *Hel:* Daughter of Loki; goddess of the dead; claims the souls of anyone who does not die in combat (all nonwarriors) and leads them to
  frozen Niflheim; she appears to be a beautiful woman from the waist
  up but is a rotting corpse from the waist down.

As these descriptions indicate, the gods took great interest in the lives
of warriors. One reason for their martial focus is unveiled in the Norse
version of the myth of Armageddon. The Vikings believed that, although
far superior to humans, their gods were not truly immortal. They could
suffer death at the hands of other divine creatures. All of the stories about
the gods culminate in a great battle between the gods of Asgard and the
evil god Loki, who is supported by various demonic creatures and giants.
This final battle, called Ragnarok, ends with the death of all the combatants (Odin and his followers defeat Loki and his wicked brood but are
themselves destroyed in the process) and the complete collapse of the
nine worlds. So, in the end, good triumphs over evil, but no one, not even
the gods, survives to savor the victory.

Viking warriors believed that if they showed great courage and
prowess on the battlefield, they would be chosen by the gods to fight by
their side in Ragnarok. They maintained that when a warrior is killed
with his (or her)[33] weapon in his hands, he is conducted up to Asgard by
beautiful shield maidens (female warriors) known as Valkyries. (You may
recall that Brynhild, in *The Saga of the Volsungs,* was also a Valkyrie.) There,
they are welcomed by Odin in Valhalla, the great warriors' hall. Valhalla
is so enormous that there are clouds beneath the roof and eagles swoop
among the rafters.

The dead heroes spend their evenings in Asgard celebrating in Valhalla with all the other fallen warriors—drinking mead, dining on the best
cuts of meat, singing songs, and generally having a very good time. There
are no stomachaches or hangovers. Then, when the sun rises, they go out
to the fields of Asgard and battle with one another to keep their warrior
skills sharp for Ragnarok. It does not matter whether they chop one
another's heads or limbs off in their practice, because when the sun
begins to set, they are all magically made whole and healthy again, fit to
return to Valhalla for another night of boisterous revelry. This pattern con-

tinues until Loki arranges the death of Balder, Fenrir the wolf breaks his magic bonds and swallows the sun, and the ultimate battle of Ragnarok is engaged.

Given these beliefs, it is not at all surprising that the Vikings of legend should so eagerly embrace their honorable deaths. Even the gods cannot avoid death, and a warrior's death is at least a ticket to Valhalla. The Viking lust for combat is thus made clear, but what is also exposed is the tremendous courage it must have taken for the early Vikings to make their many famed sea voyages. Some scholars speculate that Vikings may have sailed not only to Iceland and Greenland but even to the Americas, centuries before Columbus. And they did this despite their belief that a drowning death would condemn their souls to shiver in Hel until Ragnarok, worlds away from Valhalla, for Hel was the repository for all those who died nonmartial deaths, regardless of their character or worth.

Clearly, Viking warriors were well motivated for battle. The desire for booty, the demands of honor, the duty to family, and the dream of a glorious afterlife all drove their dedication to warrior ideals. Whether or not real-world Vikings were as committed to these ideals as their legendary counterparts, the sagas' stirring descriptions of Signy and Sigmund, Sigurd and Brynhild, Gunnar and Njal still have the power to inspire modern warriors. As one of my younger midshipmen commented after hearing the story of Signy's final sacrifice, "Now *that's* what I call an honor concept!"

NOTES

1. A historical irony, since the Normans were themselves descendants of Vikings, or "men from the North."

2. Sir George Webbe Dasent, preface to *The Story of Burnt Njal: The Great Icelandic Tribune, Jurist, and Counsellor* (London: Narrcena Society, 1907), xi–xii.

3. Dasent, *Burnt Njal*, xi.

4. Jesse L. Byock, trans., *The Saga of the Volsungs: The Norse Epic of Sigurd the Dragon-Slayer* (Berkeley and Los Angeles: University of California Press, 1990), 37.

5. Byock, *Saga of the Volsungs*, 37.

6. Terry Deary, *The Vicious Vikings* (London: Scholastic, 1994), 15.

7. See Dasent, *Burnt Njal*, chap. 8, "Thorwald's Slaying."

8. In a U.S. Naval Academy modernization of *The Saga of Burnt Njal*, I imagine Njal would be aptly drawn as a JAG (judge advocate general) officer and Gunnar, perhaps, as a Navy SEAL or a Marine Corps officer.

9. Thomas Kinsella, trans., *The Tain: From the Irish Epic Táin Bó Cuailnge* (Oxford: Oxford University Press, 1969), 25.

10. Byock, *Saga of the Volsungs*, 38.

11. Byock, *Saga of the Volsungs*, 39.

12. Byock, *Saga of the Volsungs*, 40.

13. Byock, *Saga of the Volsungs*, 47.

14. James Burke, *The Day the Universe Changed* (Boston: Little, Brown, 1985), 265.

15. Byock, *Saga of the Volsungs*, 72.

16. Brynhild's very name denotes her martial tendencies: "Bryn" means mail coat and "Hild" means battle. (Byock, *Saga of the Volsungs*, 119 nn. 82, 83).

17. Byock, *Saga of the Volsungs*, 71–72.

18. Byock, *Saga of the Volsungs*, 87–88.

19. Byock, *Saga of the Volsungs*, 89–90.

20. Byock, *Saga of the Volsungs*, 90.

21. Byock, *Saga of the Volsungs*, 67–93.

22. Dasent, *Burnt Njal*, 29–30.

23. Kinsella, *The Tain*, 75–76.

24. Although they are generally left out of the *Iliad* proper, the Homeric cycle does include scenes involving Amazon warriors who clearly do not fall in the "prize women" category, having proven their own warrior prowess just like their male counterparts. According to myth, Achilles falls in love with the Amazon queen, Penthesilea, on the battlefield, just as he delivers her a fatal blow. So perhaps it is fair to say that there were few empowered women in the tale of the Trojan War, and those who were included in the legend did not fare well.

25. Kinsella, *The Tain*, 27.

26. Dasent, *Burnt Njal*, 25.

27. When she is insulted by Njal's wife, Bergthora, Hallgerda says to Gunnar, "It stands me in little stead to have the bravest man in Iceland if thou dost not avenge this, Gunnar!" Dasent, *Burnt Njal*, 39.

28. Linda Grant DePauw, *Battle Cries and Lullabies: Women in War from Prehistory to the Present* (Norman: University of Oklahoma Press, 1998), 16.

29. Byock, *Saga of the Volsungs*, 107.

30. Dasent, *Burnt Njal*, 48.

31. For a delightful and clear account of the basic elements, deities, and legends of Norse mythology, see the *Usborne Illustrated Guide to Norse Myths and Legends* by Cheryle Evans and Anne Millard, designed and illustrated by Rodney Matthews (London: Usborne, 1986).

32. Note that, unlike the Greek pantheon, the Norse deities do include a truly evil member.

33. Remember that there are also female warriors in the Viking tradition.

5

"Never to Do Outrageousity nor Murder": The World of Malory's *Morte Darthur*

Felicia Ackerman

Higgledy-piggledy
Sir Thomas Malory
Loved battles raging un-
Til the last breath.

Landing in jail, he was
Irreconcilable,
Writing of people who
Got bored to death.

The world of Sir Thomas Malory's *Morte Darthur* is of highest importance for a discussion of the code of the warrior. Not only is battle an essential feature of Malory's world, but Malory actually provides an *explicit* code of the warrior. This is the Round Table oath (also called the Pentecostal oath), to which "all the knights . . . of the Table Round, both old and young . . . every year were . . . sworn at the high feast of Pentecost."[1] This chapter will consider the oath in principle and in practice, but first some background about Malory's *Morte Darthur* is in order.

The *Morte Darthur* is an English prose compilation, compression, adaptation, and supplementation of medieval French (in Malory's translation) and English Arthurian romances. Written by Sir Thomas Malory, it was first published (and edited) by William Caxton in 1485.[2] This chapter focuses on the two-volume Penguin Classics edition, which is based on the Caxton edition (and from which my quoted Malory passages are taken, unless otherwise indicated), as the Penguin basically preserves the language of the Caxton edition but modernizes the Middle English spelling.[3] The distinction between changing the language and changing the spelling has borderline cases, but the net effect of focusing on the Penguin is to make the quoted Malory material readily accessible to the general reader.[4] In this chapter, I take the Penguin Classics text largely as a given and use such expressions as "Malory's world" without going into such questions as to what extent the relevant aspects of Malory's world come from his sources or what editing Caxton did. Of course, when I speak of Malory's world, I mean the fictional fifth-century world of Malory's *Morte Darthur*, not the fifteenth-century world of Malory's actual life. This fictional world is fundamentally a world of the aristocracy. It does not have the full range of people that would be found in the real world. Also, although there are many writers of Arthurian material and hence many versions of Arthurian knighthood (including other versions of the Round Table oath),[5] for simplicity of exposition I will confine myself to Malory, as he is the greatest of all Arthurian writers and also the medieval Arthurian writer most widely read today.

The Penguin Classics edition's version of the Round Table oath goes as follows:

> . . . never to do outrageousity nor murder, and always to flee treason; also, by no mean to be cruel, but to give mercy unto him that asketh mercy, upon pain of forfeiture of their [the knights'] worship and lordship of King Arthur for evermore; and always to do ladies, damosels, and gentlewomen succour, upon pain of death. Also, that no man take no battles in a wrongful quarrel for no law, ne for no world's goods.[6]

The similar but not identical version in the edition of Malory described in note 2 of this chapter, the Vinaver edition, goes as follows:

> never to do outrage nor murder, and always to flee treason, and to give mercy unto him that asketh mercy, upon pain of forfeiture of their [the knights'] worship and lordship of King Arthur for evermore; and always to do ladies, damosels, and gentlewomen and widows succour; strengthen them in their rights, and never to enforce them, upon pain of death. Also, that no man take no battles in a wrongful quarrel for no love, ne for no worldly goods.[7]

How should we evaluate this oath? Three types of considerations are important. First, just as a scientific theory is supposed to yield true predictions and not false ones, the Round Table oath, like any moral code of action, is supposed to require acts that are morally obligatory and forbid acts that are morally bad. But the Round Table oath is not a code of human behavior in general. It is a code of *knightly* behavior, a code for Arthurian knights as warriors and as members of "the king's political body."[8] It has been called "perhaps the most complete and authentic record of [Malory's] conception of chivalry,"[9] "basically a code of public service,"[10] and "a peacekeeping oath with clear political and judicial implications which make it crucial to the success of Arthur's governance."[11] A list of knightly moral duties could hardly be identical to a list of moral duties for priests or for ladies, although the Round Table oath includes some universal duties, such as refraining from murder.[12] Thus, one way to evaluate the Round Table oath is by whether the things knights pledge to do and to refrain from doing fall, respectively, into "morally obligatory" and "morally bad" categories for Arthurian knights.

The Round Table oath, however, is much more than just a list of morally obligatory acts and morally bad acts for knights. It is supposed to be an oath knights actually can and will obey as a practical rule of conduct. So it must be evaluated not only in terms of its abstract correctness but also in terms of its twofold effect (both instructional and inspirational) on the fallible and limited knights who take the oath. On the instructional side, the oath must steer a middle course between being so long and/or complicated as to be not learnable, let alone usable, by the knights or being so specific as to fail "to cover a variety of situations all of which have certain salient features in common"[13] and being so general as to be uninstructive. (Caxton's preface urges readers of the *Morte Darthur* to "Do after the good and leave the evil,"[14] a useful moral exhortation in some circumstances, but hardly moral instruction in the sense of being a practical guide for settling day-to-day quandaries.) What constitutes an appropriate instructional middle course for a code obviously varies with the intellectual level of the intended users. There can be cases where providing a detailed and explicit moral code is actually harmful. Such a code may defeat its instructional purpose by being so confusing that it leads to inaction or misinterpretation. To see how such a code may defeat its inspirational purpose, imagine a society where people are permanently stuck in the moral equivalent of the "terrible twos"; they are so defiant that giving them a detailed list of their duties inclines them to behave more badly than they otherwise would. (Many people nowadays seem to have a touch of this mentality, especially when the duties appear daunting and little can be done to enforce them.) Or imagine people who are so easily discouraged that giving them a detailed list of their moral duties inclines them to give up. On the other hand, an exacting code of action can lead people to attempt feats that are beyond their powers.[15] It is hardly unknown in Malory's world for knights to bite off more than they can chew. In the final tale, where Gawain vows vengeance against Launcelot and prevents King Arthur from reconciling with him, much of Gawain's behavior illustrates this tendency, although this behavior arises from Gawain's passionate desire for vengeance, rather than from overzealousness in applying the Round Table oath. Acknowledgment that principles must be suited to the capacities of their intended followers is at least as old as Aristotle.[16] But this does not mean that the Round Table oath is overly demanding. That issue must be considered, as I will do later, in terms of the values and prevailing conditions of Malory's world. Finally, an important part of the oath's inspirational effect is bound up with its ceremonial role. The knights' yearly Pentecostal affirmation of the oath is supposed to inspire them and strengthen their resolve to follow in its path. A long oath with a series of heavily detailed and complicated qualifications might be too clumsy and unaesthetic to serve this inspirational purpose, even if Malorian knights could grasp and apply its complexities.

Assessing the Round Table oath thus requires detailed consideration of what sort of people Malorian knights of the Round Table are and what roles they play. But the cluster of roles played by a Malorian knight of the Round Table is hard to understand in modern terms. These roles are not found together nowadays. None is quite the same in Malory's world as in ours, and one has no close analogue in our society at all. To begin with what is most directly relevant to this volume, Malorian knights of the Round Table are warriors. They fight in their king's battles for his kingdom and under his leadership. The popular belief that the Round Table symbolizes full equality of the knights with one another and with King Arthur is an exaggeration. Not all seats are equally prestigious. The Siege Perilous is ordained "that no man should sit in it but he all only that shall pass all other knights"[17] (i.e., Galahad), and Pellinor also gets a seat of high honor. But although the Round Table is not fully egalitarian, King Arthur's power is far from absolute. In a crisis, Mador feels free to remind him that "though ye be our king in that degree, ye are but a knight as we are, and ye are sworn unto knighthood as well as we,"[18] and in the final tale we are told more than once that King Arthur would like to reconcile with Launcelot but that Gawain will not let him.[19] Gawain himself tells Launcelot that "if mine uncle, King Arthur, will accord with thee, he shall lose my service."[20]

A second and related Malorian knightly role will seem much stranger to the modern reader. Nowadays we are apt to take for granted our modern system of criminal justice, where the guilt or innocence of someone accused of a crime is determined by presenting the evidence to an impartial jury of his peers. In Arthur's kingdom, however, guilt or innocence is determined in a trial by battle between the accuser (or a knight fighting on his behalf) and the accused (or a knight fighting on his behalf).[21] In a sense, the judge is God, who is expected to "speed the right"[22] by providing victory to the side of the accused if he is innocent and to the side of the accuser if the accused is guilty. As part of the criminal justice system, this may strike the modern reader as bizarre. But the view that "God is on our side" is hardly unknown in American warfare, although it is not normally taken quite so literally.[23] In Malory's world, however, right is generally expected to make might and generally does. But not always. The evil and cowardly King Mark, whose "villainous deed"[24] the reader has actually witnessed, wins a trial by battle against Amant, although it is Amant, not Mark, who is "in the righteous quarrel."[25] And in a much later episode, King Arthur condemns Guenever to death by burning, refusing to let Launcelot fight for her in a trial by battle. Arthur's rationale—that Launcelot "trusteth so much upon his hands and his might that he doubteth [fears] no man"[26]—shows the limits of his faith in trial by battle.

Miscarriages of justice raise a serious philosophical problem for Malory's world. Miscarriages of justice in our world can be attributed to human fallibility. Miscarriages of justice in trial by battle, however, can hardly be attributed in Malory's world to God's fallibility. Amant's death elicits this question from two maidens: "O sweet Lord Jesu, that knowest all hid things, why sufferest Thou so false a traitor to vanquish and slay a true knight that fought in a righteous quarrel?"[27] Malory thus in effect acknowledges the traditional problem of evil, the problem of how a completely good and omnipotent God can allow anything other than the best of all possible worlds. But Malory does not attempt to solve this problem. The maidens' question goes unanswered.[28] The possibility of such wrongful victory in Malory's world is part of what makes the oath's final stricture a stricture against an offense that is more dangerous socially than merely wasting time and energy in a futile battle. And even when a wrongful cause loses, this does not entail victory for the right. Both sides can lose, as in the terrible final battle between Arthur and Mordred. (Interestingly, God attempts to "speed the right" in this instance by sending Arthur a dream in which Gawain warns him to defer the battle, but, in another illustration of the problem of evil, this attempt at averting disaster fails.)

A third and related role for Malorian knights of the Round Table is that of quasi policemen and keepers of the peace, who prevent and investigate crimes, rescue victims and potential victims, pacify rebels, and (unlike policemen in our society) lawfully sometimes mete out summary, even capital, punishment.[29] Consideration of these knightly roles shows that the Round Table oath is *not* overly demanding. The goals of upholding the kingdom, doing justice with honor and without brutality, and protecting the vulnerable are vitally important. This makes it appropriate to demand much of knights, especially given the tendency of God to speed the right and given also that the knights of the Round Table are not typically prone to defiance or discouragement (although there are exceptions). Note also that the strictures vary in the extent to which they make great demands on the knights. To require someone always to give mercy when requested or always to do women succor is to make great demands on him. To require him to refrain from murder or wrongful battles for material gain is not.

A fourth and related role is that Malorian knights are professional athletes. Their sport—jousting—is an essential part of their knightly vocation. If "[t]he battle of Waterloo was won on the playing fields of Eton,"[30] still more are the battles of Malory's world won on jousting and tournament fields. Not only do jousting and competing in tournaments "keep older knights fighting fit and . . . train young knights for battle,"[31] but these activities are in their own right a fundamental part of knighthood in Malory's world. Success in jousting and prizewinning in tournaments are ways that Malorian knights gain honor for themselves and their king. Moreover, the line between sport and battle is often unclear. What begins as a sporting joust may end as a battle with a fight to the death. In tournaments, as in battles, a victor sometimes threatens to slay his opponent unless the latter yields and asks for mercy (thereby requiring the victor to grant him mercy by the Round Table oath). Another area of overlap is that manners of sportsmanship are frequently carried over into battles where much more is at stake. A sporting knight who unhorses his opponent is supposed to be so sportsmanlike as to dismount from his own horse, thereby eschewing unfair advantage.[32] Such a notion of unfair advantage may be surprising when one is fighting for such nonsporting purposes as trial by battle or to put a stop to an evildoer. Yet this mentality pervades the *Morte Darthur*. Thus Marhaus, having been reminded in a sporting encounter with Gawain of the "courtesy [that] it is not for one knight to be on foot, and the other on horseback,"[33] applies this sportsmanlike principle to a battle with the evil giant Taulurd. Taulurd has been terrorizing the countryside and Marhaus aims to put a stop to this. Yet he decides to fight with Taulurd on foot because Taulurd is so big that "there may no horse bear him"[34] (although Marhaus does ultimately kill Taulurd after wounding him severely and causing him to flee into the water). And Launcelot, in a much later episode, handicaps himself in a trial by battle by fighting with his left hand bound and part of his armor removed. It is, in fact, a battle where Launcelot, although "technically in the right," is "morally in the wrong."[35] He is defending Guenever against the charge that her bloodied sheet and pillow indicate that she has been "a false traitress"[36] unto King Arthur by sleeping with one of her wounded knights. In fact, she has been a false traitress unto King Arthur by sleeping, not with one of the wounded knights in question, but with the wounded Launcelot. Such moral complexity is absent from an episode where Launcelot offers to "unarm me unto my shirt"[37] when fighting a knight he has seen to be a wife-killer. These handicaps are explicable as Launcelot's strategy to induce these knights to fight. But in the final tale, after Launcelot and Gawain have become enemies and "the covenant was made, there should no man nigh them, nor deal with them, till the one were dead or yielden,"[38] Launcelot dismounts after striking down Gawain's horse, and the battle between them continues on foot,[39] although Launcelot knows that Gawain needs no inducement to keep fighting. Moreover, upon hearing about how Launcelot kills thirteen of the fourteen knights Arthur himself has authorized to capture him in the final tale, Arthur's immediate reaction is the "splendidly Malorian"[40] "Jesu mercy, he is a marvellous knight of prowess."[41]

What sort of people take the Round Table oath to fulfill these knightly roles? Malory's knights are, unsurprisingly, men of action. The oath's strictures "may be interpreted as ethical imperatives designed to regulate the behavior of adventurous knights-errant."[42] "[H]e sayeth little and he doth much more,"[43] Arthur says, in explaining his decision to give Tor a seat at the Round Table, and, in fact, actions are valued much more highly than words in Malory's world. But it would be a mistake to think of Malory's knights as strong, silent types in the modern sense. Instead, the knights are what we now call emotionally expressive, given to swooning, weeping, and making "great dole." Malory's world looks favorably upon such expressiveness. For example, when Palomides comes upon Epinogrus (off the battlefield) making "the greatest dole that ever he heard man make,"[44] of course he does not recommend such present-day panaceas as therapy, support groups, or Prozac. He does not even presume to tell Epinogrus the medieval equivalent of snap out of it, look on the bright side, think about others instead of yourself. Instead, Palomides says, "Let me lie down and wail with you, for doubt not I am much more heavier than ye are; for I dare say that my sorrow is an hundred-fold more than yours is, and therefore let us complain either to other."[45]

Except for the fact that he also gives Epinogrus practical help, Palomides is doing everything wrong by present-day mental-health standards. He not only encourages Epinogrus to wallow in self-pity but also engages in emotional one-upmanship by claiming his own sorrow is greater—before he even knows what Epinogrus's plight actually is. (Upon learning, he grants that Epinogrus's sorrow is greater.) Similarly, when Tristram becomes sick in prison, he does not regard this as an opportunity for "personal growth," the way seriously ill people are often encouraged (or pressured) to regard illness nowadays. Instead, Malory tells us:

> For all the while a prisoner may have his health of body he may endure under the mercy of God and in hope of good deliverance; but when sickness toucheth a prisoner's body, then may a prisoner say all wealth is him bereft, and then he hath cause to wail and to weep. Right so did Sir Tristram when sickness had undertake him, for then he took such sorrow that he had almost slain himself.[46]

The popular present-day idea that self-pity prevents one from doing much else is emphatically false in Malory's world, where knights engage not only in justified self-pity but also in feats of arms of the highest degree. And the self-pity of Palomides, arising from the pain of unrequited love,

enables him to empathize with Epinogrus's romantic suffering and, ultimately, to aid him.

Emotional expressiveness also appears on the Malorian battlefield,
often influencing the conduct of battle. Such battlefield emotions are not
limited to the rage and excitement one might expect. Gentler emotions
can also be found. In the final tale, where Arthur and his long-favorite
knight Launcelot are at odds, Launcelot orders Bors not to slay the
unhorsed Arthur and then horses Arthur himself and implores Arthur to
reconcile. Arthur is moved to tears, "thinking on the great courtesy that
was in Sir Launcelot more than in any other man."[47] Launcelot's act illustrates the importation of manners of sportsmanship into battle. It can also
be seen as an illustration of Launcelot's love for Arthur[48] and of the often
highly personal nature of Malorian battles, which frequently arise from
personal feuds and, as in the famous Civil War ballad, can pit brother
against brother and father against son (in Malory's world, Arthur ultimately against his [bastard] son Mordred).

In addition to being highly emotional, Malory's knights are also often
impetuous and unreflective. These latter traits do not follow from emotionality. It is possible to be highly emotional yet reflective and unim-
petuous. Nor does either unreflectiveness or impetuosity follow from the
other. The dictionary definition of "impetuous" that is most relevant here
is "marked by impulsive vehemence or passion."[49] Clearly, this is not the
same as lack of reflectiveness. Unreflectiveness does not imply impulsive
vehemence or passion. It is compatible with being lackadaisical or matter-
of-factly businesslike. What may be more surprising is that impetuosity
does not imply lack of reflection. Someone can spend a lot of time pondering the ins and outs of a situation and get tired of deliberating, throw
caution to the winds, and act impetuously. It may be tempting to say that
in this case the impetuous behavior would not be grounded in reflection.
But this seems wrong. The deliberation may be precisely what grounds
the person's move to act impetuously. For example, consider a case where
preliminary reflection on alternatives yields a thicket of advantages and
disadvantages, with no course of action that is clearly superior to all others. Suppose further that the agent realizes that more reflection or more
information that is hard to get might help, but he just gets fed up with
deliberating.

Emotionality, impetuosity, and unreflectiveness are often related, however. In Malory's world, as in ours, they often accompany one another,
showing a need for a code to keep them in check. There is a familiar sort
of person who combines them, a highly emotional, impulsive, headstrong
person who plunges heatedly into action without stopping to deliberate
about the pros and cons of his behavior. For much of the *Morte Darthur*,
Gawain is such a person. In fact, unreflective, impetuous behavior is a
major force in Malory's world. Quick reactions are of course a virtue on
the battlefield, where deliberation can waste precious time. But impetu-

osity often gets Malory's knights into trouble. Perhaps one illustration is the episode in the final tale, where a knight precipitates a catastrophic battle by unthinkingly drawing a sword to kill an adder that has stung him on the foot. The knight is heedless of the risk of drawing a sword in the volatile, potential-battle situation in which he finds himself. Although this knight's behavior may be a natural, quasi-reflexive by-product of knights' training to act quickly and decisively,[50] rather than an expression of "impulsive vehemence or passion," the possibility of such disastrous misfires shows the need as well for training in self-control. At any rate, not all Malorian knights are equally impetuous, nor is any knight equally impetuous at all times. The final tale shows great variation in Gawain along this dimension, culminating in his deathbed admission that "all is through mine own hastiness and wilfulness"[51] and his long, conciliatory letter to Launcelot.

Impetuosity, distractibility, and heedlessness are not the only mental traits that inhibit success on the Malorian battlefield, as well as in other Malorian knightly roles. Another is that many of Malory's knights are not very bright. Satires exploit this, as in *Monty Python and the Holy Grail* (which includes a hilarious scene involving two guards who cannot grasp the order "Make sure the prince doesn't leave this room until I come and get him") and *A Connecticut Yankee in King Arthur's Court*.[52] To take a (literally) striking example of knightly stupidity from an early, pre–Round Table episode in the *Morte Darthur*, "[w]hen [Balan] beheld [his brother] Balin [covered in armor], him thought it should be his brother Balin because of his two swords, but because he knew not [Balin's] shield he deemed it was not [Balin]. And so they aventred [set in position] their spears and came marvellously fast together."[53] This leads to the death of both brothers and shows patent stupidity on Balan's part in failing to recognize the possibility that Balin is using another knight's shield. That is not impetuous failure to reason and think; it is stupid reasoning and thinking. Balan is apparently doing his best to achieve his desired end, which includes not harming his brother. This strengthens the claim that his error is due to low intelligence rather than to mixed motives or to such immediately correctable failings as inattentiveness.

With respect to the Round Table oath, the knights' low intelligence means that they could not grasp a heavily qualified, highly complicated code of behavior. But it also limits their ability to use good judgment in applying a simple and general code to the complicated situations they may encounter. In Malory's world, as in ours, low intelligence is a common fact of life, and a code of behavior for such a society must take into account that many of its members are rather dense.

Low intelligence, in the sense of a deficiency of basic thinking and reasoning abilities, should be distinguished from irrationality, which involves poor use of what cognitive abilities one has.[54] Irrationality can manifest itself not only in such cases of unthinkingness as that of the knight killing the adder but also in cases involving complex attitudes, including virtuous ones. For example, irrational trust in one's spouse may be a greater virtue than a rational, cold-blooded attitude toward evidence suggesting her infidelity, especially when the evidence is equivocal.

Arthur's attitude toward Guenever for a long while shows this kind of obtuseness, and as one commentator points out, "Malory implies that he was a finer man for not having suspected what was true."[55] Trust in one's loved ones can be automatic, but it can also be deliberately cultivated by selective attention, deliberate seeking of alternative explanations of evidence suggesting unfaithfulness, etc. This characterizes Arthur during part of the *Morte Darthur*.[56] By the opening of the final tale, however, Arthur has gone beyond this. He now has "a deeming, but [because of his great love for *Launcelot*] he would not hear of"[57] Guenever's affair with Launcelot.

Arthur's longtime tendency to retain faith in his queen may be reasonably counted a virtue. But this hardly seems plausible for all cases of irrational trustingness. For example, in an earlier episode, even after Launcelot knows that Meliagaunt has abducted Guenever, has accused her of treason, and is now awaiting a trial by battle with Launcelot (a knight of much greater prowess) to settle the matter, he still unsuspectingly accepts Meliagaunt's offer to take him on a tour of Meliagaunt's castle—during which Launcelot treads on a trapdoor and falls into a dungeon. Malory actually considers this trustingness a virtue. He explains Launcelot's trust here by telling the reader that "for ever a man of worship [honor] and of prowess dreadeth least always perils, for they ween [think] every man be as they [men of worship and prowess] be."[58]

The conclusion seems inescapable that, to Malory, a man of worship and of prowess is a man of poor judgment. The passage about a man of worship and of prowess invites us to admire the character of a man so honorable that he cannot conceive of dishonor in anyone else ("they ween every man be as they be"). But the evidence of Meliagaunt's wickedness is so blatant, and the obligation of trust from Launcelot to Meliagaunt is so weak, that Launcelot's trustingness here seems simply dense. (Launcelot and Meliagaunt are both knights of the Round Table, but Launcelot knows that Meliagaunt has already "cowardly and traitorly . . . set archers to slay [Launcelot's] horse."[59] Furthermore, Meliagaunt's abduction of Guenever has, to put it mildly, violated the Round Table oath's stricture "always to do ladies, damosels, and gentlewomen succour, upon pain of death.") And trustingness is not an ideal Malory consistently holds. As one scholar points out, all generalizations about Malory (except that one?) have exceptions.[60] Launcelot, the quintessential Malorian man of worship and of prowess, is not consistently trusting. In fact, there is mention, earlier in the Meliagaunt episode, that Launcelot "dread sore the treason of Sir Meliagaunt."[61] There is even an indication, in the final tale, that he does not completely trust King Arthur and needs reassurance about Arthur's trustworthiness.[62] As readers of the *Morte Darthur* will see, Malory's world has additional cases of men of worship and of prowess who do not ween every man be as they be.

Another crucial knightly trait has to do with the role of the Round Table fellowship in the lives of its members. Percival's aunt remarks that the knights "have lost their fathers and their mothers, and all their kin, and their wives and their children, for to be of [the Round Table] fellowship."[63] Of course, disloyalties, feuds, and diverting romantic entanglements are by no means unknown among the knights and in fact ultimately bring about the destruction of the fellowship. But for most of the *Morte Darthur*, the Round Table has for its members a passionate importance that present-day jargon like "male bonding" can barely begin to capture. This makes the knights receptive to a demanding oath that binds them to one another and to King Arthur. Arthur's notorious remark in the final tale, "much more I am sorrier for my good knights' loss than for the loss of my fair queen; for queens I might have enow [enough], but such a fellowship of good knights shall never be together in no company,"[64] is a particularly dramatic illustration of this attitude.

The paramount importance of the Round Table fellowship in the lives of its members has another vital consequence. It means that the knights' identities are twice defined publicly, in terms of their social role in a group that itself has a social role relative to the outside world. This is why, or part of why, the knights set such great store by their honor and repute, which Malory calls "worship" (from the Old English *weorthscipe* ["worthiness," "respect"], from *weorth* ["worthy," "worth"] and *-scipe* ["-ship"]).[65] Several Malory scholars have stressed that Malory's world is a shame-culture in the sense that shame and external sanctions matter more than guilt and internal sanctions and "[t]he important thing is not one's own knowledge of what one has done . . . but public recognition of one's actions."[66] This point has at times been overgeneralized, but it is essential to understanding the enormous importance of repute in Malory's world.

Yet another important trait of Malorian knights of the Round Table is that they are uncritical, almost reflexive Christians. This does not mean that their primary interests are religious or that they live in a state of religious fervor. Except at the end of the book and on the quest of the Holy Grail, these things are not true. What is true is that Malorian knights are not what we now call critical and independent thinkers about the basic precepts of their lives. No one raises principled objections to the teachings of the church. When Malorian knights go against (Christian) religious authority, it is never for this reason. For example, in the final tale, when Arthur's bastard son Mordred tells the bishop of Canterbury, "Do thou thy worst, wit thou well I shall defy thee,"[67] this manifests sheer headstrongness and wickedness, rather than principled disagreement with the teachings of the church. Malorian knights are likewise uncritical of the chivalric code. (A partial exception to this is the mildly iconoclastic Dinadan, but his iconoclasm is more a matter of speech than of action.) Like the teachings of the church, the Round Table oath gets violated in Malory's world, but not because of principled disagreement. Malorian knights have no ideological objection to the Round Table oath, either to its specific provisions or to the fact that it means that King Arthur is telling them how to live. When Mordred and Gawain each defy Arthur in the final tale, it is not for this reason. Nowadays, it is common to hear the view that people should develop their own moral codes according to their own consciences and no one should lay down moral rules for anyone else. Such a view of morality is totally alien to Malory's world. The knights' lack of intellectual sophistication, not to mention their eruptive emotionality, impetuosity, and unreflectiveness, will doubtless make them seem childish to many present-day readers. Different cultures have different conceptions of adult behavior. How many of us could succeed as adults in Malory's world?

Taking this background into account, I will now consider the specific provisions of the Round Table oath.

"never to do outrageousity nor murder, and always to flee treason"

It is tempting to dismiss this stricture as superfluous. Whom is it supposed to enlighten—knights who would otherwise think that "outrageousity," murder, and treason were knightly virtues?[68] To dismiss this stricture on grounds of obviousness or superfluity, though, would overlook two important points. First, part of the purpose of the oath is precisely to make it clear to the knights that they are not free to use their knightly prowess however they please. Second, as I have mentioned, the oath has an inspirational as well as an instructional function. The annual affirmation of the oath, "sworn at the high feast of Pentecost,"[69] is a ceremonial act that affirms and strengthens the knights' resolve and allegiance.

The injunction against murder raises another question. Just what sorts of killings amount to "murder" among warriors whose professional duties lead to killing under certain circumstances? Malory's concept of treason is relevant here. He tells us that "the custom was such that time that all manner of shameful death was called treason,"[70] "all manner of murderers in those days were called treason."[71] The "shamefulness" that turns a killing into treason and murder is a violation of the conventions for slaying "knightly and not shamefully,"[72] that is, it is "to take [someone] by surprise, or at a disadvantage, or to employ subterfuge."[73] This is yet another illustration of the importation of manners of sportsmanship into conflicts where much more is at stake. For example, in the final tale, Launcelot is "betrapped with some treason"[74] by fourteen knights and through subterfuge (although his trappers do not succeed in killing him).

Although in Malory's world all murder is treason, not all treason is murder or attempted murder. "Treason" also applies to an offense against loyalty and against a system of reciprocal obligation. An injunction against treason in this sense is an essential part of any warrior code where a warrior is fighting with and/or for other people. Military loyalty is fundamental to the Round Table. This makes violation of such loyalty an especially serious offense. There could hardly be a functioning military predicated on the assumption that warriors were free to betray their leader or vice versa, or that warriors were free to betray their comrades-in-arms. This sense of "treason" as disloyalty makes the Round Table oath bind the knights specifically to King Arthur and to one another. However, loyalty to one's leader does not require total obedience in Malory's world. In the final tale, Gawain is not accused of treason for rejecting Arthur's direction to bring Guenever to the fire where she is slated to be burnt or, later, for refusing to let Arthur reconcile with Launcelot. Gawain's implacability, however wrongheaded, is not disloyal to Arthur, and Gawain honorably manifests this implacability openly, not through dishonorable subterfuge.

"Treason" refers to disloyalty in other contexts as well. In feudal law, it was treason to commit adultery with the wife of one's lord or vassal, and "Lancelot's adultery with the wife of [his] king [was] high treason."[75] Launcelot, in a self-justifying speech in the final tale, acknowledges that his committing adultery with Guenever would be traitorous, although he does not admit to having done so.[76]

"also, by no mean to be cruel, but to give mercy unto him that asketh mercy, upon pain of forfeiture of their worship and lordship of King Arthur for evermore"

Pleas for mercy come in various contexts in Malory's world. Not all are relevant to the Round Table oath. When Elaine of Astolat (who may be more familiar to the general reader as Tennyson's Lady of Shalott) implores Launcelot to "have mercy upon me, and suffer me not to die for thy love"[77] by marrying her or at least becoming her lover, he is not in violation of the oath when he refuses. Nowadays, anyone threatening to die if love is not reciprocated would likely be accused of "emotional blackmail" and packed off to a therapist for a mental makeover. Such simplistic psychobabble and dismissive solutions are obviously alien to Malory's world, which honors *both* the dignity and tragedy of Elaine of Astolat's love *and* Launcelot's right to refuse it.[78] The mercy stricture of the oath requires a knight to accept a surrender and refrain from slaying a knight he has overcome in combat and who has formally yielded to him and asked for mercy. This situation can arise when the victorious knight is in any of the knightly roles I have already mentioned: warrior in a battle between armies, combatant in a trial by battle, quasi policeman and keeper of the peace, or athlete in jousts or tournaments. (It may seem ludicrous that jousts and tournaments could come to this, but, as I have mentioned, it illustrates the blurred boundary between sport and battle in Malory's world.) Mercy is a Christian virtue. Requiring mercy shows the religious underpinnings of Arthurian knighthood as embodying Christian virtues rather than resting on brute force.

Once mercy is granted, a natural question arises: what happens next? The victorious knight can have considerable leeway to set terms. In an early tournament, Tristram extracts these terms from the defeated Palomides: "First, upon pain of your life that ye forsake my lady La Beale Isoud, and in no manner wise that ye draw not to her. Also this twelvemonth and a day that ye bear none armour nor none harness of war. Now promise me this, or here shalt thou die."[79] Tristram, although a knight, is not yet a knight of the Round Table, but his behavior would be acceptable in one. In a much later episode, Launcelot, fighting on Guenever's behalf in a trial by battle, makes his defeated opponent Mador "discharge [his] quarrel [with Guenever] for ever"[80] as a condition of receiving mercy.

A common consequence of the granting of mercy by a knight in his role as quasi policeman and keeper of the peace is that the defeated opponent must present himself to the court of King Arthur. The aftermath may surprise modern readers: the former opponent may be "made . . . a knight of the Table Round to his life's end, and [given] great lands."[81] This may seem a naïve Christian approach to conflict: if you are a knight, you must give mercy when requested; your enemy is redeemable if he repents and converts to your side, but the possibility does not really arise that he might reasonably never *want* to convert to your side. (Such an approach would hardly be appropriate in a world that acknowledges what we now call pluralism and diversity.) But there is a sense in which mercy is not required across the board in Malory's world. If a knight asks for and receives mercy from his knightly opponent in a trial by battle, the person the knight is fighting for (who may be the knight himself) does not thereby automatically escape judicial, possibly capital, punishment under King Arthur's auspices.[82] In fact, the very next stricture of the Round Table oath mandates death for Round Table knights who fall short of it.

"and always to do ladies, damosels, and gentlewomen succour, upon pain of death"

Just as Launcelot does not violate the previous stricture when he spurns Elaine of Astolat's love, he does not thereby run afoul of this one. The succor that a knight is required always to do ladies, damsels, and gentlewomen does not entail granting sexual favors or reciprocating their

love. (Of course, Malory's terminology for women here illustrates my earlier point that he is basically writing about the aristocracy.) Although
women can wield considerable moral authority in Malory's world, they
are physically vulnerable and in need of knightly protection. A world
where women are dependent upon male prowess invites feminist objections that are too familiar to be interesting. Far more interesting is the fact
that this stricture of the Round Table oath turns the (female) weak into the
strong.[83] (Note the parallel with the previous stricture, which also
requires the strong to defer to the weak.)[84] This keeps women from being
"helpless before the law so long as legal quarrels could be settled only by
means of battle,"[85] any more than nonlawyers in our world are helpless
before the law to the extent that our legal quarrels can be settled only by
means of lawyers. Just as nonlawyers in our world gain legal power by
hiring lawyers, women in Malory's world gain legal power by having
knights fight on their behalf in trials by battle. In fact, since the oath
requires Round Table knights "always to do ladies, damosels, and gentlewomen succour," ladies, damsels, and gentlewomen in need of succor
have an automatic claim on the fighting prowess of even the strongest
knight. It is as if present-day Americans had an automatic claim on the
free services of the likes of Johnnie Cochran and Alan Dershowitz, and on
various other top-quality free services as well.

It is true that there are cases where women in Malory's world use the
Round Table oath "as a defense or as a weapon against their socially constructed identities."[86] But it is also true that the oath deliberately constructs women's identities in such a way as to empower ladies, damsels,
and gentlewomen with the power of even the strongest knight. The claim
that "the knightly understanding of women as powerless ironically renders them powerful"[87] is thus only part of the story. It needs to be ampli-
fied as follows. First, giving women power is a *deliberate function* of the
Round Table oath, rather than just a way women can subvert the Round
Table oath to their advantage. Second, what renders women powerful is
not just the knightly understanding of women as powerless but this
understanding *in conjunction with* the imperative that knights of the
Round Table always do ladies, damsels, and gentlewomen succor. Without this imperative, the knightly understanding of women as powerless
could be an impetus for taking advantage of them rather than for protecting and serving them.

But what if the strongest knight is unavailable? What if he is already
committed to fight for a lady's female opponent?[88] This possibility illustrates a problem with the oath. A knight can hardly fight for both sides of
a quarrel between two ladies. Or suppose in his adventurous travels
through the Malorian forest, a knight comes at once upon two ladies, each
in dire need of immediate rescue from a separate attacker. How is he to
decide which lady to aid? The oath gives him no guidance. Does he
deserve death because he cannot be in two places at once? Or is it enough

that there is *some* lady he is aiding? The oath is unclear on this point.

This stricture also raises problems in conjunction with other strictures. What if doing a lady succor requires a knight to do battle in a wrongful quarrel? Philosophers are often criticized for offering bizarre and preposterous counterexamples to moral principles that are serviceable enough for the situations people actually encounter in daily life.[89] My objection to the stricture about women is not of this sort. Problems actually arise with the daily-life application of this stricture in Malory's world, and there is no obvious, commonsense way to resolve them. Readers of the final tale can decide for themselves whether Launcelot does Guenever succor there by doing battle in a wrongful quarrel.[90] But in an earlier episode, where Guenever (wrongly) appears to be guilty of poisoning a guest at a feast, the knights present at the feast are unwilling to fight for her because "all they have great suspicion unto the queen."[91] Moreover, Launcelot, who has promised Guenever "ever to be her knight in right other in wrong,"[92] is (initially) absent. A paradox thus arises: a woman may need to *appear* to be in the right in order to get a knight to fight for her to *prove* she is in the right. Women who do appear to be in the right, however, have the power I mentioned: every Round Table knight is obliged to aid them.

Another stricture that comes into actual as well as theoretical conflict with the stricture about ladies is the stricture about mercy. The oath stipulates penalties for violating these strictures: death in the case of the stricture about ladies and social death (forfeiture of worship and lordship of King Arthur for evermore) in the case of the mercy stricture. The oath does not rank-order the strictures. But it is instructive to look at how some of the Round Table oath's strictures show their aptness by prohibiting transgressions that the knights have committed in a series of adventures leading up to the introduction of the oath. As one scholar puts it, "Malory's rules of chivalry are thus determined empirically."[93] In these preoath adventures, Gawain denies an opponent's plea for mercy and, in his quest for revenge, inadvertently kills a lady. Pellinor spurns a lady's plea for succor. Both knights receive severe criticism. Gawain even gets a reproof from his brother Gaheris using language that will later be echoed in the Round Table oath, "ye should give mercy unto them that ask mercy."[94] And Tor faces the conflict between doing succor to a damsel and granting mercy to a knight. Tor chooses the former, denying a plea for mercy. He does this partly because he has already granted the damsel's open-ended plea for "a gift"[95]—whereupon she informs him that the desired "gift" is the head of his opponent—and partly because this knight has previously declined Tor's offer of mercy. But in contrast to the criticism Gawain receives for his refusal to grant mercy in this series of adventures, Tor's actions receive only praise. Upon learning of Tor's adventures, "the king and the queen made great joy,"[96] thereby suggesting that, at least in this circumstance, they value service to a damsel over mercy to a knight.[97] Succoring women does not invariably override other considerations in

Malory's world, however. If it did, female transgressors could not be punished, let alone condemned to death, as Arthur does to Guenever. As I have indicated, Malorian knights are hardly suited to rigorous philosophical reasoning about moral dilemmas. But they are capable of seeking counsel, and many of them frequently have good judgment about moral matters. No moral code can eliminate the need for some moral judgments to be made in daily life. Requiring a pair of incompatible actions, however, is a flaw that can be avoided by better formulation of the code.[98]

"Also, that no man take no battles in a wrongful quarrel for no law [love, in the Vinaver edition], ne for no world's goods."

This stricture reinforces the idea that knightly power is something that the knights of the Round Table are not free to use however they like. They must not use their power for wrongful causes, which precludes their being mercenaries or highway robbers ("ne for no world's goods"). In the final tale, the fact that "Arthur has to *buy* a truce with [Mordred]"[99] indicates Mordred's wickedness and unknightliness. This stricture also means that knights "must never defend a guilty party in trial by battle,"[100] which, as I have indicated, clashes with the stricture about always doing ladies, damsels, and gentlewomen succor. God may speed the right in Malory's world, but, as I have mentioned, the fact that this process is not inevitable is part of what makes this final stricture an injunction against an offense that is more dangerous socially than merely wasting time and energy in a futile battle.

Despite its limitations, the Round Table oath offers a moral, inspirational, and generally serviceable code that enables Arthurian society to flourish in glory and splendor for many years. Ultimately, the Round Table falls. Is the fault in the oath or in the individuals who fall short of it or both? Why not read Malory and decide for yourself?[101]

NOTES

Felicia Ackerman, Ph.D., is a professor of philosophy at Brown University with special expertise on the subject of Sir Thomas Malory's *Morte Darthur*. She has published articles on Malory's *Morte Darthur* as well as short stories with Malorian themes. She was on my dissertation committee when I was a graduate student at Brown, and her passion and insights regarding the idealized warrior that is the knight of the Round Table have inspired my teaching of this subject to my midshipmen. She views my future warriors as the modern heirs to Malory's knights and has lectured on that subject at USNA. I asked her to guest author this chapter because her work has had such an influence on me that had I attempted to write about what she calls "Malory's world," I would have had to quote or cite her almost every other line. It seemed much better to go to the source. Felicia's deep respect for future U.S. warriors (and my students in particular) and genuine love for this project are such that I knew that her contribution would both blend with and enhance this volume. [S.E.F.]

The epigraph meets the requirements for the type of light verse known as a double dactyl. For details of these requirements, see Anthony Hecht and John Hollander, eds., *Jiggery-Pokery: A Compendium of Double Dactyls* (New York: Atheneum, 1967), 26–31. This double dactyl first appeared in my "Late in the Quest: The Study of Malory's *Morte Darthur* as a New Direction in Philosophy," in *Midwest Studies in Philosophy 23: New Directions in Philosophy*, ed. Peter A. French and Howard K. Wettstein (Malden, Mass. not : Blackwell, 1999), 312.

1. Sir Thomas Malory, *Le Morte D'Arthur* (London: Penguin, 1969), 1: 116; C 3, 15; V 120:25–27. For explanation of this form of reference, see note 3, below.
2. A different edition of Malory, the Vinaver edition, is based mainly on the Winchester manuscript. This is a Malory manuscript (believed to be in the handwriting of scribes rather than of Malory himself) discovered at Winchester College in 1934 and subsequently edited by Eugène Vinaver—a sequence of events that, unsurprisingly, transformed Malory scholarship. Although the Winchester manuscript and Caxton's edition contain basically similar material, they also have significant differences, and debate continues over which is closer to what Malory actually wrote. (For a discussion of this issue, see Robert L. Kindrick, "Which Malory Should I Teach?" in *Approaches to Teaching the Arthurian Tradition*, ed. Maureen Fries and Jeanie Watson [New York: Modern Language Association of America, 1992], 100–105; Ingrid Tieken-Boon van Ostade, *The Two Versions of Malory's Morte Darthur: Multiple Negation and the Editing of the Text* [Cambridge, UK: D. S. Brewer, 1995]; and Eugène Vinaver, ed., *The Works of Sir Thomas Malory*, 3d ed., revised by P. J. C. Field [Oxford: Oxford University Press, 1990], especially Vinaver's preface to his first edition and chaps. 2–4 of his introduction.) Reflecting his (highly controversial) view that Malory wrote eight separate romances rather than one unified work, Vinaver called his edition not *Le Morte D'Arthur* (Caxton's title) but *The Works of Sir Thomas Malory*. The general term "the *Morte Darthur*," which I use in this chapter, covers both versions. Vinaver's edition uses unmodernized Middle English spelling. There is also a text based on the Winchester manuscript and using modernized spelling (Sir Thomas Malory, *Le Morte Darthur: The Winchester Manuscript*, edited and with an introduction and explanatory notes by Helen Cooper [Oxford: Oxford University Press, 1998]), but it is abridged, with various wonderful episodes omitted.
3. For the sake of Malory scholars (whom I hope this chapter will also interest, despite the practical necessity of my including background information already familiar to them), I include references to Vinaver's three-volume *The Works of Sir Thomas Malory* for all quoted Malory passages. I am using a three-way reference system, giving first the volume and page numbers in the Penguin Classics volumes (e.g., 2:227), then the book and chapter numbers of the Caxton edition (e.g., C 14, 2), then the page and line numbers of the corresponding (and not always identical) passages in the third edition of Vinaver's three-volume *The Works of Sir Thomas Malory* (e.g., V 907:2–3), whose continuous pagination makes

specifying the volume number unnecessary. The spelling of all proper names is from the Penguin Classics volumes.

4. To appreciate the problems that the Middle English spelling can pose for nonspecialists, try to guess what *heete sone keelyth* means. None of the nonspecialists I asked got it right, even when I supplied the context, "for where they bethe sone accorded and hasty, heete sone keelyth. And ryght so faryth the love nowadayes, sone hote sone colde" (*Works of Malory*, 1119:33–1120:2). The answer is "for where they be soon accorded and hasty, heat soon cooleth. And right so fareth the love nowadays, soon hot, soon cold."

5. For a comparison of Malory's version of the Round Table oath with those of other medieval Arthurian writers, see Beverly Kennedy, *Knighthood in the Morte Darthur*, 2d ed. (Cambridge, UK: D. S. Brewer, 1992), 67–68; and Thomas L. Wright, "'The Tale of King Arthur': Beginnings and Foreshadowings," in *Malory's Originality*, ed. R. M. Lumiansky (Baltimore: Johns Hopkins University Press, 1964), 36 ff.

6. Malory, *Morte D'Arthur*, 1:115–16; C 3, 15.

7. *Works of Malory*, 120:17–24. I have used the modernized spelling in Cooper, 57, although I have not followed her substitution of "nor" for "ne."

8. Elizabeth T. Pochoda, *Arthurian Propaganda: Le Morte Darthur as an Historical Ideal of Life* (Chapel Hill: University of North Carolina Press, 1971), 84.

9. Vinaver, commentary on *Works of Malory*, 1335.

10. Pochoda, *Arthurian Propaganda*, 84.

11. Kennedy, *Knighthood*, 37–38.

12. For an interesting philosophical treatment of the relation between moral rules and social roles, see P. F. Strawson, "Social Morality and Individual Ideal," *Philosophy* 36, no. 136 (1961): 1–17.

13. R. M. Hare, *Moral Thinking* (Oxford: Clarendon Press, 1981), 36. See the discussion in this book about the relation between moral rules and human limitations.

14. William Caxton, preface to Malory, *Morte D'Arthur*, 6.

15. See Hare, *Moral Thinking*, 200 ff.

16. Aristotle, *Nicomachean Ethics*, 1106a, b. See the discussion in Hare, *Moral Thinking*, 198 ff.

17. Malory, *Morte D'Arthur*, 2:277; C 14, 2; V 907:2–3.

18. Malory, *Morte D'Arthur*, 2:378; C 18, 4; V 1050:18–20.

19. See Malory, *Morte D'Arthur*, 2:480; C 20, 12; V 1190:17–20 and 1190: 35–1191: 2; and 2:484; C 20, 14; V 1194:22–24; and 2:496; C 20, 19; V 1213:3–4.

20. Malory, *Morte D'Arthur*, 2:489; C 20, 16; V 1200:17–18.

21. This is not the only function trial by battle serves in Malory's world. Trial by battle can also be used to settle land claims and questions of which kingdom will pay tribute to the other. See the discussion in Kennedy, *Knighthood*, 46 ff.

22. Malory, *Morte D'Arthur*, 2:379; C 18, 4; V 1051:3.

23. This point was made in discussion by several actual future warriors, midshipmen at the U.S. Naval Academy.

24. Malory, *Morte D'Arthur*, 2:16; C 10, 7; V 578:26–27.

25. Malory, *Morte D'Arthur*, 2:30; C 10, 14; V 592: 26–27.

26. Malory, *Morte D'Arthur*, 2:470; C 20, 7; V 1175:20–21. See the discussion in Kennedy, *Knighthood*, 314 ff.

27. Malory, *Morte D'Arthur*, 2:30; C 10, 15; V 593:11–13.

28. For a survey of philosophical and theological responses to the problem of

evil, see John Hospers, *An Introduction to Philosophical Analysis*, 4th ed. (Upper Saddle River, N.J.: Prentice Hall, 1997), 221–30. See also Kennedy's discussion of trial by battle, *Knighthood*, 39–47, 155–61.

29. See the discussion in Kennedy, *Knighthood*, 47 ff.

30. Although this remark is commonly attributed to the duke of Wellington, the attribution is dubious. See the discussion in Elizabeth Longford, *Wellington: The Years of the Sword* (New York: Harper & Row, 1969), 16–17.

31. Kennedy, *Knighthood*, 70. See also Larry D. Benson, *Malory's Morte Darthur* (Cambridge: Harvard University Press, 1976), 168.

32. See the discussion in Kennedy, *Knighthood*, 71–72, 86–87.

33. Malory, *Morte D'Arthur*, 1:146; C 4, 18; V 160:34–35. This is not to offer Gawain's performance in this episode as a paragon of knightly sportsmanship, however. He also, most reprehensibly, threatens to slay Marhaus's horse if Marhaus fails to dismount! See Kennedy, *Knighthood*, 71.

34. Malory, *Morte D'Arthur*, 1:161; C 4, 25; V 175:29. See Kennedy, *Knighthood*, 86–87.

35. D. S. Brewer, introduction to *The Morte Darthur, Parts Seven and Eight* (Evanston, Ill.: Northwestern University Press, 1974), 20.

36. Malory, *Morte D'Arthur*, 2:438; C 19, 6; V 1132:16.

37. Malory, *Morte D'Arthur*, 1:227; C 6, 17; V 285: 24–25.

38. Malory, *Morte D'Arthur*, 2:499; C 20, 20; V 1216:18–20.

39. Malory, *Morte D'Arthur*, 2:502; C 20, 22; V 1219:27–1220: 4.

40. Mark Lambert, *Malory: Style and Vision in Le Morte Darthur* (New Haven: Yale University Press, 1975), 165. See also the discussion in Andrew Lynch, *Malory's Book of Arms: The Narrative of Combat in Le Morte Darthur* (Cambridge, UK: D. S. Brewer, 1997), 55.

41. Malory, *Morte D'Arthur*, 2:468–69; C 20, 7; V 1174:12–13.

42. Kennedy, *Knighthood*, 38.

43. Malory, *Morte D'Arthur*, 1:124; C 4, 5; V 131: 28–29. For an alternative interpretation of the remark, see P. J. C. Field, *Romance and Chronicle: A Study of Malory's Prose Style* (Bloomington: Indiana University Press, 1971), 113.

44. Malory, *Morte D'Arthur*, 2:172; C 10, 82; V 769: 12–13.

45. Malory, *Morte D'Arthur*, 2:172; C 10, 82; V 769:17–21.

46. Malory, *Morte D'Arthur*, 1:454; C 9, 36; V 540:30–36. I discuss pity and self-pity further in my "Pity as a Moral Concept/The Morality of Pity," in *Midwest Studies in Philosophy 20: Moral Concepts*, ed. Peter A. French, Theodore E. Uehling Jr., and Howard K. Wettstein (Notre Dame, Ind.: University of Notre Dame Press, 1996), 59–66; and "Flourish Your Heart in This World: Emotion, Reason, and Action in Malory's *Le Morte Darthur*," in *Midwest Studies in Philosophy 22: The Philosophy of Emotions*, ed. Peter A. French and Howard K. Wettstein (Notre Dame, Ind.: University of Notre Dame Press, 1998), 196–98; as well as in three short stories, "Have an After Eight Mint," *Moment*, April 1987, 50–57; "The Forecasting Game," in *Prize Stories 1990: The O. Henry Awards*, ed. William Abrahams (New York: Doubleday, 1990), 315–35; and "Entertain the Thought," *Witness* 16, no. 1 (2002): 42–53. (The last of these stories has a Malorian theme.)

47. Malory, *Morte D'Arthur*, 2:482; C 20, 13; V 1192:29–31.

48. This alternative interpretation was offered by a midshipman at the U.S. Naval Academy. See also Vinaver, commentary to *Works of Malory*, 1626.

49. *Merriam-Webster's Collegiate Dictionary*, 10th ed., s.v. "impetuous."

50. I owe this suggestion to Karen Cherewatuk.

51. Malory, *Morte D'Arthur*, 2:508; C 21, 2; V 1230:19–20.

52. Mark Twain, *A Connecticut Yankee in King Arthur's Court* (Berkeley and Los Angeles: University of California Press, 1979). See also Robert H. Wilson, "Malory in the *Connecticut Yankee*," *Studies in English* 27 (1948): 185–206.

53. Malory, *Morte D'Arthur*, 1:87-8; C 2, 18; V 89:9–14.

54. For discussion of this distinction, see my "Flourish Your Heart," 185–89.

55. R. T. Davies, "The Worshipful Way in Malory," *Patterns of Love and Courtesy: Essays in Memory of C. S. Lewis*, ed. John Lawlor (London: Edward Arnold, 1966), 173. See also R. T. Davies, "Malory's Launcelot and the Noble Way of the World," *Review of English Studies* 6 (1955): 360, as well as the discussion in Beverly Kennedy, "Malory's Lancelot: 'Trewest Lover, of a Synful Man,'" *Viator* 12 (1981): 424–25.

56. See Malory, *Morte D'Arthur*, 2:54; C 10, 27; V 617:10–16.

57. Malory, *Morte D'Arthur*, 2:458; C 20, 2; V 1163:22–23.

58. Malory, *Morte D'Arthur*, 2:441; C 19, 7; V 1134:28–30.

59. Malory, *Morte D'Arthur*, 2:436; C 19, 5; V 1129:29–30.

60. Field, *Romance and Chronicle*, 148. See also p. 119.

61. Malory, *Morte D'Arthur*, 2:433; C 19, 4; V 1126:10–11.

62. See Malory, *Morte D'Arthur*, 2:467-8; C 20, 6; V 1173:12–25.

63. Malory, *Morte D'Arthur*, 2:276; C 14, 2; V 906:22–24.

64. Malory, *Morte D'Arthur*, 2:473; C 20, 9; V 1184:1–5.

65. *Merriam-Webster's Collegiate Dictionary*, 10th ed., s.v. "worship."

66. Lambert, *Malory*, 179. Lambert adds that this ethos is not just depicted but also endorsed by Malory: "It is Malory himself, not just his characters, for whom honor and shame are more real than innocence and guilt. [The] *Morte Darthur* is *of* rather than *about* a shame ethos" (179; emphasis in original). See also the discussions in Brewer, introduction to *The Morte Darthur, Parts Seven and Eight*; Terence McCarthy, *An Introduction to Malory* (Cambridge, UK: D. S. Brewer, 1991), 84 ff; and Stephen J. Miko, "Malory and the Chivalric Order," *Medium Aevum* 35, no. 3 (1966): 211–30.

67. Malory, *Morte D'Arthur*, 2:506; C 21, 1; V 1228:8–9.

68. Kennedy explicates "never to do outerage" (the unmodified Middle English spelling in the Vinaver edition) as charging that the knights "never become lawless themselves" (*Knighthood*, 38). McCarthy seems to take it as an injunction against violence (*Introduction to Malory*, 73), which would presumably be limited to the wrong sort of violence, since legitimate violence is part of a knight's role. Vinaver's glossary, however, explicates "outerage" in the oath simply as "outrage" (*Works of Malory*, 1729).

69. Malory, *Morte D'Arthur*, 1:116; C 3, 15; V 120:26–27.

70. Malory, *Morte D'Arthur*, 2:378; C 18, 4; V 1050:2–3.

71. Malory, *Morte D'Arthur*, 1:338; C 8, 20; V 405:5.

72. Malory, *Morte D'Arthur*, 1:244; C 7, 8; V 305:20.

73. Kennedy, *Knighthood*, 122.

74. Malory, *Morte D'Arthur*, 2:464; C 20, 5; V 1169:14.

75. Kennedy, *Knighthood*, 9. See the discussion on pp. 9–10, 175–76, 362 n. 12.

76. Malory, *Morte D'Arthur*, 2:477–78; C 20, 11; V 1188.

77. Malory, *Morte D'Arthur*, 2:411; C 18, 19; V 1089:13–14.

78. Malory's world does not always look so kindly on those who spurn love, however. See the discussion in my "Flourish Your Heart," 210–11.

79. Malory, *Morte D'Arthur*, 1:320; C 8, 10; V 388:14–18. The condition against bearing arms or harness is not unique to Tristram; for another knight who employs it, see Malory, *Morte D'Arthur*, 2:70; C 10, 36; V 639:13–14 and 2:77–78; C 10, 39; V 646:13–5, 647:2–3.

80. Malory, *Morte D'Arthur*, 2:386; C 18, 7; V 1058:4–5.

81. Malory, *Morte D'Arthur*, 1:302; C 7, 35; V 362:35–36.

82. See the discussion in Kennedy, *Knighthood*, 298–99.

83. See the discussion in Dorsey Armstrong, "Gender and the Chivalric Community: The Pentecostal Oath in Malory's 'Tale of King Arthur,'" in *Bibliographical Bulletin of the International Arthurian Society* 1, no. 1: 293–312.

84. See my "'Always to do ladies, damosels, and gentlewomen succour': Women and the Chivalric Code in Malory's *Morte Darthur*," in *Midwest Studies in Philosophy 26: Renaissance and Early Modern Philosophy*, ed. Peter A. French and Howard K. Wettstein (Malden, Mass.: Blackwell, 2002), 1–12.

85. Kennedy, *Knighthood*, 39.

86. Armstrong, "Gender and Chivalric Community," 304.

87. Armstrong, "Gender and Chivalric Community," 303.

88. This possibility is recognized in a forerunner of the Round Table oath, administered only to Gawain, who swears he will "never be against lady ne gentlewoman, but if he fought for a lady and his adversary fought for another" (Malory, *Morte D'Arthur*, 1:104; C 3, 8; V 109:2–3).

89. See the discussions in John Martin Fischer, "Stories," in *Midwest Studies in Philosophy 20: Moral Concepts*, ed. Peter A. French, Theodore E. Uehling Jr., and Howard K. Wettstein (Notre Dame, Ind.: University of Notre Dame Press, 1996), 1–14; and Hare, *Moral Thinking*.

90. See also the discussions in the references cited in note 66, above.

91. Malory, *Morte D'Arthur*, 2:378; C 18, 4; V 1050:22–23.

92. Malory, *Morte D'Arthur*, 2:386; C 18, 7; V 1058:31–32.

93. Wright, "'Tale of King Arthur,'" 42.

94. Malory, *Morte D'Arthur*, 1:102 ; C 3, 7 ; V 106:23–24. See the discussion in Wright, "'Tale of King Arthur,'" 41–45; and Kennedy, *Knighthood*, 60–68.

95. Malory, *Morte D'Arthur*, 1:107; C 3, 11; V 112:17.

96. Malory, *Morte D'Arthur* 1:109; C 3, 11; V 114:1–2.

97. See Kennedy, *Knighthood*, 62 ff. and 137–38; Armstrong, "Gender and Chivalric Community," 300–304; and my "Always to Do," 6 ff. for additional discussion of this case.

98. See Wright, "'Tale of King Arthur,'" 62 ff; and Bonnie Wheeler, "Romance and Parataxis and Malory: The Case of Sir Gawain's Reputation," *Arthurian Literature* 20 (1993): 117–18 for additional discussion of shortcomings of the oath.

99. McCarthy, *Introduction to Malory*, 76; emphasis in original. The episode under discussion is in Malory, *Morte D'Arthur*, 2:512; C 21, 3; V 1234:30–1235:2.

100. Kennedy, *Knighthood*, 39.

101. I am indebted to many people for fascinating discussions of this material, including Dorsey Armstrong, Karen Cherewatuk, Shannon French, Kenneth Hodges, Jean Jost, Carol Kaske, Marc Ricciardi, Peter Schroeder, and students in my philosophy in literature courses at Brown University. I also presented material from this chapter at the U.S. Naval Academy and at the Thirty-Sixth Interna-

tional Congress on Medieval Studies, and I am grateful for the excellent discussion in these places as well. I dedicate this chapter to the noble memory of Cassandra Ackerman, 1986–2002.

6

Native Americans:
Warriors of the Sacred Plains

Stereotypes of Native American warriors haunt our popular culture. In song and story and especially on film the "Indian brave" has been alternately demonized and lionized as either a soulless savage who will impede the progress of civilization if not assimilated or destroyed or a noble innocent whose clear-eyed insights may contain civilization's only hope of salvation. Unsurprisingly, neither image does justice to the reality.

Native American author and activist Vine Deloria Jr. comments in his essay "We Talk, You Listen" on the unfortunate effects of the unrealistic, simplistic portrayal of the experience of North American Indians in popular films:

> One reason that Indian people have not been heard from until recently is that we have been completely covered up by movie Indians. Western movies have been such favorites that they have dominated the public's conception of what Indians are. It is not all bad when one thinks about the handsome Jay Silverheels bailing the Lone Ranger out of a jam, or Ed Ames rescuing Daniel Boone with some clever Indian trick. But the other mythologies that have wafted skyward because of the movies have blocked out any idea that there might be real Indians with real problems.[1]

Although some films have tried to depict the Indian point of view as well as that of the white invaders, they are still most often outside interpretations of the culture. More recently produced independent films such as *Pow Wow Highway* and *Smoke Signals* and documentary series such as *The Native Americans* have given indigenous Americans an opportunity to speak in their own voice. But these modern artistic efforts tend to focus more on the plight of present-day reservation Indians than on their tribes' historical struggles. So it is still the case that, generally speaking, the clearest windows into Native American culture of the past are found in what has been preserved of the oral traditions of the individual tribes.

My aim in this chapter is to peer through those windows onto the past, focusing primarily on the eighteenth and nineteenth centuries, and reflect on the ideals associated with the Native American warrior. However, since there are literally hundreds of tribes indigenous to North America, each with its own distinct culture, I cannot possibly provide any single definitive description of the "Native American warrior." Certainly, intertribal similarities exist, and yet the differences are such that, for example, transplanting a Cherokee warrior into a party of Lakota Sioux braves would be no less awkward than shoving Odysseus into a Roman legion.

I can hardly hope to describe the martial elite of hundreds of different tribes in a single chapter. But it would be unforgivable of me not to provide a profile of at least some of the extraordinary indigenous warriors who have populated the vast territory of North America. Therefore what I intend to do is to give my attention to the warrior cultures of a limited sample of Native American tribes; namely, those tribes often referred to as Plains Indians. I hope that reading about the code of the warriors of the Plains tribes will inspire you to research and compare the codes of other tribes as well.

Thomas E. Mails, author of *Mystic Warriors of the Plains,* notes, "At their population peak, around A.D. 1800, all of the Plains tribes together numbered no more than 200,000 people.."[2] Those two hundred thousand or so people were spread out across approximately thirty tribes. These tribes once dominated an enormous ribbon of land stretching down the middle of North America, from the Dakotas to the southernmost tip of Texas, and across from Colorado to Missouri. They included the Blackfoot, Cree, and Gros Ventre in the north, the Sioux, Cheyenne, Arapaho, Kiowa, and Pawnee in the central region, the Comanche and Apache tribes in the south, and the Shoshone, Ute, and Nez Perce in the Rocky Mountains.

I will use this chapter to explore and compare the warrior codes of these powerful Plains tribes. My decision to emphasize the ethos of the plainsmen was partly due to the comparative wealth of information regarding their practices and beliefs. But it was also affected by the fact that many of the myths, good and bad, associated with Native American warriors were born during the years of sustained conflict between the Plains tribes and the white settlers pushing west.

We know too little about early life on the plains, prior to European colonization. Some of the information we have about this period of American history has been pieced together from archeological evidence. But, again, the oral traditions of the tribes are also an invaluable resource. As Mails explains, "[E]ach tribe had its historians who considered it a sacred duty to instruct selected young men carefully in the traditions of the nation, just as their own teachers had taught them."[3]

The astonishing impact that horses were to have on life in the plains did not occur until the late sixteenth century when a Spanish colonizer by the name of Don Juan de Onate introduced a large number of the animals to North America. A few Spanish horses had been brought to the New World as early as 1540, but Onate's herd is believed to be the first that was large (and diverse) enough to breed and to attract the attention of the American natives:

> Some of Onate's animals escaped from their pastures; some were bartered for when the Indians saw their usefulness, and still others were stolen outright. From San Juan Pueblo [near the Rio Grande] horses spread northward to the Canadian groups of Indians; eastward onto the Plains between the Rockies and the Mississippi. With them went Spanish ideas of horse trappings and breeding, and a complete change in Indian cultures.[4]

Before the introduction of the horse, the people of the plains lived a fairly stationary existence. Each tribe was rooted to a particular territory, which included prime hunting grounds for their favorite game. These tribal lands may not have had permanently fixed or marked boundaries, but the heartlands of different tribes were recognized and generally avoided by rival tribes. Mails notes,[5] "Ordinarily small war and raiding parties were the only groups to invade the heartland of the dangerous neighboring areas—the exceptions being times when hunger drove entire tribal divisions to it."[5] The tribal people of the plains were mostly hunter-gatherers, although they also farmed some vegetables, such as corn, squash, and beans. They do not seem to have domesticated any animals for food, such as sheep or cows, in those early days, but they domesticated dogs for their labor. As Alice Marriott and Carol K. Rachlin observe in the introduction to their *Plains Indian Mythology*, "Plains Indians are generally thought of as horseback Indians chasing after buffalo or attacking white settlements, but in the beginning, in their more settled existence, the dog was their only domesticated animal."[6]

A Comanche story, passed down through the generations, tells how the Comanche people first encountered horses and learned how to manage them. According to the tale, a group of Spaniards on horseback rode into the Comanche heartland. The natives were alarmed by the pale Europeans in their strange metal armor, but were fascinated by their mounts, which they took to be large "magic dogs." They led the intruders peacefully back to their village and fed them a meal.

> When everybody had eaten, including the Comanches, the first man [one of the Spaniards] laid his face on the palm of his hand and closed his eyes, to show that he was sleepy. The Comanches gave [the Spaniards] hides to lie

on, and pretty soon all the newcomers were asleep.

"What shall we do?" asked one of the war chiefs.

"We could kill them, and take their magic dogs. That's what I'd like, to own a magic dog."

"No," said a very old man, who was wise in counseling. "Don't kill them. You wouldn't know what to do with a magic dog if you had one. Follow them when they leave here, and watch how they take care of the dogs. Then you will know better."[7]

Grasping the wisdom of the old man's advice, the Comanche warriors shadowed the Spaniards until they had a chance to learn all they needed to know about the care and control of horses. They then conducted a bloodless raid on the Spanish camp under cover of darkness, returning back to their village with their own "magic dogs."

Whether they were stolen in raids, traded for, or found in the wild after breaking free of Spanish corrals, horses were soon to be found in Native American villages all across the plains. While domesticated dogs simply had been employed to ease some of the burdens of the natives' regular lifestyle, horses suggested a means to alter the Indian way of life altogether. The horse's speed and endurance opened up a world of new possibilities.

Horses meant that tribes were no longer tied to static hunting grounds near their villages. Hunters on horseback could pursue moving herds of buffalo, and horses could help transport the villagers and their goods wherever their quarry led them. If food became scarce or conditions harsh in one territory, they could pack up the entire tribe and head for greener pastures. And as each tribe's range of travel expanded, the opportunities for trade with other tribes (and with the Europeans) also increased.

In short, the introduction of the horse converted the native people of the plains from settled villagers who lived in earth or bark lodges and supplemented their hunting with light farming into a seminomadic people who carried tepee homes with them from site to site and hunted, gathered, and traded to supply all their needs. A Cheyenne story tells how the Cheyenne first encountered horses. Comanches had stolen some horses from the Spanish and Pueblos Indians and brought them north to trade with the Cheyenne. The Cheyenne were not sure how to respond. They prayed to Maheo, their All-Spirit or Creator, who explained the effect that horses would have on his people:

"We never heard of horses," said one Cheyenne priest. "Perhaps Maheo wouldn't like for us to have them."

"Why don't you ask him?" a Comanche said. "We'll trade with you, if you're too afraid to go and get them."

. . . The Cheyenne priests all gathered in the largest house in the village, which was the medicine lodge, and they sat and smoked and prayed to

Maheo, fasting, for four days. At last Maheo took pity on them, and spoke to them through the oldest priest.

"You may have horses," Maheo said. "You may even go with the Comanche and take them. But remember this: If you have horses everything will be changed for you forever.

"You will have to move around a lot to find pasture for your horses. You will have to give up gardening and live by hunting and gathering, like the Comanche. And you will have to come out of your earth houses and live in tents. I will tell your women how to make them, and how to decorate them.

"And there will be other changes. You will have to have fights with other tribes, who will want your pasture land or the places where you hunt. You will have to have real soldiers, who can protect the people. Think, before you decide."

The priests sat and smoked and thought another four days. Then the oldest one said, "Maheo, we think we can learn the things you can teach us and our women. We will take the horses, and with your guidance we will learn the new life."

"So be it," said Maheo.[8]

This story suggests that the transition to a more nomadic lifestyle had the additional result of forcing the Plains tribes to become more martial. It is certainly not the case that there were no intertribal conflicts before the introduction of the horse. However, tribal oral histories present the impression that these conflicts were very small in scale, often consisting of no more than minor raids against rival villages. Occasionally, these raids were arranged for the purpose of seizing women from another tribe, but more often they had a more ritualistic aim. Young men on the cusp of manhood would infiltrate deep inside an enemy village to steal some prized or sacred objects, thus proving their ingenuity, courage, and potential as hunters/warriors.

I use the term "hunter/warrior" because it is clear that the warrior cultures of the Plains tribes grew out of their hunting cultures. Hunting was a male endeavor, and in most cases a man's value to his tribe (and therefore his status within the tribe) was determined by his capacity as a hunter. This is hardly surprising since, naturally, the survival of the tribe depended upon the maintenance of its food supply.

Every aspect of hunting had religious significance for the Plains people. They believed that the natural world had been created by a Great Spirit and that this Creator had given a unique spirit to everything he created. People, animals, rocks, trees, bodies of water, the sun, moon, and stars: all of these had individual spirits that made them equally worthy of consideration and respect. A plainsman could never perceive hunting to be a trivial activity because he did not regard himself as a naturally superior being entitled to kill other, lesser beings in order to sustain himself. He believed that the animals he hunted had as much right to life as he did. If he were able to kill them, it would only be because the animal itself in some sense voluntarily sacrificed its life for his (and the lives of others in his tribe). This sacrifice had to be honored and appreciated or it would not be repeated by other animals, and the hunter's tribe would starve.

Calvin Martin attempts to clarify this relationship between the Native American hunter and his prey in his intriguing treatise, *Keepers of the Game: Indian-Animal Relationships and the Fur Trade:*

> Here is a novel idea indeed: animals, in the Indian cosmology, consciously surrendered themselves to the needy hunter. . . . It is a notion completely foreign to the Western way of hunting. [Quoting Indian researcher John Witthoft:] "The white man regarded game animals as meat from which to supply his needs, as mere objects to be taken. The Indian," on the other hand, "considered the animal as an intelligent, conscious fellow member of the same spiritual kingdom. His own destiny was linked with that of the animals by the Creator, and he felt that both he and his victims understood the roles which they played in the hunt—the animal, in other words, was resigned to its fate." . . . Adrian Tanner [researching the Cree Indians] found that "a central attitude in the conduct of hunting is that game animals are persons and that they must be respected. . . . [H]unting rests on a kind of social relationship between men and animals. Throughout the cycle of hunting rites men emphasize their respect by means of symbolic expressions of their subordination to animals."[9]

A young tribesman had to earn the right to assume both the practical and the spiritual burdens of responsibility that came with being a hunter. He not only had to learn the essential arts of locating, stalking, and slaying game, but he also had to be initiated into certain sacred rites that would help him form and maintain the appropriate spiritual relationship with the animals he hunted. For many of the Plains tribes, these rites included "hunt dreaming."

Hunt dreams were visions in which the hunter made contact with the spirit of his intended quarry and persuaded the animal to lay down its life for the tribe. A successful hunt in the physical world was thought to depend on success within the "spirit hunt." Calvin Martin explains:

> When it came right down to the actual business of dispatching the game the hunter invoked all the spiritual resources at his command, first to subdue the animal's spirit, and then, anticlimactically, its body. It was the preliminary spirit hunt, as we might call it, which really mattered; by the time the hunter got around to actually bagging the animal it was as good as dead, as far as he was concerned. . . .
>
> In the "hunt dream," performed the night or several nights before the physical hunt, a man's soul-spirit reveals the whereabouts of certain game. Dreaming thus becomes a much-desired state of mind. "Anything that will induce dreaming is a religious advantage: fasting, dancing, singing, drumming, rattling, and sweat bath, seclusion, meditation, eating certain foods, as well as drinking animal grease, various kinds of medicine, [etc.]."[10]

When the widespread use of horses for hunting swept across the plains, the status of the tribes' hunters was elevated even further. Their role had always been significant, but when the tribes relied more heavily on farming or gardening for a portion of their food supply, the women who were most often in charge of producing those crops shared more of the burden of, and praise for, protecting the tribe from annihilation through starvation. As mounted hunters made buffalo meat the most essential source of tribal sustenance, elements of tribal religion that focused on agriculture faded and those that supported the hunter/warrior were enlarged.

Marriot and Rachlin comment on this ideological adjustment as it affected the Cheyenne:

> The shift from a semisedentary horticulture-gathering economy to a subsistence based principally on hunting changed not only Cheyenne material culture but also, to some extent, social organization and mythological and religious beliefs. Although the change took place, the Cheyenne still retained in their mythology and religion many elements from the prehorse days.
>
> Out on the Plains men became more economically important than women, as the hunters provided the buffalo that were the mainstay of Plains life. New men's societies developed not only to train the young men in hunting and war but also to give them the reassurance of the tribe. It was a period of shifting from a female ideology based on the Mother Earth to a male ideology based on the hunt and war.[11]

Just as Maheo predicted in the Cheyenne legend "Out of the Earth Houses," the changes wrought by the adoption of the horse produced the need for tribesmen who were as talented in protecting their people from the assaults of hostile men as from the ravages of hunger. When it came to the task of training young men to perform useful services for their tribes, the aim of tribal elders continued to be the development of each youth's physical and spiritual strength. But that strength would now be applied in a different way than it had been in prehorse days.

In the context of the hunt, Native American youths were taught to view themselves as subordinate to their game: as suppliants requesting a favor from a powerful being. The hunter's strength was necessary to inspire the animal to sacrifice its life on his behalf. He had to prove himself worthy to appeal to the animal, like a medieval knight performing brave deeds before begging a boon from his king.

The relationship between the warrior and his human enemies was viewed very differently. The warrior's intention was always to dominate his opponent completely, on both the material and the spiritual plane. Most of the Plains tribes believed that the spirit of an animal that willingly gave up its life to a hunter would either travel to a peaceful spirit world or else be reborn in this world. Either way, that animal's spirit would bear no grudge against the man who killed it. By contrast, they thought that if you destroyed a man's physical self without fully conquering his spirit as well, his spirit would continue to represent a serious threat to your own physical and spiritual well-being. The angry spirit of a fallen enemy could bring a warrior bad luck, disease, or even death.

The warriors of the plains felt that the only way for a man truly to defeat an enemy without risking postmortem supernatural harassment was to demonstrate clearly the superiority of his spirit over that of his opponent. Even after death, an inferior spirit would always fear to attack a stronger one. Therefore a great deal of their warrior training was directed toward encouraging their young men to have confidence in their own superiority of spirit.

Among the traditional stories of each of the Plains tribes there was always a creation myth that gave an account of the origins of the tribe and pointed out the distinctive aspects of the tribe's character that set it apart from other Native American tribes. These stories also had a tendency either subtly or blatantly to attest to the given tribe's superiority over all others. As these creation myths were told to the children of the tribe, they represented the first step in their warrior training.

As I mentioned earlier, the Plains tribes share the belief in a creator deity, a supernatural being who is the source of all life. This powerful entity appears in different forms and is known by different names in the stories of each tribe. Some tribes speak of the Great Spirit as an indefinable force that exists both on a higher plane and as part of every living thing on the earth, down to the smallest seed or blade of grass. The Pawnee refer to this force simply as "the Power." Some, like the Arapaho, picture the Great Spirit as the inspiration for, but not the agent of, creation. They see him as the "Man-Above," who affects life on earth through various semidivine assistants, such as a character named Flat Pipe. Others present an anthropomorphized vision of the Creator, often appearing on earth as an elderly man. The Blackfeet and Sioux refer to him simply as Old Man (or Na'pi), and Crow stories feature That Old Man Who Did Everything. Many myths also involve a complex trickster/hero figure who appears in various guises, including Coyote, Old Man Coyote, and Saynday. Sometimes this trickster/hero appears to be the Creator himself, while in other tales he seems to be a separate entity.

The creation myth of the Crow tribes highlights the importance of the virtue of bravery and is none too subtle in its suggestion that the Crow people are in greater possession of that virtue than their competitors on the plains:

> That Old Man Who Did Everything and the ducks [who were his assistants] made the world. Then they divided the world into sections by placing water here and there. They made the sky, the plants, the trees, and the animals. They made the stars and the sun and the moon. After a long while

That Old Man Who Did Everything decided that was not enough so he made the people.

He made the people out of clay as he had made everything else. He made three groups of men and women. He set them on the ground in front of him, while he made some clay arrows. He put the arrows in a row on the ground a long way away from him.

Then That Old Man Who Did Everything said to the clay people, "I do not know which group of you is the bravest. I want only brave people. I will test you to find out. Run. Run through the arrows, and the one that goes through them will be my people, and will learn many things!"

The first group started to run, but when they came to the row of arrows they were frightened and stopped in their tracks. They could not go on, and they fell to the ground.

"Get up," ordered That Old Man Who Did Everything. "Go away. You cannot be my people." Then he told the second group to run through the arrows, but they were frightened, too, and turned back.

"Go like the others," That Old Man Who Did Everything said to them.

Nobody knows anymore who these two groups of people were. They were Indians, but what Indians has been forgotten.

Now That Old Man Who Did Everything told the third group to run through the arrows, and they did. If they were frightened they did not show it.

"You are very brave people," said That Old Man Who Did Everything. "You will be my people, and I will give you helpers to teach you. Where you live shall be the center of the world."

That is why the Crows lived . . . between the mountains and the plains, and . . . why all the other tribes respected and feared them.[12]

Imagine how fierce pride would have swelled the chest of a Crow youth as he heard this tale from his elders. It must have planted the seed of what would later become a firmly entrenched conviction that the Crow deserved to be honored above all others. Surely when he became a warrior he would be able to draw additional encouragement before a raid or battle from the thought that any enemy tribe he had to face might possibly be the descendants of those unnamed Indians who were too afraid to stand up to that first deadly rain of arrows.

In a similar vein, the Nez Perce offer a story of their origin that sets them above other tribes. Unlike the Crow, however, the Nez Perce do not shrink from naming their supposedly inferior neighbors:

A huge monster from the sea, the great Iltswetsix, roamed the Kamiah Valley in north Idaho. So enormous was his appetite that he sucked everything into himself, and was soon devouring all the animals in the land. When Spi-li-yai, or Coyote (the fabled knave of Indian mythology), heard of this, he left the Umatilla country to engage in a test of strength with the monster. Upon reaching Kamiah, Coyote concealed himself under a grass bonnet and tied his body down with a wild grapevine. Then he defied Iltswetsix to pull him into his cavernous mouth. The great beast sucked and sucked, until slowly the ropes gave way and Coyote was drawn into the monster's stomach. But Coyote had not yet lost the contest. Taking a knife that he had concealed in his belt, he began to cut out the sea demon's heart, and so killed him. Then Coyote carved his way out of the monster's body.

At once Fox, who had witnessed the duel, joined him. Since Coyote did not know what to do with the body, Fox suggested that they cut it up and make people. So, from the head came the Flathead Indians; from the feet, the Blackfoot tribe; and thus from each part they made a different nation of Indians. Finally, only the heart remained. As Coyote held it aloft, the beast's blood dropped to the ground and from these drops more people sprang up. They were taller, stronger, nobler, and wiser than the others—these were the Nez Perces. The Great Spirit Chief, who rules above, was well pleased with Coyote, and, lest the people forget this wonderful deed, he turned the heart into a large stone, and it may be seen yet in the Kamiah Valley.[13]

Along with declarations of superiority, many Plains tribes' creation stories carry the message that the native people are very intimately linked to the land on which they live and therefore should be prepared to defend it. For example, the genesis story of the Lakota Sioux depicts the first member of their nation literally pulling himself up out of the soil:

Our legends tell us that it was hundreds and perhaps thousands of years ago since the first man sprang from the soil in the midst of the great plains. The story says that one morning long ago a lone man awoke, face to the sun, emerging from the soil. Only his head was visible, the rest of his body not yet being fashioned. The man looked about, but saw no mountains, no rivers, no forests. There was nothing but soft and quaking mud, for the earth itself was still young. Up and up the man drew himself until he freed his body from the clinging soil. At last he stood upon the earth, but it was not solid, and his first few steps were slow and halting. But the sun shone and ever the man kept his face turned toward it. In time the rays of the sun hardened the face of the earth and strengthened the man and he bounded and leaped about, a free and joyous creature. From this man sprang the Lakota nation and, . . . our people have been born and have died upon this plain. . . . We are of the soil and the soil is of us.[14]

This message is complemented by the equally common theme that the Creator intended certain lands for certain peoples. We find this in the Arapaho legend "How the Earth and Men Were Made," involving Flat Pipe, the Creator's assistant:

Then Flat Pipe took more earth, and made a man and a woman and a buffalo, so that they should all be together for the rest of time. He made other animals, too: deer and antelope and rabbits—everything that walks and runs. He made the war birds and the sacred birds, first the eagles and hawks, then the flycatchers, and then the songbirds.

"That is a lot of creatures," Flat Pipe said.

"Too many," Man-Above warned him. "Look, they are filling up all the space around you."

So Flat Pipe divided the land, and made an ocean; but not one as big as the first ocean on which he had floated. He made some new people, with light-colored skins, and put them on the other side of the second ocean. "Stay there," Flat Pipe ordered. "Do not bother my people on the buffalo path."

But the light-colored people did not obey him, as we all know.[15]

A tale from the Blackfoot tribe takes the further step of providing a direct mandate from the Old Man/Creator for the native people of the plains to make war on anyone who threatens their territory, including whites:

In later times once, Na'pi said, "Here I will mark you off a piece of ground," and he did so. Then he said: "There is your land, and it is full of all kinds of animals, and many things grow in this land. Let no other people come into it. This is for you five tribes (Blackfeet, Bloods, Piegans, Gros Ventres, Sarcees). When people come to cross the line, take your bows and arrows, your lances and your battle axes, and give them battle and keep them out. If they gain a footing, trouble will come to you."

Our forefathers gave battle to all people who came to cross these lines, and kept them out. Of late years we have let our friends, the white people, come in, and you know the result. We, his children, have failed to obey his laws.[16]

The tribes' beliefs about their origins provided them with two very powerful motives for making war: to assert their perceived natural superiority by dominating their neighbors and to fulfill their obligation to their Creator by defending the land with which they identified so closely.

Since war had crucial ties to their religion, it was serious business to the Plains tribes. They developed highly organized systems to train and deploy their warriors. Most formed special warrior societies that divided the males of the tribe into smaller, closely bonded units. Thomas Mails clarifies the function of these societies:

They were called Warrior Societies, and the title itself explains their main purpose. Their function, though, was really a fourfold one: they provided a club atmosphere with the luxury of participation in those mysterious activities limited to the members of a given society, they preserved order in the camp and on organized hunts, they punished offenders against the public welfare, and they cultivated a military spirit among themselves and others—especially young boys—with the ultimate aim of assuring the longevity of the tribe.[17]

Notice that an intimate connection was maintained between hunting and making war. The tribal warriors were responsible both to protect and to provide for their people. They played an additional "domestic" role.

They served as a sort of police/retribution force for the tribe, maintaining order and administering justice.

Mails observes that these warrior societies were structured in a variety of ways, following specific tribal traditions. In all cases, however, the honor of membership depended on actual accomplishment. Merit, not heredity, determined a warrior's acceptance and status within his society:

> There were two types of Warrior Societies, and historians have classified them as age-graded and non-graded societies. Simply put, membership in the age-graded societies was determined by the age of the participants. The first or lowest grade consisted of boys approximately fifteen years of age and up who had made a successful vision quest and gone on a first successful raid. The next grade might begin at age eighteen or so, with the ages for the successive steps in all instances varying with each tribe. Membership of non-graded societies had nothing to do with age. A warrior with noteworthy accomplishments or promise might be invited to join a society regardless of how old he was.[18]

A sense of pride and the perception of proven superiority were carefully cultivated within these warrior societies, as in the broader tribal context. The tribal leaders clearly understood the important role that meaningful rites of passage can play in encouraging the development of a young warrior's character and self-confidence. It was never taken for granted that a given youth would succeed in becoming the kind of warrior his people required or even that he would survive the tests intended to prove his mettle.

Acceptance into a warrior society required the achievement of certain individual milestones. Unlike many of the warrior cultures we have examined in earlier chapters, the warriors of the plains had an inward focus to their training ordeals that took them far beyond the physical. In fact, the two accomplishments most commonly demanded from would-be warriors, the vision quest and counting coup, had much more to do with spiritual strength than strength in arms.

The vision quest was a ritual performed by male members of the tribe to mark their transition from childhood to adolescence. It was certainly a prerequisite for acceptance into either an age-graded or a nongraded warrior society, but it was also a more general requirement of tribal citizenship. In some ways analogous to a modern aptitude test, the vision quest offered an early assessment of the individual's potential and likely contributions to the welfare of his tribe. Conclusions drawn from his experience could permanently affect both the participant's self-image and his community's perception of him. In a sense, the outcome of a young man's vision quest determined his identity.

The intention behind the vision quest was to allow a youth to connect to the spirit world and there seek guidance for his future. Having achieved puberty, a young man would separate from his tribe for a period of days to survive on his own in the wild. He would camp in some secluded spot where he could pray and meditate undisturbed. He would then make himself receptive to vivid dreams or visions by fasting. (Ingesting hallucinogenic substances, such as peyote, to provoke visions is more common to the tribes of the Southwest than to those of the plains.)

The youth would remain apart from his tribe until he received his vision. Only then could he rejoin his people. If he returned home for any reason before completing his vision quest, he would be shamed. He would have to attempt the ritual again, and he would be treated like a child until his quest was successful. The tribe would not trust him with the responsibilities of adulthood until he had proven himself spiritually fit.

Although the vision quest itself was a solitary activity, the interpretation of the young man's visions was not. The youth's first stop after satisfying the requirements of the quest was a visit to the tribe's religious leader, or medicine man. The medicine man was an adult member of the tribe thought to have a special ability to communicate with the spirit world. It was his duty to help the youth understand the contents of his visions. William K. Powers sketches the vital role of the medicine man in the introduction to his collection *Beyond the Vision: Essays on American Indian Culture*:

> [Each vision] must ultimately be interpreted by a wise man who has been on the quest himself and who derives his ability to interpret visions for others from an ongoing familiarity with his own spirit helpers. And the future success of the supplicant is obtainable and real only to the extent that he is able to follow the instructions and mandates from the supernaturals as perfectly and precisely as the interpretations of his mentor allow. A vision then is not only a blueprint for the future, but a theory about how one should live with himself and his relations and all the other creatures of the natural and cultural world.[19]

What might the contents of a vision have been, and what might they have revealed about a young plainsman's possible future? As they were considered sacred, the details of a specific individual's vision were seldom shared outside a medicine man's tepee. Nevertheless, some particulars of the vision quest experiences of well-known native warriors are captured by their names and associated legends. And we can extract further information about typical vision experiences from anthropological research and Indian lore.

From these sources we know that the vision quest experience for a youth of the Plains tribes generally involved a visitation from one or more animal spirits. The Great Spirit sent these animal spirits for two purposes. They were to clarify the Creator's expectations of the young man in question and guide him throughout his life as he faced the more chal-

lenging aspects of his destiny. A Blackfoot legend gives an account of how
the practice of vision quests began and describes the role of animal spirit
guides:

> Also Old Man said to the people: "Now, if you are overcome, you may go
> and sleep, and get power. Something will come to you in your dream that
> will help you. Whatever these animals tell you to do, you must obey them,
> as they appear to you in your sleep. Be guided by them. If anybody wants
> help; if you are alone and traveling, and cry aloud for help, your prayer will
> be answered. It may be by the eagles, perhaps by the buffalo, or by the
> bears. Whatever animal answers your prayer, you must listen to him."
>
> That was how the first people got through the world, by the power of
> their dreams.[20]

The first piece of information a medicine man would elicit from a youth
returning from a successful vision quest was which animal spirit(s) chose
to become manifest to him. The nature of the creature(s) that appeared to
him was thought to relate directly to key aspects of the young man's character. Animal spirit guides were not randomly assigned; their selection
always carried some significance. Which animal spoke to him was almost
as important as what the spirit had to say.

As we saw in their hunting attitudes, the Plains people were uncom-
monly humble before the animal kingdom. They had a great respect for
all creatures and were remarkably sensitive to the distinctive attributes of
each species. Every animal was associated with at least one specific excellence that a human being might easily envy. Most were seen to have several qualities worthy of human emulation.

When a warrior candidate recalled for his medicine man the catalogue
of animal spirits that appeared in his vision, the medicine man would
point out the most praiseworthy characteristics of those animals. He
would then explain that the fact that the spirits of those animals were featured in the young man's vision meant that the youth either already possessed or was expected to acquire their defining qualities himself. It was
considered a great honor to acquire an animal spirit guide or guides, and
to fail to live up to the animal spirit(s) that had chosen you was an unforgivable offense.

Although every animal had its virtues, some more than others were
readily associated with warrior values. All the Plains tribes, for example,
honored bears for their strength and ferocity, their indefatigable defense
of home and kin, and even their apparent penchant for revenge. A young
man whose vision indicated that he had been selected to be the human
ward and protégé of a bear spirit would probably be singled out as a likely future leader for his people.

Nez Perce lore records how the vision received by one of their greatest
war chiefs (Red Bear/Many Wounds) in his youth accurately predicted
the course of his warrior career:

It was during the days of youthful training and development that Red Bear went on foot to Slate Creek. . . . He lay down by the trail and slept. In a dream he beheld a great, bloodstained grizzly bear approaching. Awakening, he sprang to his feet, but no bear was to be seen. Silently he resumed his buffalo robe and dozed off, only to be aroused a second time by the same fearful vision, which vanished as he leaped erect. He again lay down and as he drowsed the monster bear appeared for the third time. This time the boy did not awaken entirely, and a voice spoke to him:

"Do not be afraid. You see my body. Blood is all over it. When you become a man, when you go to war and do fighting, you shall receive many wounds. Wounds shall cover your body. Blood like this from my body will course down your limbs. But you will not die. After these wars, and fights, because of your wounds and bloodstains people will call you Hohots Ilppilp [Red Grizzly Bear]."[21]

Intimidating carnivores such as bears, eagles, wolves, foxes, bulls, and bobcats were all predictably desirable spirit guides for the aspiring warrior. But even unlikely animals could provide inspiration. For instance, the spirit of an ordinary squirrel could show a warrior how to plan for the future (to resist the urge for immediate gratification in order to secure long-term goals) and how to use speed, agility, and familiarity with terrain to outwit a physically stronger enemy or evade an outnumbering force. Even a seemingly undignified skunk spirit guide could offer lessons on how to present the false appearance of helplessness and defeat an opponent without striking a single blow.

After drawing conclusions from the form of the spirits in the youth's vision, the medicine man's next responsibility would be to analyze the content of the message conveyed by those spirits. Sometimes, as in the case of Chief Red Bear/Many Wounds, the message was a straightforward prediction about the young man's future, providing that he lived up to his potential. In other instances, animal spirits might be expected to teach their suppliants sacred songs with secret meanings or offer expansive recommendations on such practical concerns as how a warrior should train, where he should live, or whom he should marry.

The warriors of some Plains tribes would derive their names from their animal spirit guides and openly display symbols and articles such as a feather or tooth that would expose the form of their spirit guides to everyone. Others, such as the warriors of the Cheyenne, would keep the identity of their spirit guides a closely guarded secret, believing that anyone who knew what spirits were on their side could use that knowledge against them. They feared that if an enemy discovered the form of his rival's spirit guide, he might ask his medicine man to concoct some charm to dull the spirit's influence over a battle or interfere with its ability to guide and protect its chosen warrior.

Marriott and Rachlin comment on some of the Cheyenne traditions concerning animal spirit guides:

Personal spirit guardians in animal form were also deeply respected by the
Cheyenne. Not only was there a food taboo associated with the guardians,
it was considered deeply improper to mention their names in the presence
of those they protected. An outsider might be warned, "Don't say 'crow' to
that man. It's sacred to him." How these taboos were learned about has
never been made quite clear. No one was supposed to tell who his spirit
guardian was.[22]

However the special relationship between the warrior and his animal
guardian(s) was expressed, it was faithfully cherished throughout his
entire life. Whether he openly appropriated the animal's name as his own
or clandestinely carried some token of the animal in a secret pouch or
"medicine bag," a man's spirit guide became part of his identity. An individual without an animal spirit guide was considered to be at a serious
disadvantage, doomed to struggle through life with no support from the
spirit world and therefore unlikely to succeed in any challenging endeav-
or. No wonder the completion of a successful vision quest was the foremost criterion for acceptance into a warrior society.

After the vision quest, the next most crucial rite of passage for the
young warrior was the counting of coup. To count coup on an enemy was
to approach him in battle and touch him with a special coup stick,
weapon, or hand without killing or even wounding him. Counting coup
was considered an act of great bravery and self-discipline, as the warrior
was required to deliver a precision blow to his opponent's body while
avoiding harm to himself. Such an attack was sure to infuriate, but not
incapacitate, the foe, who would almost certainly seek retaliation for his
humiliation. In short, a warrior counting coup was about as safe as a
matador taunting a bull.

The purpose of counting coup was not only to teach the young warrior
control and confirm his courage but also to allow him to assert his superiority over his enemies. Counting coup was seen as an act of spiritual
domination. It was expected that an opponent on whom you had already
counted coup would be severely weakened in his next encounter with
you by the knowledge that at least once before you were able to penetrate
his defenses.

In his personal narrative, *The Warrior Who Killed Custer,* Chief Joseph
White Bull (Pte San Hunka) from the Miniconjou band of the Teton Sioux
tribe describes his "bravest deed" as the first time that he counted coup
on an enemy from the Flathead tribe:

> White Bull counted first coup. They shot at me but didn't hit me. That was
> good. It was one of these Flatheads that I counted coup upon.
>   My father was a chief and because of this I showed no fear. It was because
> of him that I wanted to be in the thick of the fight. It was a hard thing to do
> but I accomplished it. They were all shooting at me but they didn't hit me. I

was right in the middle of things.

Afterwards they [the enemy] pursued me a long way, clear back to my own lines. It was a great fight. I did this difficult deed and count it among my coups, my friend.[23]

Even in this brief account, White Bull emphasizes several aspects of his experience that relate to the Plains Indians' concepts of honor and shame. First of all, he exposes the dangers of counting coup by stressing that the deed cannot be performed at a distance from your foe. Your enemy may shoot arrows (or, later, guns) at you from many feet away, but you must ride right up beside him, through the hail of projectile weapons, and make direct contact.

White Bull then mentions that his achievements or failures in battle necessarily will reflect upon his family. The people of the Plains tribes had great respect for both their living elders and their ancestors. They believed that the dead, though removed to a spirit world, still took an interest in earthly affairs. The spirits of deceased kinfolk could take pride in the martial prowess of their descendants, but they could also feel great shame if their posterity showed any signs of weakness or cowardice. Therefore when young White Bull rides into the thick of the battle, it is to honor his father, still living, as well as all of the former warriors of his line, who will be judging him from the afterlife.

As he remembers the pressure of the moment, White Bull reminds himself that, whatever he may have felt, he showed no fear. Maintaining a stoic aspect was very important to the native warrior. Their societies had the utmost respect for persons who could endure stress, terror, or pain without registering the impact on their countenances. Several tribes required their warriors to participate in astonishing rituals of self-torture whose aim was to prove that they could inflict tremendous pain upon themselves without flinching.

A prime example of such a practice among the plainsmen was the Sun Dance ritual. Historian Oliver LeFarge offers a vivid description of this ordeal:

> Its central feature was dancing in an enclosed area, around or facing a pole made of the trunk of a tree that had been "killed" and felled with great ceremony. The dancing was grave and extremely simple, which was true of much Plains Indian ritual dancing, the dancers hardly moving from where they started. As a rule, the "sun" dancers went without food or water through the whole time of the performance, which was often until they fell in a trance and had a vision. In some tribes, such as the Sioux, they . . . demonstrated their courage by a form of self-torture. Two parallel slits were cut in their skin, and under the strip between a stick was run, from which a string led to the central pole or to a buffalo skull or similar object. The idea was to keep jerking against the string until the strip of skin tore out.[24]

The warriors who took part in the Sun Dance (which was also a time for thanksgiving and prayers for the longevity of the tribe) were expected to remain silent and sustain a composed expression even as their resistance against the pole or the weight of the object they were dragging ripped out portions of their pectoral muscles. Even tribal women, although not warriors, were expected to be stoics. There are reports of Indian women suffering hours of labor for childbirth without uttering a single cry or exclamation. And, as among the tribes of the East, the common practice of brutally torturing prisoners of war provided additional opportunities for the people of the Plains to prove their astonishing fortitude and unflappability:

> Live, young adult, male prisoners in good condition were hard to come by. A reasonable man would sooner die fighting than let himself be taken. When a town got one, everyone was delighted. First the returning warriors cleansed themselves from the magical influences of battle, then the captive was tied to a pole in the civic center and carefully and elaborately tortured to death. This dreadful procedure had about it a curious character of a competition. The victim sang his war songs, taunted his captors, did everything he knew to infuriate them and show his superior courage. The torturers, who were mostly the women, did their best to break him down before he died.[25]

Young White Bull luckily managed to count his first coup and evade the angry pursuit of his Flathead foes. Had he been taken and tortured, he would have considered it incumbent on him to honor his family and fellow Sioux by showing no fear. Even if no members of his tribe were there to witness his final acts of courage, his ancestors would always be able to observe them from the spirit world.

Having exhibited spiritual strength, bravery, and military potential through his successful vision quest and the counting of his first coup, a young warrior like White Bull surely would be permitted to assume membership in an age-graded or nongraded warrior society. Mails expounds further on the particulars of these intratribal societies:

> Most society groups were small, numbering from ten to twenty persons, although powerful societies with as many as sixty or more members were known to exist. Usually, the society had a "charmed maximum number" which its founder had received in the vision which gave the society birth. This meant that recruits were invited only at those times when the group had sustained losses through retirements or deaths.
>
> Each society had its own name, and its own tipi or ceremonial lodge which was painted with symbols and colors given to the society founder in his original vision. . . . Society names were both descriptive and captivating. For example, the age-graded societies of the Blackfoot were named in grade order as follows: the Doves (or youths); the Mosquitoes (men who went to war); the Braves (or tried warriors); the Brave Dogs; the Kit Foxes; and the Bulls, who were the oldest in origin and held the highest standing.[26]

Marriott and Rachlin record that the Kiowa had a similar progression of society names: "from the Rabbits, which boys joined when they were six or seven and from which they graduated at puberty to the Herders or other societies, such as the Gourd Dancers and others. All aspired to membership in the Bravest of the Brave—the ten war chiefs who made up the Crazy Dog Society."[27] They also preserve a fascinating Cheyenne legend that attempts to provide an explanation for the formation and customs of one of their more unusual warrior societies, the Backward-Talking Warriors.

In the story, a Cheyenne girl is abducted by an owl after disobeying her mother's commands and leaving her home at night. She is subsequently rescued and raised by hawks. When she becomes a young woman, she wants to return to her own tribe. Her adoptive grandfather hawk (acting like an animal spirit guide) offers her advice and protective charms:

"Well, you are old enough to take care of yourself now," the hawk grandfather said. "But you must do just exactly what I tell you if you are to get back safely."

"I will," the girl promised.

Then the grandfather made her a red-painted robe, and had her make a boy's moccasins and leggings. The grandfather made her a thunder bow with lightning designs on it, and he fastened buffalo bulls' tails to the heels of her moccasins to wipe out her tracks. Last he painted her face red, and tied the skin of a prairie owl on her forehead. She was dressed like one of the Backward-Talking Warriors, who were the greatest warriors of the Cheyenne, not like a girl.

When she was ready to leave, the grandfather gave her a live mink. "Keep this inside your robe," he instructed her. "Never let go of it. . . . On the evening of the fourth day you will come to your last great danger. An old woman will come out of her lodge and call to you and offer you food. Don't eat any of the first bowl; feed it to the mink. The second time she will give you buffalo meat and you will be safe to eat that. Be sure you keep the mink with you, but let it go when the old lady threatens you."

[There follows an episode where the girl encounters and, with the help of the hawk's advice and the live mink, defeats an evil old woman bent on killing her.]

The next day the girl went on again, and that night she came to her own village. Everyone came running out to see who the handsome young man was. . . .

"Who are you? What tribe are you? Where have you come from?" all the people asked her.

At last she said, "I am the naughty girl whose mother threw her away. I have had a hard time and come through many dangers, but now I am back with my own people."

Then her mother came to her, weeping and crying to be forgiven. And some young men came to her, and asked if they could wear the same kind of clothes she had on. The girl thought a while and then she said, "Yes. But because I am a woman dressed like a man, you must always do some things backwards. If you are in a battle, and someone tells you, 'Go forward,' then you can go back." And that is how the great soldier societies of the Cheyennes got started.[28]

Whether the societies were age graded or not, moving up from one society to the next was never automatic. New challenges and additional rites of passage were always involved. Naturally, battlefield accomplishments had a lot to do with society advancement. But there were other traditions as well, some of which had an almost whimsical nature. Mails recounts that often "it was customary for young Indian braves to buy the right from their immediate elders to their sets of regalia, dances, and songs, the purchase of which gave them access to the total privileges of the club."[29]

Among the Hidatsa and Mandan tribes, this tradition of "buying" advancement became somewhat excessive, as the older warriors, or "fathers" exploited the eagerness of the younger warriors, or "sons:"

"[F]athers," remembering their own youthful desires, made the most of their advantage, professing the greatest reluctance to give up their beloved dances, badges, and rituals. Hence, the young buyers were obliged to arrive at the sellers' lodge with a great profusion of gifts and a smoking pipe, which would be accepted, but only as a token of the sellers' agreement to discuss the offer. Irrespective of the substance of the discussion, the seniors were sure to declare in the end that the initial offering was insufficient; so the buyers, as they knew they would need to do, held back a reserve supply of gifts, and in addition scurried around to coax more property from their relatives. The older men continued to act as if they were doing their juniors a great favor, until at last a proper tension was reached and began to show itself in the faces of the sons. Finally the sellers smoked the pipe again, ordering the buyers to bring food to feast their "fathers" for more successive evenings. Once more the relatives helped the purchasers to collect the food; then, on the appointed evenings, the sellers received their feasts and began to teach the buyers the songs and dances unique to their society. Continuing the extortion program, the head of the club would exhort the sons to pay generously for the emblems they were to receive. He would also urge them to imitate the example of some of the distinguished fathers as warriors. As the final evening of instructions came to an end, the insignia were turned over to the new members with proper pomp and circumstance, and a public procession and dance followed in which they advertised the fact that they were now the proud representatives of the grade just entered.[30]

For young Plains warriors, along with the general improvement in status, advancement up the ranks of the warrior societies brought with it the possibility of domestic felicity. Men were not permitted to court and acquire wives until they had proven themselves as warriors. There were several reasons for this restriction, as Mails elucidates:

Men could not marry until they had earned the right. Among the Crows, this meant they did not marry until they were either twenty-five or had counted coup, that is, touched an enemy during combat. . . . Plenty Coups, a chief of the Crows, explained that the custom was followed because a man who had counted coup or reached the age of twenty-five was considered to be strong and healthy. . . . Indians were high in their praise of the law that permitted men to marry under twenty-five only if they had counted coup. The rule made them strive to be strong and brave, and they believed that a man could be neither without good health through physical activity.[31]

Sometimes individual warrior societies would essentially "adopt" eligible young tribal women and protect them like little sisters until a suitable warrior husband could be found for them. Marriott and Rachlin comment on this practice among the Kiowa:

Each society also had a "sister": a young woman who danced with the members, and in some cases went on raids. Such women were highly regarded; they came from good families, and they had to be virgins. When a "sister" married, all members of her society had to agree in advance that the man who had asked for her was worthy of her. She could not marry into her own society.[32]

This tradition is somewhat similar to that of fraternity sisters in more modern collegiate settings, but it evokes stronger parallels within the context of the introduction of women to military service academies. At the U.S. Naval Academy, for instance, men and women live and train together in companies but are not allowed to fraternize with their company-mates. If two members of the same company wish to pursue a romantic association, one or the other of them must transfer to another company by applying for what is colloquially termed a "love chit." The common argument used to defend fraternization restrictions for mixed-gender units is appropriate to any century: such restrictions may help to prevent jealousy, sexual tension, romantic competitions, and abuses of power from destroying warrior morale.

Women warriors on the plains were extremely uncommon, but not unheard of. Where such women were found, their roles were generally limited. Warrior society sisters retired from combat when they married. Other warrior women held vital leadership or training positions behind the scenes but did not have a share of battlefield glory.

Mexican lore speaks of a secret training center in the Sierra Madres to which young Comanche warriors would be sent before returning to their tribes in the southern plains. According to legend, the commandant of this "Comanche West Point" was a woman. A story from the Osage tells of the Woman General: a white woman named Maria James who was adopted by the tribe as a child and grew to be highly respected for her astute martial advice:

Before each raid, [the male warriors] consulted her, and she told them what she thought would be the best way to approach an Indian tribal settlement or a white farmstead. Usually they followed her advice, and were glad she had given it. Even when she was an old, old woman, with grandchildren around her, the men came to her for advice.

By this time she was well known enough to be called by the whites "the Woman General." They were afraid of her good planning mind. When she died, she was buried like a man, and they piled a mound of earth over her body.[33]

The majority of the time, the women of the Plains tribes played more auxiliary parts in relation to the warrior societies. In most cases, as in many cultures throughout history, women, regardless of their potential, were allowed to serve only as support staff for an all-male military. They were not necessarily second-class citizens, however, according to some observers:

> The Indian woman was not, as is commonly thought, a drudge or a slave. White men who lived with the Indians, such as Grinnell, Schultz, and McClintock, deride this notion as an erroneous one, and avoid the use of the demeaning title "squaw." Women did do all the hard camp work. They cooked, brought wood and water, dried the meat, dressed the robes, made the clothing, collected the lodge poles, packed the horses, cultivated the ground, and generally performed all the tasks which might be called menial; but no one thought of them as servants in this. On the contrary, their position was respected and their crafts were highly valued.... [W]ives were always consulted on intimate family affairs and often in more general matters. They also shared jointly with their husbands in sacred rituals. A few women were even admitted to the band councils, and gave advice there. Assuredly, the privilege was unusual, and only granted to women who had performed a deed comparable to those of the leading men of the tribe, but it did happen.[34]

Owing to their significant contributions to tribal life (as well as for all the usual reasons), wives were an extremely desirable commodity. It is therefore not surprising that warriors could be motivated to perform great deeds in order to be thought worthy to take a bride. A Sioux story tells of a warrior named High Horse who fell in love with a beautiful young woman and became almost obsessed with winning her. He tried to get the girl's father to grant his daughter's hand in marriage by offering the father two excellent horses, but the father was unimpressed and dismissed the unlucky suitor with a wave of his hand. High Horse then several times tried to kidnap the girl but each time was discovered and sent away, dejected. Eventually, High Horse gave up in despair:

> High Horse said he never would go back to the village as long as he lived and he did not care what happened to him now. He said he was going to go

on the warpath all by himself. Red Deer said, "No, cousin, you are not going on the warpath alone, because I am going with you."

So Red Deer got everything ready, and at night they started out on the warpath all alone. After several days they came to a Crow camp just about sundown, and when it was dark they sneaked up to where the Crow horses were grazing, killed the horse guard, who was not thinking about enemies because he thought all the Lakotas were far away, and drove off about a hundred horses.

They got a big start because all the Crow horses stampeded and it was probably morning before the Crow warriors could catch any horses to ride. Red Deer and High Horse fled with their herd three days and nights before they reached the village of their people. Then they drove the whole herd right into the village and up in front of the girl's teepee. The old man [her father] was there, and High Horse called out to him and asked if he thought maybe that would be enough horses for his girl. The old man did not wave him away that time. It was not the horses that he wanted. What he wanted was a son who was a real man and good for something.[35]

Beyond the concept of earning a wife through brave deeds, there is another striking element in this Sioux tale. You may have been somewhat surprised that High Horse's brave deed was not a bold coup on an open battlefield but a stealthy raid on another tribe's horse corral. Actions that are deemed appropriate by one warrior culture may be judged immoral and dishonorable by another. The warrior culture of the Plains Indians did not see anything dishonorable in stealth. They had high praise for the warrior who was able to catch his enemy unawares and dispatch him swiftly and silently. However, the actions of a warrior such as High Horse would have been considered despicable (cowardly murder and theft) by many European cultures of the same period. Such culturally based differences in perception contributed to the European labeling of Native Americans as "savages."

Although there were some more classic battlefield engagements, most of the violent interactions between rival tribes took the form of village raids conducted by small bands of warriors. The objectives of these raids varied. Often, as in the tale of High Horse and Red Deer, the aim was to steal horses. On these occasions, little blood was shed. A raiding party attempting to make off with another tribe's stock would kill only if necessary to prevent anyone from raising the alarm and turning the whole village against the invaders.

Horse thieving was common largely because horses were the primary symbol of wealth and status in the native communities. Horses were so highly valued that they were rarely sold or traded for a quantity of lesser goods. Frequently, the easiest way for a young man to acquire his own herd was just to take one from someone else. Since stealing horses within a warrior's own tribe was strictly forbidden and would not be tolerated by any of the warrior societies, stealing an enemy tribe's was strongly encouraged.

Horse raids were not merely an opportunity to demonstrate bravery and skill. To deprive an enemy of his horses was to diminish him in every respect. It was a humiliation to have one's herd pilfered. Horses had mystical significance, and their loss was a spiritual defeat. In practical terms, a tribe without horses could not send out mounted war or raiding parties of its own, effectively hunt migrating game such as buffalo, or readily sustain their seasonally nomadic existence.

Not all raids were about horses, however. Disputes over tribal boundaries and hunting grounds, along with more petty points of contention, could create long-lasting hatreds between neighboring tribes that expressed themselves as bloody feuds. Rather than engaging in all-out wars, these rival tribes sometimes contented themselves with small-scale raids and ambushes.

When on the warpath against members of rival tribes, as in the horse-thieving raids, it was not thought dishonorable to employ the element of surprise to gain an advantage. Members of tribes with known enemies were expected to maintain constant vigilance. If they let down their guard and fell victim to a sneak attack, they were to be scorned, not pitied.

A Cheyenne story tells of a successful raid on an enemy village. The raid is sudden and vicious. Note that before they leave, the warriors collect gruesome trophies to take back to their own tribe as evidence of their night's work:

> And that night, just at twilight, they came to the enemy village. They decided that they would raid it later on, after everybody was asleep. So, very carefully, when it was very dark, they sneaked into the chief's tipi, and before he could wake they scalped him to death. They cut his head off and took it away with them.
>
> In the morning, when the people in the camp woke up, they found the chief lying there, with his head gone. They all cried and mourned and hunted around, but they couldn't even find the tracks of the raiders.[36]

Red Bear/Many Wounds, the Nez Perce warrior of whose vision quest you read earlier, used ambush tactics to kill members of a rival tribe as they themselves were heading out on raid:

> At one time when going up Little Salmon [River], at a place now called Riggins, he discovered a war band of Snake or Bannock Indians coming towards him on the trail. There was a small creek with large rocks intervening. He hid his gun and secreting himself, he waited the advance of the hated enemy. They were out for fighting or stealing horses. When they drew near, Red Bear sprang from hiding and downed the foremost warrior before his presence was fully known. In the confusion he killed others of the startled foe, who, recognizing their unconquerable enemy, swam the Little Salmon to safety.[37]

Ben Kindle's "Winter Count," a concise historical record of the experiences of the Oglala Sioux in winters from 1759 to 1925, contains many examples of stealth tactics being used both by and against the Sioux. Many of these accounts feature not only the deaths of warriors who were caught unawares but also the fate of nonwarriors, such as women, children, and the elderly, who fell victim to such attacks. Here are some sample records:

> 1772: The Sioux make a new camp and the Crows hide in the timber and kill three old women sent after wood as they are returning with the wood upon their backs. . . .
>
> 1775: About forty or fifty young people of the Sioux start out on a war party. They are concealed in the heavy timber down by the big creek. Two scouts on the hill look about and see the enemy coming down the creek, about seventy or eighty of them on foot with two Crow ahead. The Sioux mount their horses and kill the two Crow. . . .
>
> 1796: A Sioux woman going after water before sunrise with a buffalo-paunch bucket on her back is killed by a hostile Indian in hiding near the camp. . . .
>
> 1804: The Sioux stole horses from the Blackfoot, many of them curly-haired. . . .
>
> 1814: A Mandan came down to the Sioux camp and talked with his hands, telling them not to kill him. A Sioux whose brother had been killed (by a Mandan) came up to him with a concealed ax and chopped off his head. . . .
>
> 1826: An aged Sioux was scalped by the Crow Indians and he returned to camp and died. . . .
>
> 1862: A Sioux boy crossed the creek from camp and as he was coming back about nine or ten o'clock some Shoshone Indians scalped him.[38]

Once again, it was not considered a despicable or dishonorable act among the warriors of the plains to scalp or kill a noncombatant. To do so merely proved that you were clever and powerful enough to penetrate your foe's best defenses and strike at the heart of his tribe. LeFarge explains:

> Killing women and children was as highly esteemed as killing men, since to get to the non-combatants one had to go right into the town. Occasionally women and children were taken prisoner and eventually adopted into the enemy tribe. . . . [A]dult males were captured for only one reason—to torture them. Warrior prisoners were sometimes spared and adopted, but rarely.[39]

When the native people of the plains came into conflict with white settlers pushing west, many whites were horrified by the Native American warrior culture, which they judged to be uncivilized and ignoble. White propagandists defending the expansion into Indian-held territory depicted the native people as incurably savage, possessing few, if any, redeeming virtues. Raids and ambush attacks, as well as the killing of noncombatants, were presented as shameful and cowardly acts. Incendiary pamphlets and political cartoons portrayed native warriors as subhuman, fit only for extermination.

This negative characterization of native warrior values by whites is extremely ironic when set against the actual behavior of white warriors in their conflicts with the tribes. Many books have been written on the subject of the atrocities committed against the Native Americans by white settlers, the U.S. government, and its representatives, and it is not my intention to catalogue those injustices here. This chapter is about the warriors of the Plains tribes, not their white opponents, and my focus is philosophical, not historical. I will, however, briefly mention a few of the incidents of violence between the U.S. Army and the Native Americans in order that I may comment on the values of some of the significant military leaders of the Plains tribes who emerged during the so-called Indian Wars.

When the whites started to encroach on tribal lands, building homes, farms, towns, and ranches and slicing across native hunting grounds with fences, roads, and, ultimately, railroad tracks, the tribes reacted much as they had for centuries before when territorial disputes had arisen among themselves: they went on the warpath. They applied the same tactics that were used in intertribal conflict to try to chase off the whites. This included ambushes of wagon trains heading west, stealth attacks on settlements, and, on occasion, the killing or abduction of white women and children and the torture of male prisoners.

In 1881, the U.S. Secretary of the Interior reported on the continuing conflicts between the native and nonnative citizens of the plains. In her powerful condemnation of U.S. policy toward the Native Americans (originally published in 1881), *A Century of Dishonor,* Helen Hunt Jackson recorded the secretary's perceptions:

> It cannot be denied that most of the depredations committed by the Indians on our frontiers are the offspring of dire necessity. The advance of our population compels them to relinquish their fertile lands, and seek refuge in sterile regions which furnish neither corn nor game: impelled by hunger, they seize the horses, mules, and cattle of the pioneers, to relieve their wants and satisfy the cravings of nature. They are immediately pursued, and, when overtaken, severely punished. This creates a feeling of revenge on their part, which seeks its gratification in outrages on the persons and property of peaceable inhabitants. The whole country then becomes excited, and a desolating war, attended with a vast sacrifice of blood and treasure, ensues. This, it is believed, is a true history of the origin of most of our Indian hostilities.[40]

The tribes were using what were for them traditional means to defend their homeland from invasion. Unfortunately, their non-European tactics and non-Christian warrior culture caused such terror among the white population that many settlers adopted the now infamous attitude of "the only good Indian is a dead Indian." Unbelievably, they saw the natives' resistance to being driven off their land as ample justification for genocide. Historian Bob Scott, writing on the Sand Creek Massacre (about which I will say more in a moment), quotes from a letter by the Reverend William Crawford, a preacher from Denver, who was reporting to the American Home Missionary headquarters in Illinois in September of 1864:

> We are now at open war with nearly all the Indians on the plains—the Sioux, the Cheyenne, Kiowa, Arapaho and Comanche. General Curtis with a considerable force is marching toward the Blue River and a regiment of 100-day men is in Denver awaiting orders. Other companies are out on the plains. The Indians avoid open battle and only fall upon little parties of emigrants and unprotected ranches. The loss they have caused in life and property cannot well be estimated.
>
> For friends concerned for our safety, rest assured that we can defend ourselves against attack. There is one sentiment in regard to the disposition of the Indians; let them be exterminated, men, women, and children. They are regarded as a race accursed like the ancient Canaanites, devoted by the Almighty to utter destruction. I do not share these views, but my feelings have changed. The grace of God may be sufficient for them, but humanly speaking, there seems no better destiny ahead than to fade away before the white man.[41]

War with the whites turned out to be unlike any in the tribes' previous experience. Nearly every male in the tribes was a hunter/warrior, responsible for his own protection and that of his family and tribe. But the white men who moved west were not all warriors. Some were peaceful farmers, ranchers, and tradesmen who relied on the U.S. Army to defend them. The relationship between the army and the settlers and the connection to government officials back in the East were difficult for the Indians to understand. A war party could attack a settlement, and the retaliation would be led not by the survivors but by an army detachment or cavalry troop. The white invasion must have seemed like a monstrous hydra: cut off one head and the others will attack you while a new head grows in place of the severed one.

When warring tribes made peace, it was a straightforward matter. The chiefs of each tribe would meet and negotiate terms for their coexistence, with the comfort of rituals (such as the smoking of "peace pipes") to seal their bargain. The relative homogeneity of the Plains cultures made clear communication and thorough understanding possible. Similar values fostered a level of mutual respect, even if each tribe did continue to view itself as naturally superior. Intertribal competition was fierce, but it was also easily contained.

Peace agreements between Native Americans and whites were another

matter entirely. Cultural differences, misunderstanding, and miscommu-
nication were almost as damaging as the incidents of outright deception.
Settlers and local civilian authorities would sometimes attempt to seal
peace agreements with the tribes in their area, only to have their bargains
ignored by army officers sent from the East to "eliminate the threat of hostile Indians." Tribal leaders would travel all the way to Washington, D.C.,
to make pacts with U.S. government officials but would discover when
they returned to their own lands that the whites there, military or civilian,
would stubbornly refuse to honor the central government's agreements.
A treaty that was signed by one tribe would be considered null and void
by the whites because warriors from *another* tribe, not even party to the
treaty, violated its terms.

Two types of native leaders sprang from the midst of this chaos: peace
chiefs and war chiefs. The so-called peace chiefs were dedicated to reaching a settlement with the whites in order to prevent further bloodshed on
either side and perhaps permit the tribes to return to some semblance of
their former lifestyle. The war chiefs were determined to fight to retain or
restore tribal holdings and prevent future territorial transgressions by the
whites. Many men could be profiled in each of these categories. I will
mention only a sampling of the most prominent figures: of peace chiefs,
Black Kettle of the Cheyenne and White Antelope of the Arapaho; and of
war chiefs, Crazy Horse and Sitting Bull of the Sioux tribes and Chief
Joseph of the Nez Perce.

The tales of Black Kettle and White Antelope involve an incident
known as the Sand Creek Massacre, which occurred in late November of
1864. As peace chiefs, both Black Kettle and White Antelope had attended a series of meetings with U.S. government officials at Bent's Fort, on
the Upper Arkansas, four years prior to the events at Sand Creek. There
they had pledged their words that their bands of Cheyenne and Arapaho
warriors would never again go on the warpath against either the white
settlers or the U.S. military.

Helen Hunt Jackson stresses that "Black Kettle and White Antelope
wished it to be distinctly understood that they pledged only themselves
and their own bands."[42] This was a crucial caveat, because there were
many hostile bands of Cheyenne and Arapaho at this time who had no
intention of permitting themselves to be bound to a peace treaty with the
whites. These included the famous Cheyenne "Dog Soldiers."

The Dog Soldiers were members of a particularly fierce Cheyenne warrior society who had sworn that they would sooner die than be pushed off
their land by the whites. These warriors were often nothing short of suicidal in their intensity. Mails describes one of the Dog Soldiers' warrior
traditions:

If a . . . [Dog Soldier] chose, he could make a vow before a battle to drive his
pin into the ground and tie himself to it with his dog rope as the enemy

closed in. He would then remain there and fight until either the enemy was beaten or he was killed. Others could stand with him and try to save him if they wished to. A warrior who sided a pinned comrade four times gained the eminent right to free a friend in future wars; he could intervene when the warrior was about to be killed, pull the pin, lash him across the back with it, and by so doing cancel the vow.[43]

While the Dog Soldiers and others continued to war on the whites, Black Kettle and White Antelope tried to return their tribes to something like a normal existence. But this proved quite difficult. The terms of the treaties they had signed required them to keep their people off land that had been settled by whites. As western expansion continued, this meant that the tribes of Black Kettle and White Antelope were forced into the Colorado territory by their need to find viable hunting grounds.

The citizens of Colorado, as you read in the passage quoted earlier from the Reverend Crawford's letter, were already engaged in hostilities with several other tribes. Matters were so extreme by the fall of 1864 that territorial governor John Evans telegraphed the federal government, begging for assistance. The governor's wish was granted when General Samuel Curtis, who was the area's U.S. Army commander, authorized the activation of the Third Colorado, a division of volunteer "Indian fighters." The Third Colorado was soon dispatched to Evans, under the command of one Colonel John Chivington, a man notorious for his hatred of Native Americans.

Black Kettle, White Antelope, and five other Cheyenne peace chiefs met with Evans and Chivington to negotiate peace. They renewed their pledge that neither they nor the warriors under their authority would engage in any violence against the army or the citizens of Colorado. The discussion then took an inauspicious turn as the subject of the Dog Soldiers was raised and it became clear to Evans and Chivington that the peace chiefs had little power to bring peace to the region.

Scott summarizes the scene in *Blood at Sand Creek*:

In the course of the peace conference, the Cheyenne leaders admitted that their warriors had been engaging in open warfare against whites, and that the war, in fact, was still underway. Black Kettle further admitted he knew of at least two additional women and one infant who were being held as prisoners in a Cheyenne village not far from Fort Lyon [Colorado]. One of the government representatives asked why the prisoners had not already been released, and one of the chiefs—it is not recorded which one—responded that it was because the women were being held by Dog Soldiers, over whom these "peace chiefs" had no control.

Under continued questioning from Evans and Chivington, White Antelope and Black Kettle confessed that in truth they no longer had any control whatsoever over any of the young warriors of their tribes, and further, that they could not speak for younger men at this meeting. However, the chiefs promised that if these talks went well they would do everything in their power to convince the young braves to stop the war against whites. They also promised to turn the young "trouble makers" over to white authorities.

As the questioning continued, Governor Evans seemed to conclude that the conference was essentially meaningless; the chiefs were able only to say that older Indians desired peace, but admitted they had no influence over young warriors and no authority to negotiate for them. At last the impatient governor bluntly told the chiefs that they had nothing to offer, and that further talks were useless unless the chiefs could control all warriors. And the governor added that until the chiefs spoke for everyone—including the Dog Soldiers—it would not be possible to declare any truce since it would be impossible to determine which Cheyennes were friendly and which were still at war.[44]

Before these troubled times, it would have been unthinkable for younger warriors to defy the orders of their older chiefs. Respect for one's elders and for authority were cornerstones of Plains Indian culture. But the young warriors could not see the logic behind the peace chiefs' actions. The warriors did not believe that the whites could ever be trusted to live up to the terms of a peace treaty. By 1864, too many treaties had already been ignored when they interfered with the whites' perceived "Manifest Destiny" to settle the West. The peace chiefs argued that the past faithlessness of white peace negotiators should not drive the native tribes to abandon all hope for peace with the whites.

Peace chiefs like White Antelope and Black Kettle who had already signed previous treaties also felt that they could not now change their minds and lead their people to war. Their concept of honor demanded that they keep their end of the peace contract, even if the whites violated its terms. Theirs was a very demanding moral stance. They did not believe that if the white man broke his word, that gave them permission to break theirs. Their word was their bond, even if their honesty and commitment put them at a practical disadvantage.

The young warriors were too bitter about their treatment by the whites to cling to such lofty principles. What their elders saw as acting honorably, they regarded a lack of spirit. Scott cites one warrior, Bull Bear, making the following defiant declaration to White Antelope: "I am young. I can still fight. . . . My brother Lean Bear died in trying to keep peace with the whites. I am willing to die fighting the whites, and expect to do so!"[45]

Convinced that the peace chiefs could do nothing to make Colorado territory safer for white settlers, Evans allowed Chivington to plan a campaign to wipe out all the Native Americans in the region. Allegedly, Chivington publicly declared, "It simply is not possible for Indians to obey or even understand any treaty. I am fully satisfied, gentlemen, that to kill them is the only way we will ever have peace and quiet in Colorado."[46] The colonel's intentions were announced to all the chiefs, along with the halfhearted suggestion from Governor Evans that any Indians who wished to be considered friendly and remain immune to attack should surrender to the U.S. Army immediately and camp at their forts.

Taking the governor's suggestion seriously, Black Kettle and White Antelope led approximately five hundred Cheyenne and Arapaho to Fort Lyon, where they surrendered to the fort's commander, Major George Wynkoop. Major Wynkoop gave the tribes some provisions and directed them to set up their tepees some thirty-five miles away, at a site known as Sand Creek. The natives complied. Those who camped at Sand Creek were mostly women, children, and the elderly, as the majority of young warriors, still rebellious, refused to surrender to the army.

The full story of the Sand Creek Massacre has already been told in great detail in several other works, so I will keep my account concise. Several of the facts of the incident are disputed by both white and Native American historians, but I will try to present the most popular version of events.

On the morning of Tuesday, November 29, 1864, having been led to the Sand Creek encampment the night before by scouts, Colonel Chivington and the Third Colorado attacked the villages of Black Kettle and White Antelope. As soon as gunshots were fired, Black Kettle hoisted an American flag and the white flag of surrender over the camps, in an attempt to signal to Chivington that the villagers were not hostile. The attack continued. Several native warriors who had remained under the peace chiefs' authority tried to reach their horses but were headed off by soldiers of the Third Colorado.

The Indians were hopelessly outnumbered and had few weapons, having surrendered most of them to Major Wynkoop. Although every rifle they had was soon employed in defense of the camp, the fifty or so warriors who remained with their people were only able to hold off the army's assault for a short time before the battle became a massacre. Nearly all of the Native Americans present, including the women and children, were slaughtered. Only nine white soldiers were killed, thirty-eight wounded. Chief Black Kettle survived, but his wife was shot down beside him. Chief White Antelope was killed, along with eight other elder chiefs. Legend holds that when White Antelope recognized the futility and horror of the situation, he folded his arms across his chest and calmly began to chant his death song: "nothing lives long except the earth and the mountains."[47]

The influence of the peace chiefs, which had never been considerable, died in the dust at Sand Creek along with White Antelope and the other Arapaho and Cheyenne villagers. Like the Dog Soldiers, many native warriors never sought peace with the whites. Among the most successful war chiefs of the Sioux tribes were the now famous Native American leaders Crazy Horse of the Oglala and Sitting Bull, a warrior and medicine man of the Hunkpapa.

Crazy Horse was not the son of a chief, but he rose quickly to a position of leadership among the Oglala because of his impressive martial prowess and natural charisma. He always led his men from the front. He appeared to be fearless in battle, a fact which has been attributed to a vision he received when he was young in which his spirit guide promised that he would suffer no harm from the arrows or bullets of his enemies, provided that he collected no scalps, coups, or horses for himself. Only his own people could ever harm him. Crazy Horse's unusual behavior quickly gained him a reputation across the entire Sioux nation as the "Oglala Strange Man."[48]

Crazy Horse had an intense hatred for whites, fueled partly by the fact that his beloved daughter, They Are Afraid of Her, died from an illness considered to be a "white man's disease."(Diseases such as smallpox that were brought to America from Europe by whites had a devastating effect on the native population, and not all of their spread was accidental. For instance, the U.S. government intentionally sent to chiefs of the Ute tribes coats that had been sewn from blankets used to wrap smallpox victims. The disease nearly obliterated the Utes.) Crazy Horse's love for the Black Hills of the Dakotas was equally intense, and he swore he would never relinquish them to the whites. It made no difference to him whether the intruders were simple settlers or the greedy prospectors who came flooding north as soon as they heard the cry of "There's gold in them thar hills!"

By 1876, Crazy Horse had become a master strategist. Reasoning that the Sioux would have to adapt to survive, he convinced his people to alter their fighting techniques. His new approach to battle proved successful against U.S. Army Brigadier General George Crook, who had been sent by the U.S. government to conduct campaigns against the Sioux near the Power and Yellowstone Rivers:

> Crazy Horse planned his battle tactics well. He delegated the older men to stay with the lodges as guards. He emphasized that the old way of making war was no longer good. The warriors must act as one body under one leadership. There must be no coups counted, no scalps, no victory dances. Only by a concentration on killing could they hope to regain their lands.
>
> On June 17th, 1876, Crazy Horse and his fighters met General Crook at the Battle of the Rosebud. It was a hard fought battle on both sides. The Lakotas began to retreat, but Crazy Horse rallied them with cries of encouragement and they turned to follow him again into battle. The soldiers swung around and struck the rear guard of the Indians, but were breaking under the pressure of the fight. Sioux shells were gone and the Indians scattered, but Crook had been stopped in his tracks.[49]

Crazy Horse had shown the Sioux warriors that if they focused together as a unit, instead of fighting in their usual style as individual warriors, they could defeat the white forces.

Sitting Bull was another Sioux leader who demonstrated prodigious strategic insight in that crucial summer of 1876. After Crook's defeat at

Rosebud, U.S. Army General George A. Custer organized an attack on a large Sioux encampment at a place called Little Bighorn along the Powder River. He had hoped to catch the Native Americans in a trap but found himself trapped instead.

Custer marched his troops up to the Sioux lodges and sent forces around both sides of the camp, intending to encircle the inhabitants and prevent their escape. Unluckily for him, Sitting Bull had anticipated this move and had evacuated the Sioux village the night before. The Sioux warriors were gathered just outside the camp and quickly fell on Custer's men. Finding themselves almost completely surrounded, some of the soldiers were able to retreat to nearby bluffs. But the men directly under Custer's command were cut off by several thousand warriors led by Crazy Horse. Custer and his men of the Seventh Cavalry were mowed down by Sioux bullets.

The Battle of Little Bighorn was an enormous victory for the Sioux. Nevertheless, it was not enough for them to win the war against the whites. Custer's defeat, a blow to the pride of the U.S. Army, provoked wave upon wave of retaliation against the Sioux. Eventually, both Sitting Bull and Crazy Horse had no alternative but to retreat and attempt to lead their people to safety. Sitting Bull took his tribe up to Canada, and Crazy Horse led his followers deeper into the Black Hills. Many other bands of Sioux were rounded up and killed or imprisoned in army stockades.

Ultimately, in October of 1876, the chiefs of several defeated Sioux tribes signed a treaty that ceded the Black Hills to the federal government. Neither Crazy Horse nor Sitting Bull signed the document, and both refused to accept it as valid. They remained in their chosen places of refuge and continued to conduct bloody raids against the whites. Yet as winter overtook them, the plight of the still resistant Sioux became desperate. They could not hunt enough game to support themselves, and the weather was harsh and dangerous.

Crazy Horse had sworn that he would never surrender to the whites. But the lives of all his people were in jeopardy. With great reluctance and a heavy heart, the great chief led his supporters down out of the hills to join with the Sioux who had already conceded the struggle. Then he arranged to meet with General Clark, the army commander now in charge of the region.

Crazy Horse's meeting with Clark was a disaster. Clark's interpreter was a renegade Oglala Sioux named Frank Grouard, considered a traitor by his people for working with the whites, who hated Crazy Horse. Grouard intentionally misinterpreted the war chief's words. When Crazy Horse offered to help the army defeat the Nez Perce, saying, "[I]f he wishes us to go to war again and asks our help, we will go north and fight till there is not a Nez Perce left," Grouard translated it as, "We will go north and fight until there is not a white man left."[50]

After Grouard betrayed Crazy Horse, several other Sioux, jealous of his fame, also turned on him. A warrior named Woman's Dress convinced Clark that Crazy Horse would never abandon his murderous intentions toward the whites and that he had specific plans to kill another army leader, General Crook. Clark believed Woman's Dress and had Crazy Horse arrested.

As they tried to lock him in an army guardhouse, Crazy Horse pulled a hidden knife and put up a valiant struggle to break free of his captors. He was finally subdued with the help of some disloyal Brule Indians (Swift Bear and Little Big Man), and one of the white soldiers stabbed him in the stomach with a bayonet. He died of his wound a few hours later. Crazy Horse's youthful vision had been more or less correct: his death came not at the hands of his enemies but as the result of betrayal by some of his own people.

Like Crazy Horse, Sitting Bull was a proud man. He was the son of a chief but had achieved power over the Sioux nation on the strength of his own merit. When he was interviewed by a white reporter in 1881, Sitting Bull gave this account of his development as a warrior and ascent to the role of chief over his tribe:

> "When I was ten years old I was famous as a hunter. My specialty was buffalo calves. I gave the calves I killed to the poor who had no horses. I was considered a good man. My father died twenty one years ago (1860). For four years after I was ten years old I killed buffalo and fed his people, and thus became one of the fathers of the tribe. At the age of fourteen I killed an enemy, and began to make myself great in battle, and became a chief. Before this, from ten to fourteen, my people had named me the Sacred Standshotly. After killing an enemy they called me Ta TanKa I-You-Tan-Ka, or Sitting Bull. An Indian may be an inherited chief, but he must make himself a chief by his bravery."[51]

Sitting Bull shared Crazy Horse's loathing of the whites who steadily stole Sioux lands. At a meeting of Sioux warriors and chiefs in 1877, Sitting Bull made his feelings about the whites perfectly plain, supporting his anger at their incursions into Sioux territory with bitter criticism of their culture in general:

> [H]ear me, people, we have now to deal with another race—small and feeble when our fathers first met them but now great and overbearing. Strangely enough they have a mind to till the soil and the love of possession is a disease with them. These people have made many rules that the rich may break but the poor may not. They take tithes from the poor and weak to support the rich who rule. They claim this mother of ours, the earth, for their own and fence their neighbors away; they deface her with their buildings and their refuse. That nation is like a spring freshet that overruns its banks and destroys all who are in its path.
>
> We cannot dwell side by side. Only seven years ago we made a treaty by which we were assured that the buffalo country should be left to us forever.

Now they threaten to take that away from us. My brothers, shall we submit or shall we say to them: "First kill me before you take possession of my Fatherland."[52]

After he led his people to Canada following the Battle of Little Bighorn, they stayed there in relative comfort for four years. By 1881, the story of Sitting Bull started to resemble that of Crazy Horse, with one startling difference. Like the followers of Crazy Horse, Sitting Bull's people found that there were no longer enough buffalo to allow them to survive in their place of exile, so they, too, traveled back south and surrendered to the U.S. Army. It was in 1885, a few years after his surrender, that Sitting Bull's life took an unexpected turn. Historian Mildred Fielder explains:

> By 1885 he had quieted his animosities towards the whites so greatly that when the world famous Buffalo Bill Cody approached him with an invitation to join his Wild West Show, it didn't take much persuasion. He toured the United States and several foreign countries with the Wild West Show. Buffalo Bill billed him as "Enemies in '75, friends in '85." The Wild West Show presented Indian war dances, bucking bronchos and a western rodeo, buffaloes and a simulated prairie fire, even an Indian village with a sham battle between Indian tribes. It was a great success, particularly in London where they played for British royalty.[53]

To the relief of those who honored him as a noble war hero, Sitting Bull did not remain with the Wild West Show forever. By 1890 he became involved in an effort to reassert Sioux rights to their ancestral lands. The Sioux who had been forced onto reservations, where they were constantly visited by Christian missionaries bent on converting them, instead adopted their own faith, known as the Ghost Dance religion. This religion held that a Native American messiah would arrive who would reunite the warriors of all the tribes and lead them against the whites to reclaim their lost territories in the Black Hills. When Sitting Bull heard of the Ghost Dance movement, he decided to join it and try to once more lead his people to victory, as he had done against Custer.

It was not Sitting Bull's fate to lead his people again. Word reached General Miles of the U.S. Army that Sitting Bull intended to rejoin his people, and General Miles immediately ordered Sitting Bull's arrest. Sitting Bull was with a band of warriors, including his own son, Crowfoot, when a group of Indians who were friendly with the whites and under the command of Major Fechet, a subordinate of Miles, came to arrest him. The Sioux warriors fought bravely, but Sitting Bull was killed, along with thirteen of his supporters.

Chief Joseph of the Nez Perce was another great warrior who resisted the power of the white man as long as he could but was finally overwhelmed by the hopelessness of his cause. As a young man, Joseph had promised his dying father, who had been a chief of his tribe, that he would always fight for his tribal homeland. Joseph's own account of this deathbed pledge is preserved:

[M]y father sent for me. I saw he was dying. I took his hand in mine. He said: "My son, my body is returning to my mother earth, and my spirit is going very soon to see the Great Spirit Chief. When I am gone, think of your country. You are the chief of these people. They look to you to guide them. Always remember that your father never sold his country. You must stop your ears whenever you are asked to sign a treaty selling your home. A few have their eyes on this land. My son, never forget my dying words. The country holds your father's body. Never sell the bones of your father and your mother." I pressed my father's hand and told him I would protect his grave with my life. My father smiled and passed away to the spirit-land.[54]

Later in his life, Chief Joseph tried to explain to U.S. commissioners his and his people's refusal to leave their own territory and accept life on a reservation:

[T]he Creative Power, when he made the earth, made no marks, no lines of division or separation on it, and that it should be allowed to remain as then made. The earth was his mother. He was made of the earth and grew up on its bosom. The earth, as his mother and nurse, was sacred to his affections, too sacred to be valued by or sold for silver and gold. He could not consent to sever his affections from the land that bore him. He asked nothing of the President. He was able to take care of himself. He did not desire Wallowa Valley as a reservation, for that would subject him and his band to the will of and dependence on another, and to laws not of their own making. He was disposed to live peaceably.[55]

But the Nez Perce were not permitted to live peaceably on their own lands any more than the Sioux. And so Chief Joseph led his people to war. He recognized, as had Crazy Horse, that the traditional fighting methods of his people would not produce many victories over the U.S. Army. He organized and disciplined his troops, earning the admiration even of his enemies. General Shanks, who fought against Joseph and his men, was awed by the warriors' order and skill:

Joseph's party was thoroughly disciplined; . . . they rode at full gallop along the mountain side in a steady formation by fours; formed twos, at a given signal, with perfect precision, to cross a narrow bridge; then galloped into line, reined in to a sudden halt, and dismounted with as much system as regulars.[56]

The Nez Perce, under Joseph's leadership, fought many times against the soldiers of the U.S. Army. They won three major battles, fought more than a dozen smaller engagements that could be considered draws, and were only defeated in one large-scale confrontation. Chief Joseph was hailed as the "Indian Napoleon." Nonetheless, in the end, he and his people suffered the same fate as all the other native tribes who tried to oppose the progress of the whites. Chief Joseph's final surrender speech is one of the most famous ever spoken:

> I am tired of fighting. Our chiefs are killed. Looking Glass is dead. The old men are all killed. It is the young men who say yes or no. He who led the young men is dead. It is cold and we have no blankets. The little children are freezing to death. My people, some of them, have run away to the hills, and have no blankets, no food; no one knows where they are, perhaps freezing to death. I want time to look for my children and see how many of them I can find. Maybe I shall find them among the dead. Hear me, my chiefs. I am tired: my heart is sick and sad. From where the sun now stands, I will fight no more [forever].[57]

In time, all of the Plains tribes were either destroyed or required to restrict themselves to government-selected reservations. Many of these reservations, of course, still exist today, and modern Native Americans continue to strive to preserve their culture and resist assimilation into the world of their conquerors. For many, the spirit of resistance, the warrior spirit, endures. And some even maintain hope that the native people of the plains will yet regain their former strength and retake the land that once was theirs. Most Native Americans, however, now turn their energy more to the urgent task of searching for ways to ease the social and economic struggles facing the tribes today than to reliving the battles of the past.

Modern warriors, whatever their heritage, can glean lessons from both the positive and the negative aspects of the culture and traditions of the warriors of the Sacred Plains. One of the most relevant of these is the importance of rigorous rites of passage for warriors-in-training. Such rites help warriors bond and build trust with one another, while also allowing the individual warrior to feel the pride of accomplishment and the confidence that comes with knowing one has endured what others could not.

Well-conceived rites of passage enhance individual dignity; they do not damage it. It is both ridiculous and cruel to protect future warriors from rites of passage on the grounds that such rites may cause them physical or emotional distress, when we have no intention of protecting them from much greater physical and emotional distress in their careers or in combat. The specific skills and abilities that warriors need to succeed in responding to modern threats will continue to evolve, but as long as war involves killing and dying, there will be a need for warriors who *feel like warriors.* Mind you, reaching that goal may not quite require reviving the Sun Dance ritual, as some of my students have gamely suggested.

NOTES

1. Vine Deloria Jr., *"We Talk, You Listen"* (New York: Macmillan, 1970).

2. Thomas E. Mails, *Mystic Warriors of the Plains* (Garden City, N.Y.: Doubleday, 1972), 12.

3. Mails, *Mystic Warriors,* 29.

4. Mails, *Mystic Warriors,* 7.

5. Mails, *Mystic Warriors,* 20.

6. Alice Marriott and Carol K. Rachlin, *Plains Indian Mythology* (New York: Thomas Y. Crowell, 1975), 3.

7. "The Magic Dogs," from Comanche oral history, retold by Jean Edwards, Comanche, in Marriott and Rachlin, *Plains Indian Mythology,* 91.

8. "Out of the Earth Houses," from Cheyenne oral history, retold by Belle Martin, Cheyenne, in Marriott and Rachlin, *Plains Indian Mythology,* 96–97.

9. Calvin Martin, *Keepers of the Game: Indian-Animal Relationships and the Fur Trade* (Berkeley and Los Angeles: University of California Press, 1978), 115–16.

10. Martin, *Keepers of the Game,* 120–21.

11. Marriott and Rachlin, *Plains Indian Mythology,* 77.

12. Marriott and Rachlin, *Plains Indian Mythology,* 32–33.

13. Helen Addison Howard and Dan L. McGrath, *War Chief Joseph* (Lincoln: University of Nebraska Press, 1941), 28–29.

14. Frederick W. Turner III, ed., *The Portable North American Indian Reader* (New York: Viking, 1973), 125–26.

15. Marriott and Rachlin, *Plains Indian Mythology,* 28.

16. Turner, *North American Indian Reader,* 164.

17. Mails, *Mystic Warriors,* 37–39.

18. Mails, *Mystic Warriors,* 40.

19. William K. Powers, *Beyond the Vision: Essays on American Indian Culture* (Norman: University of Oklahoma Press, 1987), 5.

20. Turner, *North American Indian Reader,* 162.

21. Turner, *North American Indian Reader,* 230.

22. Marriott and Rachlin, *Plains Indian Mythology,* 42–43.

23. James H. Howard, trans. and ed., *The Warrior Who Killed Custer: The Personal Narrative of Chief Joseph White Bull* (Lincoln: University of Nebraska Press, 1968), 43–44.

24. Oliver LeFarge, *A Pictorial History of the American Indian* (New York: Crown, 1956), 167.

25. LeFarge, *Pictorial History,* 33.

26. Mails, *Mystic Warriors,* 40.

27. Marriott and Rachlin, *Plains Indian Mythology,* 38.

28. Marriott and Rachlin, *Plains Indian Mythology,* 45–47.

29. Mails, *Mystic Warriors,* 42.

30. Mails, *Mystic Warriors,* 42–43.

31. Mails, *Mystic Warriors,* 32.

32. Marriott and Rachlin, *Plains Indian Mythology,* 9.

33. Marriott and Rachlin, *Plains Indian Mythology*, 121.

34. Mails, *Mystic Warriors*, 31.

35. Turner, *North American Indian Reader*, 134–35.

36. Marriott and Rachlin, *Plains Indian Mythology*, 79.

37. Turner, *North American Indian Reader*, 231.

38. Martha Warren Beckwith, trans., "Ben Kindle's Winter Count," in *North American Indian Reader*, ed. Turner, 135–57.

39. LeFarge, *Pictorial History*, 31–33.

40. Helen Hunt Jackson, *A Century of Dishonor: A Sketch of the United States Government's Dealings with Some of the Indian Tribes* (New York: Harper, 1885).

41. Bob Scott, *Blood at Sand Creek: The Massacre Revisited* (Caldwell, Idaho: Caxton, 1994), 119–20.

42. Jackson, *Century of Dishonor*, 83.

43. Mails, *Mystic Warriors*, 49.

44. Scott, *Blood at Sand Creek*, 122–23.

45. Scott, *Blood at Sand Creek*, 125.

46. Scott, *Blood at Sand Creek*, 131.

47. Scott, *Blood at Sand Creek*, 150.

48. Mildred Fielder, *Sioux Indian Leaders* (Seattle: Superior, 1975), 11–13.

49. Fielder, *Sioux Indian Leaders*, 16.

50. Fielder, *Sioux Indian Leaders*, 22–23.

51. Fielder, *Sioux Indian Leaders*, 40–41.

52. Turner, *North American Indian Reader*, 255.

53. Fielder, *Sioux Indian Leaders*, 51.

54. Howard and McGrath, *War Chief Joseph*, 85.

55. Howard and McGrath, *War Chief Joseph*, 102.

56. Howard and McGrath, *War Chief Joseph*, 153.

57. Turner, *North American Indian Reader*, 232.

7

Chinese Warrior Monks:
The Martial Artists of Shaolin

Religion has been a factor in shaping the traditions of most of the warrior cultures we have examined so far, from the Vikings to the knights to the Native Americans. The warrior training of the Buddhist monks of the Shaolin Temple in the Henan province of China, however, not only reflects the influence of their religion but also is integral to their practice of it. Gung Fu, the Chinese martial art developed by the Shaolin monks beginning in the sixth century A.D., was originally conceived to help its practitioners achieve Buddhist enlightenment. That it also aided the monks' survival when hostile forces threatened their sanctuary was a secondary benefit.

Before we step inside the Shaolin temple and evaluate the code of the warrior monks, I first should review some basic Buddhist beliefs. It is notoriously difficult to capture the substance of Asian religions in the language of the West, but I will nevertheless attempt a thumbnail sketch to elucidate the key concepts of Buddhist ideology. I believe the best approach to Buddhism for beginners is through the life story of Buddha himself.

Unlike the figure of Jesus Christ in Christian doctrine, Buddha is not a god or an aspect of a god. He was born Prince Siddhartha (a name meaning "one whose goal is accomplishment")[1] Gautama, the son of King Suddhodana, a wealthy ruler in India. The year of his birth is sometimes disputed but is often recorded as 560 B.C. His mother, the queen, died seven days after giving birth to the infant prince. King Suddhodana asked prophets to predict the future of the boy for whom his beloved wife had given her last measure of strength, and he was told that Siddhartha would either follow in his father's footsteps and become a powerful and respected monarch or else would forsake all claims to his father's kingdom and become an enlightened spiritual leader who would show humanity the way to end its suffering.

The king was more concerned with securing a successor for his throne than with putting an end to human suffering, so he asked the prophets how he might encourage his son to choose the royal path. He was told that Prince Siddhartha would one day become king only if he could be kept from ever observing human misery. To accomplish this end, King Suddhodana ordered three lavishly appointed palaces to be constructed for his son. No one who was sad, ill, or aging was allowed to enter these palaces, and guards were placed at every entrance to ensure that nothing and no one from the outside world that might possibly expose the existence of human suffering to the young prince could ever pass the thresholds.

Prince Siddhartha enjoyed his sheltered, luxurious life for many years, completely ignorant of the true conditions of life. When he was twenty-nine, he married a beautiful woman named Yasodhara, and the happy couple soon conceived a child. Before becoming a father, Siddhartha decided he should have a look at the world outside his palace walls. The prince informed the king that he intended to instruct his charioteer, Chandaka, to take him on a brief tour of his father's kingdom. The king was alarmed, but reluctantly approved the plan after making elaborate arrangements to guarantee that Siddhartha would encounter nothing that might disturb him anywhere along his preselected route.

At first, the king's preparations seemed successful. Everywhere Siddhartha went he saw only young, happy, healthy people who cheered him and threw flowers at his chariot. Then in a village along the way, the prince suddenly observed what was to him a very startling figure: an old man, weak and withered, leaning on a cane for support. Somehow the king's guards had overlooked the old man, who had heard the commotion of Siddhartha's approach and had hobbled out of his cottage to discover the source of all the fuss.

Prince Siddhartha immediately asked his charioteer to account for the old man's appearance. Chandaka explained that the villager was simply suffering the natural ravages of advanced age, just as Siddhartha himself would one day do. As Siddhartha attempted to process this shocking information, the king's guards finally noticed the elderly intruder into their carefully choreographed scene and quickly ordered Chandaka to return the prince to his palace.

Siddhartha's curiosity was now fully aroused, and he insisted on taking three further journeys into the real world. Despite the king's best efforts, each of his son's subsequent outings also produced a shattering revelation. On his second trip, Siddhartha met a man battling disease. Chandaka informed the prince that everyone, including royalty, can fall prey to illness. On his third visit, Siddhartha saw a corpse, prompting Chandaka to clarify that all people, whatever their rank or station, are mortal creatures who will one day die.

After these first three tours the prince's heart was filled with compassion for his fellow humans and sympathy for their distress. He could no longer find bliss in the artificially ideal environment of his palaces. Even the birth of his son, Rahula, could not bring him joy, because every time he looked at the weak and helpless little baby, he envisioned the boy's future experience as inescapable suffering and inevitable death. If such was life, why should the start of a new life be an event worthy of celebration?

Having finally been exposed to the brutal realities of human existence, Siddhartha became obsessed with finding some meaning in such an existence. He resolved to go on yet another outing in search of further revelations. On this fourth tour, he encountered an ascetic, a monk who had voluntarily forsaken all material possessions and earthly pleasures in an effort to achieve clarity of mind and tranquility of spirit.

The monk's dedication persuaded the prince that he, too, should pursue the deeper understanding that eluded him by abandoning the comforts of his home and committing all his energy to the quest for spiritual enlightenment. It was a bitter thing for Siddhartha to turn away from his beloved family, knowing that they might not understand his reasons for leaving them. But he felt compelled by a higher calling to try to answer the burning questions that now plagued his mind: Why do human beings suffer? Can their suffering be ended or avoided? Is there a purpose to it?

For six years Siddhartha endured the harsh life of an ascetic. He joined five other ascetics, and they lived out in the wild, without shelter from the elements, drinking only rainwater and eating so little as to be always on the edge of starvation. In this way, the formerly pampered royal spent month after month meditating on the meaning of life, abiding the intense physical pain of exposure and severe deprivation.

At the end of these six years, Siddhartha came to the conclusion that such excessive self-denial was not the way to further his pursuit of a solution to the problem of human suffering. Abruptly, he gave up the ascetic manner of life, inspired by the analogy between a person and the strings on a musical instrument. If you overtighten an instrument's strings, they will snap and produce no music. If you let them hang loosely, again they cannot be played. But if you adjust them properly, they can fulfill their function and bring forth beautiful notes. Similarly, Siddhartha Gautama reasoned, human beings who wish to achieve their potential should avoid the extremes both of self-denial and of self-indulgence.

To the disgust of the other five ascetics, Gautama walked to a nearby river, bathed himself, and accepted a bowl of rice milk offered as charity by a young girl from a nearby village. He savored the taste of his first real meal after so many days of hunger. Then, sensing that he was on the edge of an epiphany, he went and sat beneath a fig tree to reflect on the human condition once again.

As he turned his mind inward, he saw existence as an endless cycle of life, death, and rebirth. A person's soul or spirit, he believed, was an eternal part of the universe that could be reincarnated many times into many different mortal forms: humans, animals, and even insects might possess reincarnated souls. As long as these souls remained attached to mortal beings, they would be susceptible to all the potential pain of earthly existence.

In a surge of understanding, Siddhartha grasped the four Noble Truths of Buddhism. It was in this moment of enlightenment that he became a Buddha. These were the four Noble Truths that became clear to him:

- the Noble Truth of suffering *(dukkha)*
- the Noble Truth of the origin of suffering
- the Noble Truth of the cessation of suffering
- the Noble Truth of the Eightfold Path to the cessation of suffering

The first Noble Truth is that life on earth is painful. As we go through life, we experience physical pain from injury, illness, and aging in addition to mental and emotional pain from such sources as frustration, rejection, cruelty, neglect, disgust, and loss. We are never completely satisfied because we never get everything that we want.

The second Noble Truth is that if we carefully examine the source of our suffering, we will recognize it to be the result of grasping or craving *(tanha)* after things we do not have. Injuries, illness, and aging torture us because we desire perfectly sound, healthy, youthful bodies. We experience frustration and rejection when we are denied what we crave, cruelty and neglect when we are not treated as we believe we deserve, disgust when the world fails to reflect our wishes, and loss when that which we value proves not to be eternal.

The third Noble Truth draws the conclusion that if tanha (grasping, craving, and desiring what we do not have) is the source of dukkha (suffering), then the way to put an end to dukkha is to extinguish tanha. According to the Buddha's reflections, souls become trapped in the cycle of reincarnation because they are too attached to their earthly desires. Their goal should be to free themselves from that cycle, cease to exist as an individual soul, and return to a state of oneness with the universe, known as Nirvana.

Nirvana is described as an ideal state because to be one with the universe is to permanently escape tanha and its consequence, dukkha. The universe is not susceptible to grasping and craving. It has no unfulfilled needs and desires. The universe, being infinite, contains everything and so wants for nothing. By breaking the cycle of rebirth, the Buddhist loses his or her individual existence but gains the universe.

The critical question, then, is, how is the release from the cycle of rebirth supposed to be achieved? The answer to that question is the fourth

Noble Truth, which identifies the Eightfold Path that leads to the cessation of suffering. The eight components of this path are right speech, right action, right livelihood, right effort, right mindfulness, right concentration, right view, and right thought. These eight points are at the core of Buddhist philosophy.

The first three points—right speech, right action, and right livelihood—essentially prescribe moral behavior (*shila*). To embrace right speech is to avoid such offenses to truth as lies, gossip, and slander, which are generally employed in the service of selfish aims (an aspect of tanha). Right action requires not only eschewing conduct that causes harm, like killing, raping, or thieving, but also performing good deeds that model virtues like charity, benevolence, and generosity. Right livelihoods are those that do no harm to others (a person attempting to stay on the Eightfold Path should not become a loan shark or paid assassin, for example) and those that do not bar the road to enlightenment.

The principles contained in these three points are also summarized in the five precepts to which Buddhists adhere:

- Do not take or destroy life.

- Do not take what is not given.

- Do not engage in any sexual misconduct.

- Do not speak falsely.

- Do not indulge in the consumption of intoxicating or mind-altering substances (i.e., drugs and alcohol).

The next three points of the Eightfold Path pertain to the practice of meditation (*samadhi*): right effort, right mindfulness, and right concentration. Mental discipline is critical for the Buddhist adherent. Buddha's experiences as an ascetic taught him that the mind could be trained to transcend the demands of the body. But with his enlightenment he came to embrace a more harmonious dualist vision. He saw that the mind should not be a mere tyrant, roughly repressing physical desires and ignoring natural corporeal needs. Rather, it should be a teacher, firmly guiding a reformation of the appetites to produce a well-balanced self, the unification of an equally wholesome body and mind.

The final two points of the Eightfold Path are right view and right thought. These both relate to the attainment of wisdom (*prajna*). Buddha believed that true wisdom could only be found in the achievement of an unfiltered connection to the whole of existence. What separates us from the rest of the universe is our sense of ourselves as individuals: our egos and our attachments to specific aspects of life on earth. Therefore, for the Buddhist, to have the right view is to let go of the perception that you are a distinct, unique entity. To have right thought is to no longer think of yourself as something apart from the rest of creation, to no longer divide the world into categories of "me" and "things that are not me." Abandoning your sense of self is the last step on the path to Nirvana.

The following Buddhist story illustrates the doctrine of nonattachment and its essential role in the quest for enlightenment:

> Kitano Gempo, abbot of Eihei temple, was ninety-two years old when he passed away in the year 1933. He endeavored his whole life not to be attached to anything. As a wandering mendicant when he was twenty he happened to meet a traveler who smoked tobacco. As they walked together down a mountain road, they stopped under a tree to rest. The traveler offered Kitano a smoke, which he accepted, as he was very hungry at the time.
>
> "How pleasant this smoking is," he commented. The other gave him an extra pipe and tobacco and they parted.
>
> Kitano felt: "Such pleasant things may disturb meditation. Before this goes too far, I will stop now." So he threw the smoking outfit away.
>
> When he was twenty-three years old he studied I-King, the profoundest doctrine of the universe [and made some successful predictions about the future using I-King]. . . .
>
> "If I perform such accurate determinative work with I-King, I may neglect my meditation," felt Kitano. So he gave up this marvelous teaching and never resorted to its powers again.
>
> When he was twenty-eight he studied Chinese calligraphy and poetry. He grew so skillful in these arts that his teacher praised him. Kitano mused: "If I don't stop now, I'll be a poet, not a[n enlightened] teacher [of Buddhism]." So he never wrote another poem.[2]

This story emphasizes the idea, central to Buddhist philosophy, that no effort or accomplishment on earth has any value unless it assists in the achievement of enlightenment. The Buddhists' goal is to avoid being reincarnated, to break free of the cycle of rebirth and the attending pain of mortal existence. This goal cannot be reached so long as they dedicate their energy to any earth-bound struggles or identify themselves with any pursuit other than the pursuit of enlightenment.

The modern-day Buddhist monks of Tibet practice the art of mandalas as an exercise in nonattachment. These mandalas are elaborate and stunningly beautiful circular designs made with brightly colored grains of sand. The creation of each mandala requires many hours of intense concentration. Yet as soon as the work is completed, it is destroyed: the sands are scattered to the wind. It is a symbolic reminder that the universe is in constant flux. Elements of the universe may be drawn together in temporary unions to form temples or mountains or human bodies, but eventually those elements will be shaken apart, either to assume another form or to merge with the infinite.

Buddha's teachings concerning the path to enlightenment and the doctrine of nonattachment spread from India to China via Buddhist missionaries during China's Han dynasty (206 B.C.–A.D. 220). There were many such missionaries, but only one carries the significant distinction of being credited both with the establishment of the Ch'an (or Zen) school of Buddhism in China and with being the father of gung fu, the Chinese martial art. That one is the Indian monk Bodhidharma, who reached Southern China sometime around A.D. 500.

Bodhidharma (also known to the Chinese as P'u-t'i-ta-mo, or just Tamo) was highly respected as the "twenty-eighth patriarch."[3] In other words, he was believed to have been the twenty-eighth man to have received the original teachings of Buddha, passed down as an oral tradition from teacher to disciple. Owing to this distinction, after he arrived in China, Bodhidharma was reportedly summoned to a personal audience with Emperor Wu of the Liang dynasty.[4]

There are several conflicting accounts of Bodhidharma's meeting with Emperor Wu. While they differ in detail, they all seem to suggest that Bodhidharma took the emperor to task for allowing Buddhism in China to drift away from the core revelations of Buddha. Bodhidharma had observed many richly ornate Chinese temples dedicated to Buddha in which Chinese Buddhists worshiped with elaborate rituals. He felt that these extravagant settings and practices could only serve to trap the mind in temporal reflections, rather than lifting it to a more spiritual plane.

The Zen approach to Buddhism, championed by Bodhidharma, not only rejects ornamentation and ceremony as unnecessary distractions that hamper right concentration but also challenges the idea that enlightenment can be obtained through the study of sacred texts. Bodhidharma asserted that the truth of Buddhism could best be found not in books but inside oneself. Seeking enlightenment through research, rather than through the mental discipline of meditation, could itself represent a form of attachment to the mundane.

In his book *Buddhist China*, early-twentieth-century scholar Reginald Fleming Johnston draws a revealing parallel between Bodhidharma's account of Zen Buddhism and Christian teachings in the West that also encourage an inward search for spiritual awareness. Johnston also outlines some of the positive and negative effects of Bodhidharma's introduction of Zen Buddhism into China:

> "You will not find Buddha in images or books," was the teaching of the venerable Tamo. "Look into your own heart: that is where you will find Buddha."
>
> The Chinese word for "heart," it should be noted, has a very complex significance, and we often come across religious or philosophical passages in which the word might more appropriately, though even then inadequately, be rendered by "mind." The Chinese term is hsin, and this may be regarded as the key-word of the Ch'an Buddhism which has for many centuries dominated Chinese religious thought. . . .

Tamo's system has been described as "the Buddhist counterpart of the Spiritual Exercises of St. Ignatius Loyola"; but there are other Christian saints
and mystics with whom he may be compared even more fittingly. . . .

No less readily would Tamo have welcomed a kindred spirit in St. Paul,
who rejected "tablets of stone" in favour of "the fleshy tablets of the heart";
or in St. Augustine, who, in words which contain the essence of Tamo's own
teaching, bade men look for truth in the depths of their own being. . . .

. . . [I]t must be admitted that in China the results of Tamo's teachings
have been both good and bad. On the one hand they are partially responsible for the decay of learning in the Chinese monasteries. Tamo's advice was
taken too literally. Books were neglected, and monkish energy concentrated
itself on ecstatic meditation. In many cases religious zeal died away for
want of substantial nourishment, and there is reason to suspect that some of
the monks who believed themselves to have attained the exalted state of
mystical union were apt to confuse that state with the less honourable condition of physical somnolence. On the other hand, the influence of Tamo
and his successors undoubtedly tended to save Chinese Buddhism from the
evils of priestcraft and "clericalism" and from a slavish worship of images
and relics, dogma, and sacred books. . . . There are monks in China to-day
who would not be sorry to see the temples cleared of every image that they
contain; and there are many others who would plead for the retention of the
images only for the sake of those simple-minded and unenlightened souls
who cling to the material symbol because the truth that it symbolizes is
beyond their grasp.[5]

Bodhidharma tried to explain to the emperor Wu that the truths of Zen
Buddhism could not be taught the way that calligraphy or mathematics
are taught. In his fascinating and detailed treatise, *The Bodhisattva Warriors*, Shifu (Master) Nagaboshi Tomi makes a useful reference to a lesson
in the *Ching Te Chuan Teng Lu* that illustrates the "wordless doctrine" of
Ch'an Buddhism favored by Bodhidharma:

[I]t is said that Shakyamuni had assembled his monks for a lecture but that
few of them had been able to understand its inner meanings, they all sat
there pondering what it was they were supposed to be understanding. After
what seemed an embarrassingly long period of waiting, Shakyamuni, who
knew well how puzzled his monks were, stood up, picked up and held aloft
a flower. The monks were even more confused by such an action. Suddenly
one of the elder disciples named Maha Kasyapa stood, and looking directly
at Shakyamuni, burst into a great smile. At that point, it is said, Shakyamuni Buddha knew that Maha Kasyapa alone had understood his words.[6]

Maha Kasyapa grasped the meaning of the master's gesture directly. It
was a flash of insight similar to Buddha's own critical epiphanies about
the nature of existence. That sudden, total comprehension is the essence
of Zen.

Bodhidharma's Zen teachings are sometimes called the philosophy of
"no mind." While in China, Bodhidharma gave a sermon on Zen that

attempts to clarify how an adherent should seek to free himself from the bonds of karma:

> Language and behavior, perception and conception are all functions of the moving mind. All motion is the mind's motion. Motion is its function. Apart from motion there's no mind, and apart from the mind there's no motion. But motion isn't the mind. And the mind isn't motion. Motion is basically mindless. And the mind is basically motionless. But motion doesn't exist without the mind. And the mind doesn't exist without motion. There's no mind for motion to exist apart from, and no motion for mind to exist apart from. Motion is the mind's function, and its function is its motion. Even so, the mind neither moves nor functions, because the essence of its functioning is emptiness and emptiness is essentially motionless. Motion is the same as the mind. And the mind is essentially motionless.
>
> Hence [Buddhist teachings] tell us to move without moving, to travel without traveling, to see without seeing, to laugh without laughing, to hear without hearing, to know without knowing, to be happy without being happy, to walk without walking, to stand without standing. . . . "Go beyond language. Go beyond thought." Basically, seeing, hearing, and knowing are completely empty. Your anger, joy, or pain is like that of a puppet. You can search, but you won't find a thing. . . . [O]nce you know that the nature of anger and joy is empty and you let them go, you free yourself from karma.[7]

It was clear that the Zen form of Buddhism did not appeal to the emperor, and Bodhidharma soon left the imperial palace. He traveled to Henan province, where he paid a visit on the Buddhist monks of the Shaolin temple. But he was not impressed with what he saw. In Bodhidharma's opinion, the monks of Shaolin had strayed quite far from Buddha's Eight-Fold Path. The majority of their time and attention was devoted to activities such as the performance of rituals, the creation of artistic works dedicated to Buddha, and the careful study of sacred texts, all of which Bodhidharma judged too conducive of attachment to earthly concerns. He felt that the monks were worshiping Buddha and memorizing his teachings instead of trying to be like Buddha themselves and truly understand what he taught.

Bodhidharma also derided the monks for their inability to meditate for any length of time without succumbing to fatigue. Either in disgust with the monks' weakness or in order to provide them with an object lesson on right concentration, he departed from the Shaolin temple and went to live in a nearby cave, where he sat in deep meditation for nine years. As the (presumably embellished) story goes, sometime during this period Bodhidharma took the extreme measure of cutting off his eyelids to prevent himself from losing focus and drifting asleep. It has also been said his lidless gaze was so intense that it bored a hole in the cave wall. Artistic representations of Bodhidharma often depict him with bulging, lidless eyes to commemorate these aspects of his legend.

The monks of Shaolin were awed and shamed by Bodhidharma's superior meditative skills. Several monks approached the mouth of the cave to petition Bodhidharma to instruct them in the Zen form of Buddhism, but Bodhidharma steadfastly refused to see anyone, reportedly insisting he would take on no disciples "until . . . Heaven makes the snow red."[8] Finally, a monk named Hui-k'o appeared at the entrance to the cave, bearing a sword in his right hand. With one swift, resolute movement, Hui-k'o swung the blade and sliced off his own left arm. His blood stained the snow red, and Bodhidharma, moved by the monk's devotion, agreed to become his teacher. (Out of respect for Hui-k'o's sacrifice, the monks of Shaolin to this day bow to the image of Buddha with right arms only raised to their chests in a gesture of prayer.)

Many of the secrets that Bodhidharma conveyed to Hui-k'o involved the manipulation of an individual's internal energy, or *chi*, for the purposes of strengthening, healing, and defending the body. This is important so that the body's natural vulnerabilities will not impede the pursuit of enlightenment. In the tradition of Zen Buddhism, a person's chi is his or her essential life force. The epicenter of one's chi is the abdomen (which is one reason why many statues of Buddha present him with a large belly, symbolizing an abundance of chi), but it radiates out along certain paths to all parts of the body. The ancient healing art of acupuncture is based on the belief that it is possible to map the channels of chi throughout the body and use small needles to redirect the energy and balance its flow.

In *Shao-Lin Chuan: The Rhythm and Power of Tan-Tui*, Simmone Kuo acknowledges the significance of the belief in the existence of chi in Bodhidharma's teachings:

> The emphasis on *chi* is another of Bodhidharma's contributions to the artless art and scienceless science of empty-hand combat techniques.
>
> The cultivation of *chi*, the vital energy flow, was Bodhidharma's primary concern in meditation. He emphasized the acquisition of control over this internal force and the use of its power to mold superior human beings. "Breath" is the flywheel of life, based on respiration. But the flow of the *chi* starts from the feet, develops in the legs, is directed by the waist, moves up to the spine, then to the arms, hands, and fingers. These are the channels of the flow of *chi*. When the *chi* is well-channeled, the whole body becomes alive, and when the *chi* is released, the whole body becomes one unit in action.[9]

Through Hui-k'o, Bodhidharma passed on to the monks of Shaolin a series of highly demanding physical exercises known as the "eighteen routines of Shaolin wushu, designed to help the monks focus and control their chi.[10] These exercises honed the monks' limberness, strength, endurance, agility, and balance. They included such activities as slapping water out of a bucket or pounding a bowl of iron pellets with their bare hands hundreds of times a day, performing elaborate movements while perched precariously atop plum-flower stakes above sharpened wooden spikes, withstanding fierce blows to the abdomen from sawed off tree trunks wielded like battering rams, standing on their heads for hours, hanging themselves by the neck or feet, and even suspending heavy stone weights from their testicles.

Bodhidharma's exercises taught the monks that mental discipline and the harnessing of their chi could allow them to overcome the previously assumed physical limitations of their bodies. After they practiced Bodhidharma's methods for a sufficient time, the monks found that they could perform seemingly impossible acts. These included breaking large slabs of stone or thick pieces of wood with their bare hands, licking fiery-hot iron shovels, and balancing their bodies unharmed on beds of nails or the tips of battleworthy spears.

Bodhidharma and his disciple Hui-k'o did not enable the monks to attain these amazing skills so that they could feel superior to other men. They were not teaching mere tricks to dazzle, frighten, or impress non-practitioners of their art. The monks' grueling regimen of astounding physical challenge was carefully conceived to serve two seemingly competitive ends, both equally crucial to the monks' survival: to help the monks defend their temple from attack (be it by beasts, brigands, or trained imperial brigades) and, at the same time, to support and in no way derail each monk's personal spiritual journey of enlightenment. In other words, Bodhidharma offered the monks means that were not in conflict with Buddhist teachings to resist any threat to the sanctuary that they needed to live a life dedicated to those teachings.

What the monks actually learned was the original martial art of gung fu. It combined ancient Chinese and Indian grappling and boxing techniques (*wushu*) with Bodhidharma's own "iron body" training. The moves of Shaolin wushu require intense concentration and precision, along with balance, agility, and grace, while the iron body training consists of repetitive exercises that build strength and endurance, integrated with breathing methods that focus the chi. Thus as the monks practiced their art, they simultaneously learned to be in harmony with themselves and with their surroundings, to practice right effort and right concentration (components of the Eightfold Path), and to recognize that the success of any meaningful endeavor depends primarily on the unseen inner strength of the one who strives.

Potential students of gung fu could seek admittance to the temple as young as five or six years of age. Both males and females were welcome (the Shaolin order had nuns as well as monks). The opportunity for enlightenment was certainly gender neutral, and physical disparities were utterly irrelevant. (How could a woman be rejected for, say, lacking the upper body strength of a man, when Bodhidharma's first disciple was accepted only after he gave up one of his arms altogether?) It was spiritual commitment that mattered for initial entry, not physical form.

There were three ranks of martial monks at the temple: students, disciples, and masters. Those most recently arrived, the students or novices,
were made to spend the majority of their time performing the labor-inten-
sive menial chores necessary to sustain day-to-day life for all the temple
residents. These tasks had to be assigned to someone, but they did not simply fall to the students because they were the "low men on the totem pole."
It was hoped that their humbling assignments would help the young students begin to let go of their egos and abandon their concerns for their own
self-interest or advancement. They were instructed to accomplish each task
with as much efficiency and perfection as humanly possible so that they
would live fully in every moment (or, as a martial-arts-trained high school
drama coach of mine liked to repeat, "Be here now!"), not clouding their
minds with memories or regrets from the past or dreams or worries for the
future. Students who became angry, bored, easily frustrated, forgetful,
clumsy, or rude would not attain the rank of disciple.

The senior monks at the temple who had already mastered the skills of
gung fu and internalized the philosophy underlying them were the ones
who selected those students whom they deemed worthy to become disciples and receive the dangerous secrets of Shaolin wushu. It was a great
honor to be taken on as a master's disciple; however, it was by no means
an advancement that brought an easier or more comfortable life than that
endured by the students.

The disciple's day began well before dawn (modern Shaolin monks rise
at 0400) with several hours of deep meditation. As Xing Yan explains in
Shaolin Kung Fu, "In meditation a monk sits still, with his mind, heart,
eyes and ears ignoring his surroundings. He holds his ground despite
roaring thunder and swords pressed at his throat."[11] After a meager
morning meal (consumed, like all of their meals, not seated around a table
but standing or crouching in muscle-straining poses), the disciples began
their iron-body exercises to toughen everything from their skulls to their
fingertips to their groins. Xing Yan expounds further on the iron-body
methods of Bodhidharma, using the example of finger training:

> The monks begin by thrusting their fingers into a jar filled with rice 50 to 100
> times a day. Two to three months later, they shift to using sand, not quitting
> even though it is extremely painful to the fingers. When the skin peels off
> and new skin appears, they practice in iron sand 300 to 500 times daily. In
> this way, a hard layer of callus eventually forms on the finger tips. As the
> calluses thicken, the thrusting power of the fingers increases, enough to
> bore holes in a wall. This is a will-tempering exercise; in fact, all the skills of
> the Shaolin hard exercise are learned this way. The monks practice day and
> night, rain or shine, in short, the year round. . . . A saying at the temple goes,
> "A palm can smash bricks after three years' training, a single finger can
> make a hole in a wall in 10 years' time, a fist will become as hard as an iron
> hammer after 30 years' practice, and a hand can break a wooden column in
> 40 years' time."[12]

These painful routines were complemented by additional exercises to help the monks control their breathing, manipulate their chi, and familiarize their bodies with the basic boxing, blocking, and dodging movements that would ultimately evolve into a smooth fighting style. Their days ended with more meditation and, finally, sleep to restore their strength for equally torturous tomorrows.

As their training progressed, the monks eventually received guidance on how to combine their new talents in ways that would allow them to effectively ward off and deliver blows in battle. Shaolin wushu is not limited to one prescribed set of movements in a single style. There are numerous gung fu styles, many of them inspired by natural fighters from the animal kingdom. For example, there are tiger and snake styles, as well as styles that imitate the monkey or the praying mantis. There are also styles that commemorate skills of particular humans. For instance, the style known as "drunken boxing" is said to be derived from the movements of the protagonist in a tragic Chinese tale. The man in the story left home one night to celebrate with friends the recent birth of his son. When he returned from his revelry, inebriated, he discovered that bandits had murdered the baby, along with his young wife. Wracked with grief, he consumed more and more alcohol, until he became a constant drunk. Yet despite his altered state, he successfully plotted and executed a plan of revenge against the perpetrators of the crime. The villains he pursued were caught unawares because they mistakenly believed that his intoxicated state had rendered him harmless.

The drunken boxing style, like the animal forms, is enhanced by its unexpected elements. Like nature itself, gung fu fighters find strength, beauty, and balance in the blending of opposites (hard/soft, male/female, yin/yang). A soft and subtle strike can project massive power; a broad, forceful kick can be landed with delicate precision. The monks who studied at Shaolin could acquit themselves stunningly in a single style or flow from one to another within a single fight. They also learned how to handle many different weapons (as many as forty-five or more), from the long army lance to the fan.

Before a disciple could become a master, he had to overcome one final challenge. Known as the "hall of the wooden men" or "the Corridor of Death," this merciless test required the disciple monk to make his way through a passage containing over one hundred wooden mechanisms that would randomly release deadly weapons in his path. A monk with less than perfect reflexes could not hope to survive. Blocking the exit at the end of the corridor was an enormous iron cauldron containing red-hot coals. The cauldron had no handles. The only way for the monk to move it and make his escape was to use his bare arms. As he lifted the cauldron out of his way, the searing metal burned symbols of the temple into the flesh of his forearms. He was branded with a tiger on one arm and a dragon on the other. These scars were thereafter a permanent reminder that, using the hard-won skills of a master martial artist, he had conquered a truly impressive rite of passage.

How did the monks deploy their extraordinary skills in a manner compatible with their Buddhist ideals? The answer is not immediately obvious. Fighting to defend the Shaolin temple suggests an attachment to earthly concerns, while resorting to deadly or extremely destructive force to settle any dispute does not instantly imply an enlightened perspective. What was the warrior code of the soldier monks, and was it ideologically consistent?

To begin with, a dedicated Buddhist monk would of course not fight for any material prizes, such as territory or wealth, nor would be do battle for ego-driven goals like fame or glory. Buddhists do not fight for Buddha the way that Christian Crusaders claimed to fight for Christ. They are certainly encouraged to spread the teachings of Buddha around the world but not to try to convert anyone at a sword's point. These restrictions, however, still leave room for martial monks to fight in self-defense (providing that they do not care more for their physical survival than for their spiritual enlightenment) and for the defense of others. The focus for each Buddhist monk, warrior or not, is selfless nonattachment. If a monk can concentrate on the fight itself without investing himself in either its cause or its outcome, combat can be no more detrimental to his spiritual development than tending a garden or preparing a meal.

Nonattachment is not the only Buddhist principle at stake, though, when monks become warriors. Buddhism holds all life sacred. Human, animal, even insect life is cherished. How then could the monks of Shaolin justify training in a potentially deadly martial art?

First, it is important to understand that Buddhism does not promote a concept of sin like that found in the Judeo-Christian tradition. In Buddhist thought, an individual's spirit, the nonphysical part of his or her person, is inherently pure and cannot become tainted or stained by any action performed by the physical body. The spirit's purity is untouchable, but it can become weighed down with a burden of negative karma if the individual eschews the Eightfold Path and gives in to grasping and craving (tanha). This is what perpetuates the cycle of reincarnation.

Killing that is done as an act of malice (i.e., murder) is an expression of tanha and produces negative karma that can keep the soul from reaching Nirvana. But killing that is not related to grasping and craving does not necessarily shackle the soul to the material plane and prevent its release into infinity. Bodhidharma himself addresses this point in one of his sermons on Zen Buddhism, translated by Red Pine in *The Zen Teachings of Bodhidharma*:

> Despite dwelling in a material body of four elements, your nature is basically pure. It can't be corrupted. Your real body is basically pure. It can't be corrupted. Your real body has no sensations, no hunger or thirst, no warmth

or cold, no sickness, no love or attachment, no pleasure or pain, no good or bad, no shortness or length, no weakness or strength. Actually, there's nothing here. It's only because you cling to this material body that things like hunger and thirst, warmth and cold, and sickness appear.

Once you stop clinging and let things be, you'll be free, even of birth and death. You'll transform everything. You'll possess spiritual powers that can't be obstructed. And you'll be at peace wherever you are.

. . . Regardless of what we do, our karma has no hold on us. . . . [I]t's only because people don't see their nature that they end up in hell [endless reincarnation]. As long as a person creates karma, he keeps passing through birth and death. But once a person realizes his original nature, he stops creating karma. If he doesn't see his nature, invoking buddhas won't release him from his karma, regardless of whether or not he's a butcher. But once he sees his nature, all doubts vanish. Even a butcher's karma has no effect on such a person.[13]

The second important thing to keep in mind when debating whether it is consistent for Buddhist monks to be martial artists is that the monks who trained at Shaolin were determined to use their powers only when no peaceful option was available to them. They never sought conflict but fought only in response to another's aggression. In that respect, they are entirely unique among the warrior cultures examined in this text.

The warrior monk would be considered most successful who never allowed himself to be forced into a situation in which he had to exchange blows with an opponent. Next best would be the monk who had to fight but subdued his enemy without harming him. Deadly force was only to be used in extreme circumstances, to protect innocents or prevent additional deaths on either side.

Just as some argue that it is impossible for someone to be both a dedicated warrior and a dedicated Christian, there surely will be those who maintain that the monks' apparent reconciliation of Buddhist beliefs with their martial lifestyle rests on mere rationalizations. I find the interpretation and application of religious doctrine to be an extremely complex and profoundly personal matter, so I choose to leave such determinations to the reader's discretion. Suffice it to say, while neither Christianity nor Buddhism advocates violence as a means for solving problems or settling disputes, both acknowledge that the imperfections of this world (and the people in it) can produce evil, suffering, or wrong actions. This acknowledgment may help support the view that using imperfect methods, even violent ones, to resist evil, reduce suffering, and redress wrongs is at least both understandable and forgivable, if not laudable, when peaceful alternatives seem not to exist.

The monks of Shaolin never fought any large-scale battles on the order of the Roman legions. Their opponents were most often rogue bandits or hired thugs in the service of corrupt local warlords, seeking to strip the temple of its wealth or harass the helpless peasant farmers who were tenants on the monks' land. Occasionally the monks took part in some more historic exploits, but details are sketchy. Most notably, in 1553 (during the reign of Emperor Jai Jing), a group of forty monks under the leadership of three master-level warrior monks named Yue Kong, Zhi Nang, and Zi Ran battled a group of Japanese pirates.[14]

Japanese pirates made frequent raids up and down China's eastern coast. These pirates viewed the Chinese as subhuman and thus showed no compunction in treating them with unspeakable cruelty. Chinese historians Geng Zhi and Liang Yiquan describe some of the Japanese atrocities:

> They plundered and killed. They shaved the heads of the men and made them [serve] as their guides and porters and do chores for them. During a battle they put the Chinese [prisoners] in front [as a human shield]. They forced the women to weave and cook during the day and raped them during the night. They poured boiling water on their babies for sport.[15]

Armed with seven-foot iron staffs, the monks managed to kill or incapacitate over thirty of the pirates, while dozens more were granted mercy after they attempted to flee but were encircled and halted in their tracks. This was quite a tribute to the monks' talents, considering that the pirates were well armed with broadswords and other edged weapons and fought with no moral restraint. The monks' vigilance purportedly discouraged further piratical raids along the coast for a number of years.

In an earlier incident, thirteen Shaolin monks executed a flawless stealthy operation to rescue a Chinese prince, Li Shimin, from a power-hungry warlord named Wang Shiyun.[16] Li Shimin later became Emperor Tai Zong of the Tang dynasty. Tai Zong never forgot his debt to the warrior monks, granting them relative autonomy during his rule. This was, however, one of the few times in their history that the monks of Shaolin enjoyed a good relationship with their imperial lords.

Because their Buddhist devotion superseded any loyalty to human authorities, the monks were often at odds with the emperors of China, who seemed to fear the monks' secret arts. The temple itself was raided and burnt several times by imperial troops, including once during the Boxer Rebellion. The monks and nuns resisted these attacks as well as they could, with varying success.

In a story recounted by Geng Zhi and Liang Yiquan, a warrior nun named Lu Siniang, trained at Shaolin, even goes so far as to assassinate an emperor, Emperor Yong Zheng of the Qing dynasty (1662–1723).[17] According to the tale, Lu Siniang's father, Lu Liuliang, was an eminent Confucian scholar who refused to serve the Qing dynasty after it overthrew the Ming dynasty. Lu Liuliang even wrote essays that challenged the new emperor's right to rule. As punishment, Emperor Yong Zheng ordered every member of the Lu family killed. Only young Lu Siniang, who was away from home when the imperial troops arrived, survived.

Thirsting for revenge, Lu Siniang sought admittance to the Shaolin temple and ultimately became the disciple of a one-armed nun named Master Guang Ci. Guang Ci had formerly been Princess Chang Ping of the deposed Ming dynasty. The Qing emperor Yong Zheng had cut off one of her arms as a warning before allowing her to leave the imperial palace. The maimed princess fled to Shaolin and spent the rest of her life training in the martial arts, in search of inner peace.

Under Master Guang Ci's care, Lu Siniang eventually became a master of gung fu herself. She left the temple and journeyed to the palace of the emperor, sneaking into his very bedchamber in the dead of night:

> Emperor Yong Zheng stood up and drew his sword. Hacking down, he noticed the assassin was a beautiful girl about 15 or 16, glaring at him with arched brows and piercing eyes, three steps away. . . . The emperor brought down his sword. The girl fenced and at the same time kicked the emperor at his wrist. The emperor felt shooting pain, as if the hand had been cut off. Lu Siniang ripped away the sword from the emperor's hand. Retreating hastily, the emperor demanded, "What do you want?"
>
> "I want your head!" the girl said.
>
> The emperor moved over to his bed and drew another sword from it. But the girl was quicker. She swung her sword and the emperor's head rolled down onto the ground.[18]

While this story is a gripping testament to the power of gung fu, it does not necessarily showcase the truly nonattached, internally harmonious Buddhist warrior in action. The passionate desire for vengeance is not especially Buddhist, nor is actively seeking a physical confrontation (let alone planning an assassination). Still, Lu Siniang did not kill the emperor for any glory or material gain, and she did prevent him from perpetrating any additional crimes against the Chinese people.

With such a tempestuous history behind them, what was the ultimate fate of the Shaolin warriors? Amazingly, despite its centuries of conflict with national authorities, the Shaolin order has survived even to the present day. Tracing the more recent past of the warrior monks, we find that the communist revolution of the 1950s drove Shaolin gung fu underground. Practicing martial arts was declared against the law, but a few masters continued to offer clandestine training in the mountains, under cover of darkness. In the 1960s, the Shaolin temple itself was once again burned by young Chinese soldiers, and three monks who stubbornly took up residence in the ruins were arrested and imprisoned by the communist authorities. Oddly enough, within a generation the temple was rebuilt by those same authorities, who belatedly decided it was a national treasure.

Today, Shaolin is once more home to warrior monks and nuns who train in iron-body techniques and traditional gung fu. Both Chinese nationals and foreigners (at least thirteen years old) can study martial arts at a government-run school established beside the temple in 1987. The temple and the monks have become a huge tourist attraction. Billed as "The Shaolin Warriors," some of the modern monks tour outside of China, demonstrating gung fu and performing feats of chi manipulation on stage in front of live audiences in places such as Europe and the United States. Gung fu has given birth to many other martial arts, as well, but the original form of the art is still practiced and taught all around the globe.

For some, the image of gung fu, once so integrally linked to the noble quest for spiritual enlightenment, has been tarnished by its association with two very different worlds: the Chinese underground and Hollywood. Unfortunately, many members of the criminal Triad gangs who terrorized Beijing (much like the Mafia in other countries) after World War II were trained in at least the techniques, if not the ideology, of gung fu. In the 1960s and 1970s, desperate Chinese authorities had to hire other expert martial artists to help ordinary policemen contend with these extraordinary felons.

When most Westerners think of gung fu (or, as it is often written, kung fu), they probably picture neither Shaolin monks nor members of the Triad gangs. Instead, the images that come to mind are of film and television celebrities such as Jackie Chan, David Carradine, Chuck Norris, Yon-Fat Chow, Michelle Yeoh, Jet Li, and, perhaps most of all, the peerless Bruce Lee. These stars were indeed trained in the Chinese martial arts (either classic gung fu or its derivatives), and some may also have chosen to embrace its attendant philosophical tenets and spiritual elements. Bruce Lee, for example, was a genuine scholar-warrior, well versed in both Western and Eastern philosophies. (Lee, who was an author as well as an actor and filmmaker, actually created a new martial art which he termed Jeet Kune Do, or "the way of the intercepting fist.") He gained notoriety by displaying his precision movements and astounding martial prowess in films like *The Chinese Connection* and *Enter the Dragon* and the television series *The Green Hornet*, but his interest in gung fu was far from superficial. Nevertheless, purists have often criticized Lee and those who have followed in his cinematic footsteps for committing what they deem the dishonorable act of revealing the secrets of gung fu on celluloid for a profit.

For the monks and nuns of the Shaolin temple, the study of gung fu today, as in the past, is not about, as one of my students so delicately put it, "kicking butt." Although they carefully craft their bodies into lethal weapons, Shaolin warriors do their best to avoid any external conflicts. They believe that the most important battle the gung fu warrior will ever face is the internal struggle to detach from the desires of his ego and release his soul from the cycle of reincarnation. They have no interest in fame, territory acquisition, power, or wealth and only seek justice through just means. For them, no ends linked to earthly concerns could possibly justify means that might derail their spiritual development. The defeat of a thousand enemies would be worse than meaningless if accomplished without right action, right effort, right mindfulness, right concentration, right view, right thought, etc. Handed down from Bodhidharma and his one-armed disciple Hui'ko, the Shaolin warrior's code is truly exceptional in that its intention is to produce warriors who have no interest in making war.

This attitude is embodied in a Chinese parable by fourth-century B.C. Zen master Chuang-Tzu:

> Chi Hsing-tzu was raising a fighting cock for his lord. After ten days, the lord asked, "Is he ready?" Chi answered, "No, sir, he is still vain and flushed with rage." Ten days passed, and the prince asked about the cock. Chi said, "Not yet, sir. He is on the alert whenever he hears another cock crowing." When the prince's inquiry came again, Chi replied, "Not quite yet, sir. His sense of fighting is still smoldering within him." When another ten days elapsed, Chi said to the lord: "He is almost ready. Even when he hears another crowing, he shows no excitement. He now resembles one made of wood. His qualities are integrated. No cocks are his match—they will at once run away from him."[19]

NOTES

1. C. Scott Littleton, ed., *Eastern Wisdom* (New York: Henry Holt, 1996), 60.

2. Paul Reps, comp.,, *Zen Flesh, Zen Bones: A Collection of Zen and Pre-Zen Writings* (New York: Doubleday, Anchor Books, 1939), 80.

3. Reginald Fleming Johnson, *Buddhist China* (London: John Murray, 1913), 83.

4. There are some who question whether this meeting ever indeed took place. If it is pure fiction, its role in the legend of Bodhidharma is nevertheless significant, as it stresses Bodhidharma's commitment to the Zen approach to understanding Buddhism.

5. Johnson, *Buddhist China*, 83–86.

6. Shifu Nagaboshi Tomio (Terence Dukes), *The Bodhisattva Warriors: The Origin, Inner Philosophy, History and Symbolism of the Buddhist Martial Art within India and China* (York Beach, Maine: Samuel Weiser, 1994), 266.

7. Red Pine, trans., *The Zen Teachings of Bodhidharma* (New York: North Point Press, 1987), 43–45.

8. Geng Zhi and Liang Yiquan, *Shaolin Martial Arts* (Beijing: China Reconstructs Press, 1987), 3.

9. Simmone Kuo, *Shao-Lin Chuan: The Rhythm and Power of Tan-Tui* (Berkeley, Calif.: North Atlantic Books, 1996), 117.

10. Xing Yan, ed., *Shaolin Kung Fu: Treasure of the Chinese Nation, The Best of Chinese Wushu* (Beijing: China Pictorial Publishing House, 1996), 16.

11. Xing, *Shaolin Kung Fu*, 80.

12. Xing, *Shaolin Kung Fu*, 80.

13. Pine, *Teachings of Bodhidharma*, 39–41.

14. Geng and Liang, *Shaolin Martial Arts*, 18.

15. Geng and Liang, *Shaolin Martial Arts*, 17.

16. Xing, *Shaolin Kung Fu*, 39.
17. Geng and Liang, *Shaolin Martial Arts*, 22.
18. Geng and Liang, *Shaolin Martial Arts*, 23.
19. David Schiller, *The Little Zen Companion* (New York: Workman, 1994), 91.

8

The Soul of the Samurai:
Duty, Devotion, and Death

Bushido. The Way of the Warrior. Just as the Christian knights of medieval Europe bound themselves to a code of chivalry, the samurai of Japan, knights of the East, committed their lives to the code of Bushido. Like chivalry, Bushido reached beyond the battlefield, touching every aspect of the warrior's existence, from the sacred to the mundane. His reputation as an honorable man depended as much on his courtly deportment as on his courage and martial prowess. Any false move, from ordering his men to senseless slaughter to bumping a superior's dinner table with a sheathed weapon, could cast him and his entire clan under the darkest cloud of disgrace. Once he was shamed, his only hope for redemption was to make the ultimate sacrifice.

The history of Japan is like a beautiful sword whose finely edged blade, though splattered with blood, still catches the sun. The island nation has rarely been at peace, either internally or with its neighbors, yet it has never neglected its spiritual development or abandoned its passion for philosophy, poetry, and the arts. There were no Dark Ages for Japan to mirror those experienced by the citizens of Western Europe. The Japanese retained their reverence for the transcendental even as they engaged in devastating civil strife, executed unheralded acts of aggression, and perpetrated unspeakable atrocities in the service of imperialist expansion.

To try to understand how a people could hold life at once both so cheap and so dear, we must consider the role of religion in shaping Japanese values. Of the three commonly identified periods of Japanese history—classical Japan, A.D. 500–1200; feudal Japan, A.D. 1200–1868; and modern Japan, 1868–present—our primary interest is in the feudal age, which saw the flowering of the samurai warrior culture. Through these centuries, Japan was influenced by overlapping waves of religions, including Shinto, apparently native to Japan's shores, and Buddhism, Taoism, and Confucianism, carried over the water from India and China.

We will begin our study of these religions with Shinto, which may be indigenous to Japan and has had an undeniable impact on her people. Shinto claims no founding prophet or sacred texts. Its precise origins are unknown, but its central tenets have been passed down from ancient times, primarily as an oral tradition. Basic to Shinto is the belief in the *kami*. Kami are natural spirits or life forces found in everything from human beings to trees, from animals to objects, and from the sun to the wind. The teachings of Shinto describe how these kami relate to one another and prescribe methods for worshiping kami.

Sokyo Ono, in collaboration with William P. Woodard, explains something of the nature of Shinto worship in the introduction to the book, *Shinto: The Kami Way*:

> In its general aspects Shinto is more than a religious faith. It is an amalgam of attitudes, ideas, and ways of doing things that through two millenniums and more have become an integral part of the way of the Japanese people. Thus, Shinto is both a personal faith in the kami and a communal way of life according to the mind of the kami, which emerged in the course of the centuries as various ethnic and cultural influences, both indigenous and foreign, were fused, and the country attained unity under the Imperial Family.[1]

The catalogue of kami is extensive. Some, such as the kami of fertility and growth, are somewhat abstract in essence, while others, such as the kami of the sun and of the moon, resemble gods and goddesses familiar to the West from the pagan mythology of Greece and Rome. Not all kami are created equal; there is a spiritual hierarchy. The most powerful kami is the sun, known as the goddess Amaterasu (or Ama-terasu-o-mikami). Her dominance has striking significance in Japanese culture because the imperial family claims to be descended from her divine line.[2] According to legend, Emperor Jimmu, the first recorded Japanese ruler, was the great-grandson of the powerful kami god Ninigi-no-mikoto, the immortal guardian of the island of Japan, who was himself the grandson of the supreme sun goddess Amaterasu.

Shinto encourages ancestor worship, and it promotes the idea that the honored dead continue to observe and pass judgment on the living, holding them to high standards of ethical behavior. One of the general lessons of Shinto is that you can never hide your transgressions. You are as transparent to the kami world as you are to yourself. The most basic Shinto shrines feature a polished mirror as their only ornament, to encourage those who come to worship to pursue self-awareness and make sincere evaluations of their own shortcomings.

Inazo Nitobe, a Japanese expatriate writing on Bushido in 1899 for the benefit of curious European and American scholars, interprets the moral aspects of Shinto:

> Shinto theology has no place for the dogma of "original sin." On the contrary, it believes in the innate goodness and God-like purity of the human soul, adoring it as the innermost sanctuary from which divine oracles are proclaimed. Everybody has observed that Shinto shrines are conspicuously devoid of objects and instruments of worship, and that a plain mirror hung in the sanctuary forms the essential part of its furnishings. The presence of this article is easy to explain: it typifies the human heart, which, when perfectly placid and clear, reflects the very image of the Deity. When you stand, therefore, in front of the shrine to worship, you see your own image reflected on its shining surface, and the act of worship is tantamount to the old Delphic injunction, "Know Thyself." But self-knowledge does not imply, either in the Greek or Japanese teaching, knowledge of the physical part of man, not his anatomy or his psycho-physics; knowledge was to be of a moral kind, the introspection of our moral nature.[3]

From Shinto the samurai warriors of Japan gained a strong sense of moral obligation to their ancestors, to their island, and to their divinely generated imperial family. The legacy of Shinto is diversely reflected in fierce Japanese nationalism, delicate artistic celebrations of natural beauty, and exacting and uncompromising codes of behavior. It can further be seen in self-sacrificial filial and feudal loyalty. Belief in kami transforms the samurai's every act of defense—of his family, his lord, his emperor, or his homeland—into the fulfillment of a sacred trust.

Around A.D. 500 (at the time that Bodhidharma was beginning his mission to the Shaolin monks), the leaders of ancient Japan became interested in the culture of their powerful neighbor, China. To satisfy their sudden inquisitiveness, they sent peaceful representatives to observe Chinese ways. On their return, these "explorers" reported that Chinese civilization was significantly more advanced that that of Japan. This was quite a blow to Japanese national pride, but initial distress was rapidly replaced by strategic planning, followed by immediate action. Historian Scott F. Runkle explains:

> The most promising Japanese youths, carefully selected by the government, were sent on the extremely perilous sea journey to the distant, magnificent Chinese capital. . . . There they stayed for several years at a time, diligently studying China's arts, sciences, philosophy, laws, architecture, governmental structure, and even urban organization.[4]

This calculated exposure to Chinese thought spawned a kind of renaissance in Japan. The state was reorganized from a collection of independent clans jockeying for power under the supposedly overarching but often ineffectual rule of the imperial family into a highly structured feudal system. The emperor, like a king or queen in medieval Europe, technically owned and controlled the entire island of Japan. But he divided the land among a class of wealthy aristocrats who were the leaders of the most dominant Japanese clans. Each of these landed lords, or *daimyo*, was served by a number of samurai, who, like European knights, were responsible for defending their daimyo's person and property and for administering his laws. Farmers and craftsmen toiled for the samurai and their lords, producing goods and cultivating the soil. Members of the lower, peasant class were treated like property by the "noble" classes and were used as menial laborers, foot soldiers, or household servants. Similar to the serfs and thralls of Europe, these Japanese peasants had no rights and no voice in the government.

In A.D. 710 a stunning new Japanese capital was erected at Nara, patterned after the Chinese capital of Ch'ang-an. There, Runkle notes, "The emperors and their courts avidly continued to import and imitate Chinese culture; their writing, poetry, arts, gardens, architecture, sports, even their cooking, had to be as close to the Chinese model as possible."[5] Less than a century later, in A.D. 794, a second, even more magnificent capital was established in Kyoto. Kyoto remained the seat of the imperial family for the rest of the classical period. In A.D. 900, the emperor Daigo set up Japan's first university in the capital city, and by A.D. 1000 the population of Kyoto had swelled to approximately half a million people.[6] Over a period of five hundred years, Japan had transformed itself from an unsophisticated and chaotic tribal nation into an orderly, educated, and imposing civilization.

When Japanese students adopted Chinese script and began to study the work of Chinese scholars, they became entranced by the ideas they discovered in Chinese philosophy and religion. Buddhism, especially in its Zen form (as discussed in chapter 7), captivated the Japanese and was quickly blended with their native Shinto. The Buddhist principle of nonattachment would become a great influence on the samurai. Buddhist temples and monastic institutions sprang up all over Japan, and the image of the smiling, serene Buddha was seen everywhere. The more elaborate rituals sometimes associated with Buddhist worship (those that disgusted Bodhidharma) appealed to many of the Japanese people as a way of adding power and pomp to their relatively simple Shinto practices. Early anxieties that adopting Buddhism would anger the kami who guarded Japan swiftly gave way as "it became clear that Buddhism was not a threat to the harmony of the native *kami* but was an effective complement to the *kami*."[7]

Two other Chinese imports also became part of religious life in Japan during the classical period: Confucianism and Taoism. Religious historian H. Byron Earnhart comments on how these religions related to Buddhism and Shinto in his comprehensive text, *Religion in the Japanese Experience:*

Shinto and Buddhism are the major organized religions in Japan; the influence of Confucianism and religious Taoism have been more subtle and diffuse. Neither Confucianism nor Taoism has ever constituted a full religious organization with priests, scriptures, regular worship services, and other ecclesiastical aspects. In general, Confucianism entered the stream of social ethics and government rationale, whereas Taoism pervaded the realm of everyday religious observances such as astrology and fortune telling. Some Japanese scholars and popular lecturers advocated Confucianism as a system of thought and code of ethics, occasionally in conjunction with other teachings. Most Japanese people, however, implicitly felt the Confucian rationale in their social conduct and in their support of the government.[8]

The essence of Taoism is not easily captured in prose. It is a Taoist belief that all existence is composed of opposites that are capable of harmonizing with one another to form a perfectly balanced, unified whole. Almost everything in the natural world contains some combination of both yin and yang. Yin is understood to be the feminine, soft, cool, moist, dark, passive element, while yang is the masculine, hard, warm, dry, light, active element. Both have equal power and are equally revered. The prescriptive aspect of religious Taoism directs believers to seek harmony both within themselves and between themselves and the rest of the world. This goal, however, cannot be achieved by struggling to achieve it. Balance is found only by surrendering all resistance to the organic flow of life, which is known as the Tao, or "the Way."

Taoism has many points in common with Roman Stoicism (discussed in chapter 3). Like the Stoic, the Taoist considers most of the goods coveted by humans to be both impermanent and outside the reach of an individual's control. The Taoist surrenders himself to the Tao just as the Stoic embraces fate. Both prize inner peace over any material rewards, accolades, or opportunities to grab power or prestige. Neither has any fear of death, regarding it as simply a return to nonexistence that should inspire neither terror nor mourning.[9] The words of the fourth-century-B.C. Taoist teacher Chuang-Tzu in response to criticism that he did not weep when his beloved wife passed away could easily have been uttered, after only minor modifications, by Stoic sages Epictetus or Marcus Aurelius:

> "To live with your wife," exclaimed Hui-tzu, "and see your eldest son grow up to be a man, and then not to shed a tear over her corpse—this would be bad enough. But to drum on a bowl and sing; surely this is going too far!" "Not at all," replied Chuang-tzu. "When she died I could not help being affected by her death. Soon, however, I remembered that she had already existed in a previous state before her birth, without form or even substance; that while in that unconditioned condition, substance was added to spirit; that this substance then assumed form and that the next state was birth. And now, by virtue of a further change she is dead, passing from one phase to another like the sequence of spring, summer, autumn and winter. And while she is thus lying asleep in eternity for me to go about weeping and

wailing would be to proclaim myself ignorant of these natural laws. Therefore I refrain."[10]

The third Chinese religion to seep into Japanese culture was Confucianism. Founded by the Chinese philosopher Confucius (or Kung) in the
fifth century B.C., Confucianism stressed the moral significance of a person's behavior within certain important human relationships. Confucius
identified the five most critical relationships as those between (1) ruler
and subject, (2) father and son,[11] (3) husband and wife, (4) older brother
and younger brother, and (5) friend and friend. He advised that your conduct within these key relationships defined your character. Confucius
taught that your behavior within these relationships should at all times be
guided by principles of love, loyalty, and respect.

According to the doctrine of Confucius, both people in each of the five
relationship pairings have specific obligations to one another. For example, a father is supposed to teach and train his son in the ways of the
world and support him until he is old enough to be out on his own, while
a son is supposed to honor his father, obey his commands, and care for
him in his old age. But Confucian relationships do not work like standard
Western contracts, in which the failure of one party to meet its obligations
typically voids the contract for both parties. Confucius did not allow one
party's breach to justify the other's. So if a father neglected or failed to
provide for his son, that did not in any way alter the son's standing obligations to his father. In this respect, the moral standards of Confucius
resemble those of the peace chiefs of the Plains Indians (see chapter 6).
Peace chiefs such as Black Kettle and White Antelope believed that they
were honor-bound to uphold the treaties that they signed with the whites
regardless of broken trust on the other side.

Confucian influence is plainly apparent in the way members of the
samurai class were expected to relate to their employers, the daimyos, as
well as to their peers, family members, and servants. Many points of the
Bushido code stress a samurai's obligation not only to those above him in
his chain of command or in the general social hierarchy but also to those
who rank beneath him yet are bound to him by one of the five Confucian
relationships. Unfortunately, those who did not fit in any of the relationship pairs seem to fall outside the samurai's sphere of moral obligation
altogether.

The classical period in Japan that dawned with the Japanese discovery
of the empire of China eventually succumbed to a decadent decline. Runkle characterizes the imperial court at the end of the first millennium in
less than flattering terms:

> Kyoto became effete and ostentatious in time. Men of quality rouged their
> cheeks, powdered their faces, and made liberal use of perfume, while ladies
> not only painted their nails but also gilded their lower lips. . . . The extrav-

agances of Kyoto's glittering court finally exhausted the state treasury, and a courtier's taste in composing a superb tanka [a thirty-one-syllable poem] did not compensate for his growing incapacity and indolence as an administrator. And while luxury and refinement obsessed the rich, the poor in the neglected provinces had to resort more and more to crime; . . . Worst of all, the elegant courtiers swarming around the emperor had lost their martial virtues, and they and their monarch were soon helpless against the growing incursions of rough, provincial lords, with their private armies.[12]

Recognizing the weakness of the imperial family, the leaders of the provincial clans tried to wrest control of Japan away from the court at Kyoto. Civil wars broke out, with the country mainly divided between the supporters of the Taira clan and those of the Minamoto clan. In 1185, the Minamoto clan and their followers were triumphant, and their leader, Yoritomo, became the first legitimate shogun, or supreme military ruler, of Japan.

As shogun, Yoritomo was the de facto ruler of Japan, although he did not actually depose the emperor. Shinto and Confucian beliefs had too strong a hold on the Japanese people for them ever to have permitted the Minamotos to do away with imperial family and its traditions. Instead, the emperor was kept in place as a figurehead for the nation, just a symbol with little real power left to wield. Yoritomo invoked the emperor's name when issuing orders to the clans, but those orders, it was widely understood, came from the mind of the shogun, not from the imperial court.

The Yoritomo shogunate ushered in the feudal era of Japan, the age of the samurai. No longer looking to China for its exemplars, Japan bred its own unique martial culture. Historian Milton W. Meyer describes the evolving Japanese military state:

[The] emerging dominance of the military over civilian authorities had continuing significance in Japanese national life. Japan turned its back upon the Chinese example of the supremacy of the educated civilian bureaucrat in political affairs. In the Japanese tradition of a ruling, hereditary, and landed aristocracy that stressed military strength, Japan was more nearly like Western Europe than China. . . . As a descendant of the ancient mounted warrior . . . and the aristocratic armored knight, the retainer [samurai] of Yoritomo re-emerged in the twelfth century as a man of military prowess. Armed with bows and arrows, the mounted warrior wore armor consisting of small strips of steel held together by leather thongs. He fostered ideals of bravery and loyalty, and the extra-family ties that existed between him and his lord ranked higher than family bonds (quite unlike China where the family remained the strongest social unit).[13]

The code of these new samurai knights melded the values of Shinto, Confucianism, Taoism, and Zen Buddhism. Its driving principle was the deep-seated conviction that the only way to live a meaningful life was to free yourself from the fear of death. Zen Buddhism taught the samurai that enlightenment could be obtained while one was engaged in any worthy endeavor that permitted the practice of the vital components of the Eightfold Path (see chapter 7), such as right effort, right mindfulness, right action, and right concentration. Attaining the Buddhist goal of complete nonattachment was equally possible for a man training to be a warrior as for one practicing to perform an ancient and elaborate tea ceremony. As long as the activity was not in itself an expression of attachment to, and continuing desire for, finite, earthly ends (such as wealth, position, or power), it did not matter so much what you did as how you did it. The correct way to do anything, from displaying proper dinner etiquette to piercing a target with an arrow from your bow, was to seek utter perfection. To experience even an instant of perfection in any context was to glimpse the infinite perfection of the universe, and that was an end in itself. Your purpose was not to achieve some further, mundane goal, such as impressing your host or felling your opponent. Such things might follow as a matter of course, but they were not supposed to be the true Buddhist's motivation for chasing perfection.

The most profound perfection for the warrior to pursue was perfect peace with death. Samurai were instructed always to keep the reality of their mortality in the forefront of their minds. Thus the first lesson of the *Budoshoshinshu*, an instruction book for young men training to be warriors, is "Make Life Replete, Constantly Thinking of Death."[14]

A Japanese warrior named Daidoji Yuzan, who lived from 1639 to 1730, at a time when samurai culture was at a low ebb, wrote the *Budoshoshinshu*, or warrior's primer, to preserve samurai values. Political restructuring in 1600 after a period of prolonged civil war had reduced many samurai to *ronin*, or knights with no daimyo to serve. These masterless warriors were considered a potential threat to public safety and so were ordered to assume roles in the government as bureaucrats: clerks and accountants. Japan was at peace, but her once proud warriors, now trapped in mind-numbing "desk jobs," were losing their identity. In an attempt to combat this decay and resurrect the spirit of the samurai, Daidoji Yuzan set himself the task of recording the once orally transmitted tenets of the Bushido code. He assembled these into a book of fifty-six lessons, which he explained were "for the understanding of those intending to be warriors."[15] By examining these lessons, we too can gain a clearer understanding of what was demanded of the Japanese samurai.

The titles of the *Budoshoshinshu's* fifty-six lessons, as translated by American scholar William Scott Wilson, are:

1. Make Life Replete, Constantly Thinking of Death
2. Do Not Forget Preparedness for Battle
3. Learning Is Also Important for the Warrior in Times of Peace
4. Be Devoted, Even to Negligent Parents

5. A Sense of Shame Will Uphold Justice
6. In the Mind, the Way; in Form, the Law
7. Choosing a Horse
8. Gossip and Back-talk Are Inexcusable
9. Do Not Place a Foot in the Direction of the Master
10. When Thinking of the Battlefield, One Cannot Be Indolent
11. Do Not Be Spoiled by Length of Service
12. The Law of Borrowing the Lord's Authority
13. Ability and Diligence
14. Exceed Others in Some Way
15. The Moment of Death is Important for a Warrior
16. Scholarship and Refinement, Too, Can Occasionally Be of Great Harm
17. Do Not Mix Personal Feelings with Duties
18. Old Hands and Dirty White Garments
19. Distinctions in Family Relations
20. Forbidden Slander of a Former Lord
21. Rules for a Guardian
22. The Spirit of "Even Though a Warrior Doesn't Eat . . . [He Will Still Use a Toothpick]"
23. Frugality, Too, Is for the Sake of Service
24. A Splendid Entrance, but Plain Living Quarters
25. Companions in Play Are Unnecessary
26. It Is Shameful Not to Know Clan History
27. Braggarts, Not Slanderers
28. Both Contradiction and Flattery Are Failure of Duty
29. Discerning a Brave Man from a Coward
30. There Is Nothing So High-Priced as a Warrior
31. Do Not Forget Sensitivity toward the Discomfort of Others
32. The Warrior Who Strikes His Wife Is a Coward
33. Complete One's Duties within the Day: One Second Ahead Is Uncertain
34. The Warrior's Duty Is to Protect the Farmer, Craftsman, and Merchant
35. Cherish the Family Crest of One's Lord
36. Keep a Respectful Distance from the Administration of Financial Affairs
37. Undertaking Promises Easily Will Bring One to Ruin
38. Do Not Forget the Subordinate's Mind
39. A Man of Low Rank Should Not Have a Wife and Child
40. Always Aspire to Distinction and Merit
41. Loyalty Includes Longevity
42. The Crime of Stealing a Stipend Is Grave
43. Even If One's Stipend Is Diminished He Should Make No Complaint

44. Accept Difficult Orders Positively
45. Do Not Oppose Even the Unreasonable Words of One's Lord
46. The Principle of Horsemanship
47. When on an Official Journey, Safety Is First
48. When Accompanying One's Lord
49. The Everyday Care of Armor
50. Consideration for the Equipment of One's Servants
51. Be Thorough in the Disciplined Practice of the Martial Arts
52. Encountering a Commotion When Accompanying One's Lord
53. Being Present when One's Lord Cuts Down an Attendant
54. It Is Disloyal to Complain about Labor Lost
55. The Responsibility of Counseling Strategy Is Grave
56. Great Loyalty That Surpasses *Junshi*

Daidoji Yuzan explains in lesson 1 that holding the idea in your mind that your death may be imminent will have positive effects on both your performance and your character. On the practical front, if you accept that death can cut you down at any moment, you will be less likely to let your personal responsibilities languish unattended. This point is echoed in lesson 33, "Complete One's Duties within the Day: One Second Ahead Is Uncertain":

> [I]f one thinks that the world will go on without change and that he will have unlimited time in which to perform his duties, as time passes he will become bored with things, his mind will slacken, and his spirit will become negligent. He will put off until tomorrow not only his lord's more unpressing concerns, but also those that should be briskly talked over and brought to a conclusion, and thus matters will pile up and be neglected.[16]

Keeping your potential death in mind will also improve your character by inspiring you to treat those with whom you have special relationships as you would if you believed you might never see them again: "when before his lord receiving orders or looking on his parents with thoughts that it may be for the last time, . . . his concern for them will be sincere."[17]

Daidoji presents attentiveness to the possibility of death as an antidote to all pettiness, intemperate behavior, inappropriate ambition, greed, and selfishness. He argues that the warrior who accepts the potential nearness of death will not allow himself to be drawn into minor altercations over matters of little importance, nor will such a man waste his precious hours at mindless social gatherings or in pursuit of excessive food, drink, or sexual amusement. He will not dissipate his energy by committing any of his time or efforts to ill-conceived campaigns for power or fame but will instead try to leave behind a noble legacy by serving the interests of others. According to Daidoji, reflections on his own impending demise will not be paralyzing to the samurai. Instead, they will propel him to excellence.

The second lesson of the *Budoshoshinshu*, "Do Not Forget Preparedness for Battle," can be associated not only with the first lesson but also with lesson 10, "When Thinking of the Battlefield, One Cannot Be Indolent." Both lesson 2 and lesson 10 warn the warrior in training against the dangers of becoming too complacent in times of peace. When conflict and danger are present, it is less of a challenge for a samurai to maintain the appropriate level of vigilance and intense commitment to his work. On the other hand, if a samurai lives quietly for months or even years without being tested in combat, he may lose his edge and become too comfortable performing below his peak capacity. Such slackness, Daidoji insists, is anathema to the true warrior.

Recall the religious influences on the samurai code: Buddhism, Taoism, Shinto, and Confucianism. The samurai who becomes a listless drone in his master's employment, doing only the minimum he must to get by, has clearly forgotten the Buddhist and Taoist teachings of nonattachment. By their lights, fulfilling his responsibilities as a samurai is only worthwhile insofar as doing so offers him an opportunity to embody the components of the Eightfold Path and achieve spiritual balance. If he permits himself to cut corners, overlook flaws, and rationalize bad habits, he is clearly failing to practice right effort, right concentration, right mindfulness, etc. Nor is he promoting harmony either within himself or between himself and the rest of the world. Rather than flowing smoothly with the Tao, his soul will find itself weighed down by mundane, egocentric concerns, like the heavy chains that burdened Jacob Marley's ghost in Dickens's classic "A Christmas Carol."

The lax warrior is also a moral failure by the standards of Shinto and Confucianism. Both religions require practitioners to place a premium on loyalty and filial piety. The samurai who lets his defenses down leaves not only himself but also those he serves open to attack. Even if by good luck his lackadaisical manner produces no dire results, the mere fact that he has ceased to take his obligations as seriously as he ought will reflect poorly on his entire clan, from his living relatives all the way back to his most distant ancestors.

To avoid all of this, Daidoji advises the samurai to prepare each day as if he expected a battle before sunset. The warrior should keep his sword at his side and his senses as sharp as its blade. He should be aware of his surroundings and expect the unexpected. At the same time, he should never complain when required to do trivial chores that might seem beneath the dignity of a great warrior. As Daidoji notes, such "peacetime duties . . . are easy indeed," especially when compared to the hardships endured by warriors on long campaigns.[18] To carp about soft assignments just because they are tedious both insults the memory of those who have truly suffered and casts doubt on the warrior's own fortitude: "if one approaches his unexacting duties with a faltering heart, how will he be able to bear the pains of battle or travel?"[19]

Lesson 3 also deals with how warriors should behave when not embroiled in urgent martial endeavors. It instructs that "learning is also important for the warrior in times of peace." Samurai were encouraged not only to acquire skills of obvious pragmatic worth, such as horsemanship, archery, and the sword arts, but also to study literature, philosophy, religion, and the fine arts. The recommended curriculum included reading works known as "the Four Books, the Five Classics, and the Seven Books," which were *The Great Learning, The Doctrine of the Mean, The Analects, The Mencius, The Book of Changes* (or the *I-Ching*), *The Book of Documents, The Book of Poetry, The Spring and Autumn Annals,* and seven military classics.[20] Japanese culture valued the well-rounded warrior-scholar, equally comfortable with the calligraphy brush and the bow. Samurai were even supposed to find time for crafts and artistic expressions that required creativity and sensitivity to natural beauty, such as watercolor painting, flower arranging, and origami. Miyamoto Musashi, Japan's most famous swordsman and author of the classic strategy text *The Book of Five Rings,* wrote in his autobiographical introduction, "Although I was committed to my sword, I was also dedicated to learning painting, sculpture, and poetry."[21] Still, lesson 16 cautions that "scholarship and refinement, too, can occasionally be of great harm." Daidoji's point here is again one of balance. As members of the nobility, warriors should be learned and refined. But they must not so devote their lives to memorizing texts or perfecting tea ceremonies that they are no longer up to snuff as swordsmen or archers. The martial arts must always be their primary focus.

The theme of the importance of gentlemanly behavior runs throughout the *Budoshoshinshu.* Several lessons emphasize the need for the warrior to keep up appearances and act according to the rules of etiquette. No matter how grim the circumstances, a samurai should always look his best, from the styling of his hair to the shine on his horse's harness. The samurai took their sense of style so to heart that they even took pains to look good dead. The samurai were avid head collectors (like the Celts of chapter 4). It was part of the postbattle ritual to neatly prepare and present the mounted and labeled heads of one's enemies to one's daimyo. Therefore, warriors preparing for battle would take a moment to sprinkle or dust sweet-smelling perfume on their scalps, so that when their helmets were lifted off their severed heads, their vanquishers would enjoy the waft of a pleasant scent.

Lesson 6, "In the Mind, the Way; in Form, the Law," provides details of a gentleman's code for the samurai class that covers everything from bathing and shaving to how to carry a decorative fan.[22] Lesson 22, "The Spirit of 'Even Though a Warrior Doesn't Eat . . . [He Will Use a Toothpick],'" praises an older generation of warriors who were too genteel to discuss openly matters relating to money or sex and who would not use any deprivation as an excuse for letting standards slip. And lesson 31, "Do Not Forget Sensitivity toward the Discomfort of Others," instructs that even as the samurai ignores any inconveniences (or worse) to himself, he should not be insensitive to the feelings and needs of others. Here the *Budoshoshinshu* gives the example of keeping the noise down in one's room when someone dwelling in the same building is ill, even if the sufferer is a stranger. And, of course, there were exacting rules that governed how a warrior should behave as a guest or when hosting others. Like the ancient Greeks, the feudal Japanese took guest-host relations very seriously. A warrior with a rude manner would not find favor among his fellow warriors, no matter what his prowess with arms.

As the lessons at which we have already looked indicate, the character of warriors living under the Bushido code was judged holistically. The samurai were not meant to compartmentalize their lives in any way with the intention of protecting some areas from moral scrutiny. Nor was it considered irrational or unjust to use information gathered from the study of one aspect of a warrior's life to extrapolate and draw conclusions about how he was likely to perform in other arenas.

This style of holistic judgment via inferences drawn across disparate sectors of experience can be seen in several *Budoshoshinshu* lessons, such as lesson 4, "Be Devoted, Even to Negligent Parents," and lesson 29, "Discerning a Brave Man from a Coward." Lesson 4 first makes the Confucian case that every person has a moral duty to treat his or her parents well and care for them in their waning years. According to the Confucian conception of obligation, nothing the parents do to their children or fail to do for their children can in any way diminish their children's obligation to them. Having made this clear, Daidoji goes on to argue that it is possible to tell how a samurai will treat his daimyo by observing how the warrior treats his own parents. He gives no credit to the man who is devoted to loving parents, because this presents no challenge. On the other hand, the man who is devoted to negligent parents receives high praise, his behavior giving proof that he comprehends how the requirements of the key Confucian relationships are supposed to breed unconditional commitments:

> A warrior with such a disposition will have a good understanding of the Way of loyalty and duty when serving a lord. He will labor in true loyalty, not only when his lord's power is flourishing, but even when his master has met with something unexpected and is in trouble. . . . Although the words *parent* and *lord, filial piety* and *loyalty* are different, in the sincerity of the mind they are one. . . . It is, then, unreasonable to say that a man may be unfilial to his parents yet loyal and correct to his lord.[23]

Compare this view with those that arise in modern debates about the relevance of evidence of misconduct in "private" spheres to assessments of an individual's worthiness to assume responsible roles in public life (e.g., in government or military service).

Lesson 29 contains the assertion that just as a man's loyalty and integrity can be tested in one role and the results trusted to predict how he will acquit himself in any role, his potential courage on the battlefield can be projected accurately by analyzing his daily actions, even in the most peaceful of settings. So Daidoji writes, "A man's ordinary life at peace reflects his courage or cowardice just like a mirror."[24] His rationale is that the sort of sustained moral courage and strength of character that it takes to live each day resisting temptation and avoiding vice in all its forms is fundamentally the same quality of the soul (or mind) needed to support physical courage in combat.

The idea that virtues learned and practiced in one realm of life can be transferred with ease to any other flows throughout the Bushido code. From this follows the further belief that cataloguing a person's habits of character in one context will produce conclusions that can reliably be applied to any context. This conception of virtue is not uncontroversial in Western thought, although, interestingly enough, it is shared by many of my Western warriors in training. For example, one of the midshipmen in my fall 2001 "Code of the Warrior" course, Lora Gorsky, wrote the following in a term paper on samurai values: "Among these values, . . . is the *accurate* [my emphasis] idea that performance in one area of your life reveals core characteristics that inevitably permeate all other areas of your life."

The Greek philosopher Aristotle spoke of the habituation of virtue and would have agreed that once a man acquired a quality like courage, he could be expected to display it whenever the need arose in defense of a noble cause. Immanuel Kant, however, defined courage differently and maintained that a man could be extremely courageous in the service of a bad cause or for purely self-interested ends. If such a man were not in possession of a good will, he could not be counted upon to eschew cowardice when courage might go unrewarded. Whether virtues are generally conveyed unaltered from one potential application to the next is to some degree an empirical question, requiring data from the real world. Drawing from your own observations and anecdotal evidence, you may be sympathetic to, or skeptical of, such suggestions. Whatever my intuitions on the subject, I cannot provide sufficient compelling facts and examples either to support or to reject the claim that men who lack integrity in their private dealings with family and friends tend also to be less trustworthy when practicing their profession of arms, or that men who are extravagant, intemperate, and self-indulgent in peacetime are more likely to be cowards and shirkers in war. What is important is to recognize that the samurai believed these things to be true and guided themselves accordingly.

Lesson 15, "The Moment of Death Is Important to a Warrior," expresses a related point. Just as lessons like lesson 29 require the warrior to be consistently virtuous in both his public and private lives, this lesson challenges the warrior to display the same virtues in death (e.g., courage, loyalty, commitment to duty) that he did in life. Even death is no excuse for slackness in observing the samurai code. On the contrary, Daidoji warns, the man who behaves poorly at the hour of his demise may be remembered for that weakness alone, whatever his past glories: "if, in his final moments he is so panicky that he loses consciousness or otherwise faces his end poorly, all his former good behavior will become as water."[25]

The samurai is told specifically how he must approach death in order to avoid shame. If he is about to be beheaded on the battlefield, he should proudly and calmly declare his name and lineage to the one who has vanquished him, so that his head can be labeled correctly when it is severed and mounted for presentation to his enemy's lord.[26] If he is fading away from a fatal wound, he must use his last strength to give clear and useful parting instructions to his subordinates, "ignoring his wounds and meeting his end as though it were an everyday occurrence."[27] Unlike the Viking warriors of chapter 3, the samurai did not think it shameful for a warrior to die peacefully in his bed. If struck down by a fatal illness during a time of peace, a samurai could still meet his fate *as a warrior.* He could achieve this by showing no fear and by using his final moments to pass down wisdom to his children regarding the loyal service they, too, will owe their masters until their dying days.[28]

Lesson 15 concludes by reminding the warrior-to-be that he should cultivate "a resolution to die," as advocated in lesson 1, long before the grim reaper begins to stalk him. Given such a resolution, the precise form his death takes will be irrelevant:

> Say a person . . . did not establish a resolution to die [before coming down with a fatal illness]. With such a cowardly disposition how could this man face the battlefield and meet with an enemy that bore him no grudge at all? Nor could he be struck down splendidly in battle with only thoughts of not being lacking in righteousness. Thus, for a man who is constantly aware of what it means to be a warrior, dying of illness in bed can be said to be an important, unique event in the one life we receive.[29]

In other words, if the warrior is resolved to die and is confident in his righteousness, it should not matter to him whether his end comes from battle or bacteria.

The psychological motivation for the samurai to remain true to such unforgiving standards and never lapse into a self-indulgent state, even on the precipice of death, came at least in part from the greater fear of shame. Shame was an incredibly powerful force in samurai culture. To be shamed was to be cast out, separated from all social goods. And an individual's shame infected the lives of everyone in his clan. If a samurai committed a disgraceful act, such as disobeying a superior's command, he would not be the only one to suffer. His entire family would be ostracized for his dishonor. If he had unmarried sisters or daughters, no suitors would court them. Friends would break off contact and withdraw support. All social status, the foundation of identity in their Confucian- and Shinto-influenced world, would be lost.

The *Budoshoshinshu*'s fifth lesson, "A Sense of Shame Will Uphold Justice," contains a narrative that illustrates the role that shame is supposed to play in the psyche of a samurai. In this tale, a samurai is traveling somewhere with an acquaintance who is not a friend or a comrade-in-arms or anyone else with whom he might share a special relationship. This acquaintance asks the samurai to carry some money for him, just until their paths diverge. However, before that point in their journey is reached, the man unexpectedly dies of natural causes, having told no one of the money he entrusted to the samurai. The just thing for the samurai to do is obviously to return the money to the man's relations. The lesson describes three distinct ways he may be led to that conclusion.

First, the samurai may simply recognize immediately that it is his duty to return the money. He may not seriously consider any alternative. This is the ideal. Second, he may consider keeping the money for himself, and even begin to construct a rationalization to make himself feel good about that choice. Yet before he can fully commit himself to such an unjust action, he will find himself overcome with shame and so will decide that he would not be able to live with himself (or ever again gaze into the mirror at a Shinto shrine) if he kept the dead man's cash. Or, third, he may succeed in persuading himself that hanging on to the money is not a crime worthy of any mental self-flagellation. But then he might imagine what would happen if anyone ever found out about his action. Even if he is not privately ashamed of himself, others could still bring him public shame. Thus, once again, the fear of shame will drive him toward the just action.[30]

The powerful notion of "saving face" not only underlies the personal ethics of the samurai, it also provides the backbone for their relationship with their lords. To show proper loyalty to one's daimyo is not just to follow his commands and perform well in his service. It is also crucial to save face *for* one's employer. Shielding one's master from shame is even more important to a samurai than avoiding shame himself. In the end, protecting one's master and oneself from shame are one and the same, since nothing could bring greater shame to a samurai than to allow his master to suffer any humiliation on his watch.

The samurai's efforts to protect his master's reputation required sacrifices both small and great. Lesson 24, "A Splendid Entrance, but Plain Living Quarters," recommends that the money a samurai sets aside for housing himself and his family should be apportioned so that the majority of it goes toward making his home appear lavish on the exterior and in the formal entryway where guests are greeted. The actual living quarters should have only the barest necessities.[31] This is done to give visitors the impression that the samurai's daimyo is wealthy and generous to his staff, whether or not that is truly the case. Lesson 53, "Being Present When One's Lord Cuts Down an Attendant," is similarly motivated but considerably more demanding. It describes a situation in which a daimyo attempts to take the life of an insolent servant but fails to strike a deadly blow. To save his lord any embarrassment, the loyal warrior is supposed to step in and say, "'The blow from your sword has greatly weakened him. Allow me to finish him off,' and quickly stab the man to death."[32]

A great deal of the Bushido code is clearly calculated to help those who wielded the political power in feudal Japan—the shogun and his daimyo—to control the potentially dangerous physical power of their samurai. Just as the knights of the West were taught to regard any rebellion against their rulers as not merely traitorous but *blasphemous*, the samurai were carefully indoctrinated to regard even the slightest insubordination or challenge to their lord's authority as the mark of a degenerate character. A samurai owes his daimyo absolute loyalty, obedience, and respect at all times. And again, as in all Confucian relationships, no failure or weakness on the part of his master can alter the samurai's obligations to him.

Several lessons in the *Budoshoshinshu* deal explicitly with how a warrior should behave toward those in authority over him when their behavior is not what the warrior might wish. For example, lesson 43 instructs the warrior that "even if one's stipend is diminished, he should make no complaint." Here Daidoji describes how a daimyo in reduced circumstances will sometimes resort to "borrowing" from the funds that he would normally use to pay his samurai their yearly wages. According to the *Budoshoshinshu*, a samurai who has his income reduced in this way "should humbly comply and never let even a hint of complaint slip out in his conversations with wife and children, much less in front of others."[33] Furthermore, he should not consider leaving his lord and going to seek more profitable employment elsewhere (as a ronin, or masterless samurai—similar to a lordless knight, or "freelancer," in Europe) until his master's finances improve. He should not even try to improve his situation by pawning possessions or asking for loans, because such actions would both draw attention to his master's distress and place the samurai himself in a compromised position. The samurai (and his family, dependent on him) is simply to economize as best he can and wait the trouble out, doing his best to conceal it from the world to protect his lord's reputation.

While protecting his master's pride is paramount, the *Budoshoshinshu* warns strictly against the warrior allowing his own pride to interfere with his mission of service. In many other warrior cultures (including some of those discussed in previous chapters), pride is allowed, even encouraged, in the warrior as long as it does not become excessive (i.e., hubris). After all, warriors are supposed to have confidence in their martial prowess and make an effort to be superior to their foes. The *Budoshoshinshu,* too, urges the samurai in lesson 14 to "exceed others in some way." Of course, even the possession of objective superiority in certain areas does not necessitate a lack of humility.

Lesson 11, although entitled "Do Not Be Spoiled by Length of Service," is mostly about comparing the life of a samurai to that of a Buddhist priest. The conclusion of the lesson is that while both vocations require tremendous character and sacrifice, the priest's path is actually more demanding than the warrior's. Daidoji argues that while some mediocre warriors manage to rise up through the ranks of the samurai just by meeting minimum requirements and not attracting negative attention, priests cannot be promoted to higher positions in a Buddhist temple without passing exacting examinations at every level, administered by "various scholars and famous instructors," and requiring constant, intense study. Thus he concludes that "the discipline of warriors in training is far inferior to that of priests."[34]

The reason for including this comparison between priests and samurai in a book of lessons for young warriors must be to combat the arrogance that can sometimes develop in those who have earned their way into an elite group. Knowing that you have endured trials that would have overthrown weaker spirits and that you have honed abilities far above those of the common throng may cause you to undervalue the achievements of people in other fields. Lesson 11 admonishes warriors not only to show proper respect for those who pursue excellence in nonmartial occupations but also to open their minds to the idea that those who have followed different paths may have something to teach the samurai about sacrifice and commitment.

The need to keep self-importance in check is stressed directly and indirectly throughout the Bushido code. Lesson 38, "Do Not Forget the Subordinate's Mind," contains timeless advice for leaders of any stripe. One reason that changes are often slow to occur in hierarchical institutions is that the same people who resented their treatment at the hands of those ranked above them when they were subordinates behave just like their former oppressors when they achieve higher rank themselves. Having escaped the lower strata, they dismiss their underlings' concerns as brutally as if they had never shared them.

The *Budoshoshinshu* certainly does *not* advocate collapsing the hierarchy (or "flattening out the organization," as it might be phrased today) so that those of lower rank can be given a stronger voice ("360-degree feedback" was not a concept embraced by feudal Japan). Daidoji does, however, see two distinct benefits that arise from remembering how one felt as a subordinate. First of all, since a subordinate is eager to improve his position, he is likely to have less trouble maintaining his motivation to excel than someone who has already been promoted. Recalling—and re-creating—how he felt as a subordinate could help a senior samurai maintain his intensity. Second, if a warrior of high rank makes an effort not to block from his mind his own experiences in the lower ranks, that first-hand knowledge will give him insights that will help him judge the abilities of his subordinates fairly and use them accordingly, neither overlooking talents nor favoring those who do not deserve it.[35]

Daidoji's concern that more advanced samurai may have difficulty keeping up the same consuming commitment to serve they had as their younger selves stems in part from an acknowledgment of the fact that higher-ranking samurai have more potential distractions in their lives from responsibilities outside the warrior sphere. Thus lesson 39 orders that a man of low rank should not have a wife and child. Daidoji does not mince words, calling it "madness" for a junior samurai whose occupational demands are high and his income low to attempt to support a family.[36] He concludes:

> Thus, while a warrior of low rank is still young, if he will increase his vigor, endeavoring solely in the labors of his duties night and day, he will come up in the world appropriately according to his lord's will. Judging the proper time to raise a family he will be able to consider the matter of descendants later.[37]

Incidentally, this is not the only place in the *Budoshoshinshu* where Daidoji gives the young warrior advice about how to manage his domestic affairs. Lesson 32, "The Warrior Who Strikes His Wife Is a Coward," presents an unequivocal condemnation of domestic abuse. As always, the samurai culture's holistic conception of character is at work here. A warrior capable of insulting or beating his wife is not expected to be capable of appropriate conduct in other contexts, as required of a gentleman under the Bushido code. It is also deemed against the nature of a true warrior to derive any satisfaction from using his strength against someone who cannot fight back: "[T]he unfair act of seeking out an opponent who is unable to resist is absolutely not the deed of a valiant warrior. The man who loves to do the things a valiant warrior hates and does not do is said to be a coward."[38]

Controlling one's temper is a theme of several other Bushido lessons, as is maintaining what would today be called "a good attitude." Lesson 17, "Do Not Mix Personal Feelings with Duties," teaches the samurai-in-training to set aside grudges for the sake of harmony in the ranks. If a warrior finds himself assigned by his master to work with a man he hates (even with good cause), he should take the initiative to make peace with the man—an exercise in humility and nonattachment—so that they can have a productive working relationship.[39] Lesson 44, "Accept Difficult Orders Positively," points out that even a successful mission can afford a warrior only tarnished honor if it was undertaken reluctantly, sullenly, or without "manly" enthusiasm.[40] The reason for this revolves, like so much in samurai culture, around public perception. As Daidoji wisely observes, if a person undertakes a challenging or risky assignment with a sour attitude and still manages to complete it, people are likely to assume that mere luck, not effort or skill, carried the day. And if the same person fails in his mission through simple bad fortune, others will believe the fault really to be his.

If a samurai were issued orders that he regarded as not just difficult but actually misguided, he would be very limited in his response because of the primacy within his code of the prohibition on challenging authority. Lesson 28, "Both Contradiction and Flattery Are Failure of Duty," suggests that a warrior's proper reaction to hearing his master make a poor decision should be to keep his mouth shut about it. He should not try to flatter his superior by pretending to agree with his views. But contradicting his master or arguing with him is not an option. All the samurai can do is hope the lord will come to change his opinion on his own.[41]

The samurai were expected to place loyalty and obedience above all other considerations, including concerns for the protection of both their master's interests and their own. This is echoed again in Lesson 45, "Do Not Oppose Even the Unreasonable Words of One's Lord." This lesson restricts a warrior from voicing any direct protest even when his master unfairly reprimands or falsely accuses him. He is told to "listen with all humility and abashment to the words of the lord whom he is serving, no matter how unjust or upbraiding they may be."[42] The most he is allowed to do on his own behalf is to discreetly "ask the chief retainers, elders, or stewards to intercede . . . after the matter has passed."[43] That is only permitted, however, in cases where the undeserved punishment with which the warrior is threatened will actually permanently remove him from his master's employment by dismissal or death.

Even after a samurai was dismissed from a lord's service, either honorably or dishonorably, he was required to continue to be loyal, as we see in lesson 20, "Forbidden Slander of a Former Lord." This lesson charges that a warrior should not speak ill of anyone he has served, regardless of what grounds he may have for doing so and even if the lord in question has been publicly shamed for his wrongdoing. Rather, samurai should display their respect for all those of higher social rank, regardless of their individual qualities, and seek consolation in the likelihood that they will have an opportunity sometime during their martial careers to serve good masters as well as bad ones.[44]

The final lesson of the *Budoshoshinshu*, "Great Loyalty That Surpasses *Junshi*," ties together the threads of loyalty and death woven through all fifty-six lessons. Daidoji speaks of the ultimate expression of servile devotion: *junshi*, or the act of committing ritual suicide when one's master dies. He cannot hide his admiration for those willing to commit junshi, an act by which the warrior with one stroke fearlessly embraces death as a

Buddhist should and proves his selfless commitment to a crucial Confucian relationship. Still, Daidoji is compelled to officially condemn it since it was made illegal in 1663. In place of traditional junshi, he urges the dedicated samurai to honor his fallen lord by performing one last, great act of service for the lord's clan.

The *Budoshoshinshu* closes with a utopian vision of how Japan would be if more samurai were faithful to the code of Bushido:

> If there were only one such deeply resolved warrior at the side of every feudal lord, thoughtful only of putting his life on the line for his master and being his safeguard, . . . evil and treacherous men with the minds of devils and vicious spirits would hesitate to act, and, perverse and unrighteous deeds would cease to be done.[45]

One of the most famous Japanese stories illustrating Bushido in practice is the tale of the Forty-Seven Ronin. Although details vary in different tellings, the central events purport to be historical, not fictional. The story begins in the year 1701, during the Tokugawa shogunate. Lord Asano, a wealthy daimyo, was given the customary but rather expensive honor of making (and funding) all the preparations to entertain a delegation from the imperial court in the shogunate palace at Edo. To make sure he arranged everything correctly, Lord Asano consulted frequently with another daimyo, Lord Kira, who served as a kind of protocol officer to the shogun. Lord Kira, however, was a greedy man who liked to take advantage of his position by collecting lavish gifts in return for his expertise. When Lord Asano failed to provide Lord Kira with what he deemed to be a sufficient bribe for his assistance, Lord Kira insulted Lord Asano (as it is usually recounted, by calling him cheap, miserly, and uncouth).

If Lord Asano had been insulted in his own home, his loyal retainers—his samurai—would have struck Lord Kira down before Lord Asano could even draw his blade. They would then accept any consequences of the act themselves, thus shielding their daimyo from any discomfort, shame, or punishment. Alone in the shogun's palace, Lord Asano had no choice but to respond to the insult himself. Drawing his katana, he attempted to decapitate Lord Kira but succeeded only in wounding him on the shoulder and forehead.

Lord Asano's actions were disgraceful in two respects. First of all, it was a crime even to unsheathe a blade in the shogunate palace without the shogun's permission, let alone to attempt murder. Second, it was considered shameful under any circumstances for a warrior to fail to cut down an opponent whom he intended to kill, ideally with one blow. As lesson 53 of the *Budoshoshinshu* ("Being Present When One's Lord Cuts Down an Attendant") suggests, it reflected very poorly on Lord Asano's martial prowess that he merely wounded Lord Kira.

Perhaps because he knew of Lord Kira's character flaws, the shogun not only permitted Lord Asano the dignity of committing seppuku to redeem himself and protect the honor of his clan but also instructed the officials overseeing Lord Asano's suicide to shield him from the knowledge that Lord Kira's injuries were not fatal. Lord Asano performed his death ritual well, and he died comforted by the false belief that he had struck his enemy a mortal blow.

When his faithful samurai learned what had befallen Lord Asano, so far from their aid, many of them wanted to commit the act of junshi at once, despite the act's illegality. However, in line with the final lesson of the *Budoshoshinshu* (lesson 56, "Great Loyalty That Surpasses *Junshi*"), this notion was quickly supplanted by the desire first to seek vengeance against the author of Lord Asano's downfall, Lord Kira. Forty-seven of Asano's former samurai—now masterless ronin—devised a secret plan to throw Lord Kira and his retainers off their guard until the moment for revenge was ripe.

For an entire year, the forty-seven sacrificed every appearance of honor, feigning a complete lack of concern for their deceased master. Some, such as samurai Oishi Suranosuke, even abandoned their wives and children and pretended to be irresponsible drunkards. Like Signy in the Icelandic *Saga of the Volsungs* (discussed in chapter 4), all of the ronin placed their commitment to their revenge above every other consideration. Under the Bushido code, their quest for vengeance, or *kataki-uchi*, could end only one way: with them laying Lord Kira's severed head on Lord Asano's tomb.[46]

When Lord Kira and his men had been lulled into a false sense of security, believing that Lord Asano's former retainers were men of weak character who posed no threat, the forty-seven ronin struck. They conducted a surprise assault on Lord Kira's home, slaughtering his ill-prepared samurai. Lord Kira himself fled in terror and hid inside a coal shed. The ronin hunted him down, pulled him from his hiding place, and sliced off his head.

Their vengeance complete, the forty-seven ronin surrendered to the shogunate authorities. Although officials at every level of the government expressed sincere admiration for the lengths to which the forty-seven had gone out of loyalty to their fallen lord, in the end no one was willing to bend the rigid Tokugawa laws that forbade the murder of members of the daimyo class. The penalty for their actions was death. In a show of respect, the authorities permitted the ronin to take their own lives. All forty-seven of the men, who reportedly ranged in age from a seventeen-year-old to a vassal in his seventies, calmly disemboweled themselves, finding final redemption—and a permanent place in Japanese legend—in the act of seppuku.

The employment of ritual suicide is at once one of the most impressive and most disturbing aspects of samurai culture. The details of seppuku (also known less formally as hara-kiri, or the cutting of the belly) often hold a strange fascination for Westerners who have been trained to condemn the taking of one's own life as a sinful usurpation of divine authority. The samurai were by no means the only warrior culture to consider suicide an honorable choice, at least in certain circumstances. The Celtic queen Boudicca took her own life rather than be captured by the Romans when they eventually crushed her bold but ill-fated rebellion in Britain. The Romans themselves condoned suicide as a way to escape disgrace, preserve one's dignity, or deprive one's enemies of any satisfaction. Yet seppuku stands out both for its uses and its actual procedure, which to my mind is rivaled only by self-immolation as one of the most painful ways to end your life.

The most common use for seppuku was to redeem oneself after a shameful act. As we know, a samurai could fall into disgrace for anything from an overt act of cowardice in combat to a trivial (by nonsamurai standards) breach of etiquette at a formal dinner. If performed correctly, ritual suicide could rescue the fallen warrior and his clan from the dire consequences of dishonor. Through seppuku, the slate could be wiped clean, just as if the transgression had never occurred. Another reason for committing ritual suicide has already been discussed: junshi, or following one's master to the grave.

Although the popularity of junshi diminished after it was declared illegal in the seventeenth century, the practice was not easy to stamp out completely, especially since the courts could not prosecute the corpse of a man who illegally performed it. A form of junshi survived even into the twentieth century, when defeated Japanese soldiers in World War II assisted in the suicides of their commanders and then killed themselves in turn:

> Modern episodes drawn from the archives of World War II provide startling examples of the reactions of the Japanese military man (as well as those of great numbers of Japanese civilians) when faced with the possibility of capture. From the centuries-old performance of *hara-kiri* by numerous commanders who used their swords to make the traditional first cut before being shot in the head or beheaded by their lieutenants, to the less ritualized suicides of lower-ranking officers after they had beheaded their own soldiers: from the individual suicides of soldiers who pressed grenades against their bodies or balanced them on top of their heads, carefully replacing their caps before the explosion, to the mass suicides of Japanese soldiers and civilians—an orgy of self-destruction was the salient characteristic of Japanese behavior when confronted with defeat and the prospect of capture.[47]

The vicious treatment of prisoners of war by the Japanese in World War II is made more understandable, though no less despicable, by linking it to samurai traditions. The samurai held that only a man with no honor would allow himself to be taken prisoner by his enemies. Suicide was always considered the more noble and courageous choice. Samurai who surrendered were held in contempt, which made it easier for their captors to rationalize cruelty toward them. Unfortunately, the belief that prisoners of war lay down their honor with their arms outlived the samurai themselves.

Perhaps the most intriguing motive some samurai had for committing seppuku was simply to make a point. The *Budoshoshinshu* leaves no doubt that samurai had very few avenues to explore if they objected to a superior's decision or action or pattern of behavior. They could not just say, "You are doing the wrong thing, sir. You must pursue a different course," regardless of what even the superior himself stood to lose by his misguided moves. If a samurai really wanted to protest something his superior (e.g., his daimyo) did—whether it was to falsely accuse the samurai of a crime or to waste his (the daimyo's) family fortune, or to order his troops to certain, wasteful slaughter—the samurai's best bet to make his master rethink his plans was to commit ritual suicide (called *kanshi* when used for this purpose). No one could question either the sincerity or the selfless devotion of the samurai who was willing to commit kanshi to make his superior see reason.

To understand the significance and possible effects of an act of kanshi, imagine it transposed into a Western setting. At the bloody battle of Gettysburg in the U.S. Civil War, Southern general Longstreet identified General Lee's plan for Pickett's Charge as folly but was ineffectual in conveying his reservations to his beloved superior. Suppose that as a last resort, Longstreet had said to Lee, "Sir, I see that you are resolved upon this disastrous course. I have ordered my men to prepare for battle exactly as you directed. However, to show how strongly I feel that you should reconsider your decision, I will now slowly disembowel myself."

What exactly were the grisly details of this act that the samurai were willing to perform to erase shame, avoid capture, express ultimate devotion, or register protest? In its most traditional form, the ritual of seppuku began with the samurai who was to perform the rite presenting himself before a solemn audience of observers, which could include members of the samurai's clan, his daimyo, fellow samurai, and perhaps representatives from the imperial court, if the samurai was high-ranking or his offense had been especially grave. He would be dressed in his finest, formal embroidered silk robes, and his grooming would be impeccable. A servant would attend him, and by his left side would be his second, or *kaishaku*. This man would in most cases be another samurai and a close, trusted friend of the samurai performing the rite.[48]

The samurai's servant would bring him a tray that held a piece of white silk, a cup of sake (a rice-derived alcoholic beverage), and perhaps some writing materials. The samurai would pray, asking for the strength and will to perform the ritual correctly. Then he would drink the sake, draw his short sword (the *wakizashi*), and wrap the white silk around part of its blade, near the hilt. Next, the samurai would kneel down, taking care to tuck the ends of his long sleeves under his knees. This was done so that when his lifeless body finally collapsed, it would fall neatly forward, rather than sprawling backwards in an undignified way. He would open his clothing to reveal his belly and gather himself, sometimes with meditation, achieving a quiet calm before making the first incision. His kaishaku would continue to stand on his left, now with his bright katana blade drawn.

The samurai would first thrust his wakizashi deep into the center of his abdomen. (Recall that the Buddhist monks of chapter 7 regarded the abdomen as the seat of a person's life force, or chi.) Next he would slice the blade across, from the left to the right. He would then return the weapon to the center of the incision and make another cut up towards his sternum. He would do all of this without a single cry of pain. Once he removed the long dagger from his body, it would be retrieved by his servant, who would see to it that the now blood-soaked silk was given to the samurai's family as a token of remembrance.

Now slowly dying, the samurai could show additional grace and fortitude by finishing off his suicide with a flourish. Some samurai used their last moments to compose short but poignant death poems, which could even be written in their own blood. And, for those with an even more extreme bent, as historian H. Paul Varley notes, "By some it came to be considered an appropriate gesture of bravado or defiance to draw out part of the entrails and to leave them hanging in the wound."[49]

The ritual concluded at last with the kaishaku swinging his razor-sharp sword, the *katana*, to sever the samurai's neck. It was a grave responsibility to perform the role of kaishaku. He was there to end the samurai's suffering but also to safeguard his friend's honor. If at any point in the ceremony the samurai appeared to lose his resolve or seemed about to abandon the required stoicism and scream out in pain, the kaishaku would let his blow fall early, to help the samurai save face. There was also another challenge, as Varley observes: "Ideally, the second [the kaishaku] did not cut entirely through the neck, but left just enough flesh and skin to hold the head to the body and to prevent it from rolling grotesquely away."[50] A samurai had to show decorum, even in death.

While samurai warriors were the only ones officially granted the privilege (for so it was seen) of committing seppuku, men of other ranks were known to try to imitate the act. Women of the samurai class (e.g., the wives of samurai) were allowed to commit a form of ritual suicide, although it differed from that of the samurai men. It usually involved the woman slicing into the jugular vein at her neck. This was a quicker, less painful way to achieve the same ends as were offered by seppuku. However, there are stories of samurai women who chose more spectacular methods of suicide. One of the most famous of these comes from the period of civil war between the Taira and Minamoto clans. The Taira clan was wiped out in the sea battle of Dan-no-Ura. Rather than surrender to the victorious Minamoto, the women of the Taira clan plunged themselves into the waters of the straits of Shimonoseki and fiercely resisted attempts by the Minamoto to rescue them. All but one succeeded in drowning themselves.[51]

Some might consider the practice of seppuku to be the "dark side" of samurai culture. Examining the ritual highlights the brutal, uncompromising qualities of the samurai code that may both appall and impress the modern mind. Surely there is at least a pragmatic flaw in a system that could lead a warrior culture's most courageous and committed members to make the ultimate sacrifice to save, not land or lives, but face.

More uncontroversially open to criticism is the behavior of samurai who did not make an effort to honor the code that they espoused. Corrupt samurai betrayed their culture's values in several ways, most related to the abuse of power. Although Bushido called on the samurai to defend the ordinary citizens of the nonwarrior classes (e.g., lesson 34 of the *Budoshoshinshu*, "The Warrior's Duty Is to Protect the Farmer, Craftsman, and Merchant"), it was sadly common for Japanese peasants to find themselves the playthings of samurai cruelty, caprice, or excess.

A dramatic example of this is the centerpiece of contemporary British philosopher Mary Midgley's well-known essay challenging the logic of moral relativism, entitled "Trying Out One's New Sword:"

> There is, it seems, a verb in classical Japanese which means, "to try out one's sword on a chance wayfarer." (The word is *tsujigiri*, literally "crossroads-cut.") A samurai sword had to be tried out because, if it was to work properly, it had to slice through someone at a single blow, from the shoulder to the opposite flank. Otherwise, the warrior bungled his stroke. This could injure his honour, offend his ancestors, and even let down his emperor. So tests were needed, and wayfarers had to be expended. Any wayfarer would do—provided, of course, that he was not another samurai.[52]

More regular ill-treatment came in such forms as forcing lower-class women into unwilling prostitution, overtaxing and driving peasants off the land, and employing draconian punishments to control the masses through fear.

Aspects of the samurai code that pertained to interactions with superiors and peers were treated with greater reverence, yet those whose only concern was with the mere appearance of respectability could subvert them, too. Just as Bushido discouraged battling those weaker than oneself, it demanded that combat between equals be fought in an entirely straightforward fashion. A true samurai always challenged his enemy openly; stealth was considered beneath contempt. Nevertheless, the final resolution of power plays and feuds between rival clans often resulted as much from the use of shadowy methods such as bribery and assassination as from overt armed conflict.

Many times, the men—and women—secretly hired to carry out samurai "dirty work" such as spying, assassination, and sabotage were members of an entirely distinct warrior culture that developed parallel to that of the samurai, but with few values in common: the ninja.

> We are referring to a group of people, the ninja, whom the bushi [warriors under the Bushido code] employed to execute, with their particular weapons and supposedly occult methods, missions of dubious morality or of extreme difficulty, thus sparing the warrior the embarrassment of openly violating the norms of his own code of conduct (Bushido), which demanded that he behave as a soldier and gentlemen, facing his enemies openly without resorting to dishonest ruses.[53]

Like the samurai, the ninja underwent intense martial training that was grounded in spiritual beliefs, valued their honor more than their lives, and sought perfection in every mission. However, the spiritual beliefs emphasized in ninja training were missing the Shinto and heavy Confucian influence that made the samurai such fierce defenders of Japan's rigid, hierarchical social order. Ninja warriors came from a variety of classes within Japanese society (a ninja could be a ronin or a merchant's-daughter-turned-warrior) and served a variety of classes, as well. A daimyo might hire a ninja to engage in espionage against his neighbor, or a poor farmer might beg a ninja to protect him from a tyrannical landlord.

The ninja concept of honor, far from requiring the warrior to declare himself and his intentions before engaging battle, depended on the preservation of his anonymity and near invisibility. Individual ninja neither sought nor received any recognition for their accomplishments. While the victories of a samurai brought additional glory to his master, those for whom the ninja toiled in secret could only be destroyed if their connection to the ninja were exposed. A daimyo caught sending ninja to deliver secret messages, steeped in political intrigue, would soon find himself baring his neck to his kaishaku. A peasant discovered seeking ninja services would most likely forfeit not only his own life but also the lives of his entire family. A ninja warrior showed his loyalty by refusing to reveal from whom his order came, even under torture. To guarantee that they could never be traced back to those they served, ninja were even trained to disfigure their own faces and commit swift, nonritualized suicide rather than submit to capture.[54]

We know that the samurai would sooner die than shame himself (and his clan, and his ancestors) by failing to perform as expected against the enemies of his daimyo. Yet his martial methods were restricted by the same sense of honor that fueled his efforts. No samurai was ever supposed to retreat or show any sign of weakness in the face of his foes, or attempt to gain an "unfair" advantage on the field by employing deceptive, stealthy, or guerilla tactics.

The ninja, in contrast, were taught to set such niceties aside and exploit every opportunity to further the interests of their clients:

> [T]he Ninja's mission had to be completed by any means, fair or foul. To the samurai, losing face, or humiliation, was unacceptable. . . . The Ninja, however, would crawl before the enemy, humiliating himself as a short-term necessity for the sake of the long-term goal of completing a mission.[55]

A ninja warrior would not hesitate to "run away and fight another day" or pretend to defect to his opponent's cause. There are even tales of female ninja assassins who married or became the mistresses of their intended targets, biding their time for months or years before slipping poison in their lover's sake, a venomous snake between his sheets, or a sharp knife in his back.

The fact that any samurai or daimyo would come to the conclusion that his best course of action was to contract for ninja assistance behind the scenes is an acknowledgment of the price of clinging to an inflexible warrior tradition. The Bushido code left no room for the warrior to adapt to changing times or explore new styles of fighting. The only way a samurai could try out ninja tactics and remain a samurai was to become a hypocrite, upholding his traditions in public while privately undermining them. Open departure from the ways of the past was virtually unthinkable, as any innovations were thought to endanger the noble values that were the source of a samurai's strength.

In truth, the samurai class managed to survive several potential threats to its culture and traditions, including the introduction of guns. Muskets were brought to Japan by Portuguese traders in 1542, but they, along with all artillery, were relegated to use by foot soldiers in large engagements: "firearms . . . never became very popular as weapons of individual combat in feudal Japan."[56] The samurai clung to his beloved katana, with all its rich symbolism. The katana sword was both elegant and deadly. It was a symbol of the soul of the samurai. As Thomas McClatchie observed in 1873, "There is, perhaps, no country in the world where the sword, that 'knightly weapon of all ages,' has in its time, received so much honour and renown as it has in Japan."[57]

In the end, however, the samurai encountered a storm they could not weather: the arrival of Commodore Matthew Perry of the U.S. Navy and the opening of Japan to the West in 1868. Admiral Perry's landing on Japanese shores helped create the conditions that thrust the country into a crisis of identity. The ruling Tokugawa shogunate represented those who wanted to preserve the Japanese feudal system unchanged, while a powerful contingent of lower-ranking samurai spearheaded a push to reinvent Japan as a modern, industrialized nation. Ultimately, it was the shogunate that crumbled. The emperor remained enthroned, but, as before, the real power lay elsewhere:

> [R]eal governing power . . . was assumed by a small group of men, composed chiefly of activist samurai, who became an enlightened oligarchy

dedicated to transforming Japan into a strong modern nation on European and American lines. . . . [T]he oligarchs soon realized that the retention of an hereditary and privileged warrior class was incompatible with the needs of a modern society. Hence in the early 1870s they abolished the special rights of the samurai and decreed broad social and legal equality for the mass of the Japanese people.

Thus the samurai as a clearly identifiable class were eliminated from history.[58]

Of course, the legislation that wiped away the special rights of the samurai could never erase their legacy and enduring status as symbols of Japanese martial excellence. Their influence can be traced through Japan's twentieth-century warfare and twenty-first-century business practices. The age of the samurai ended long ago, yet in many ways Japan is still steeped in the values of Bushido. A famous Japanese saying that survives to the present day compares the samurai to the stunning yet short-lived cherry blossoms that fade quickly, only to return in dazzling form year after year: "As among flowers the cherry is queen, so among men the samurai is lord."[59]

NOTES

1. Sokyo Ono and William P. Woodard, *Shinto: The Kami Way* (Tokyo: Charles E. Tuttle, 1962), 3–4.

2. Bloodlines are as important in Japanese culture as they were to the Vikings, discussed in chap. 3. And, as in the case of the Vikings, this has been a source of intense racism in Japan.

3. Inazi Nitobe, *Bushido: The Warrior's Code* (Santa Clarita, Calif.: O'Hara Publications, 1979), 19.

4. Scott F. Runkle, *An Introduction to Japanese History* (Tokyo: International Society for Educational Information Press, 1976), 7.

5. Runkle, *Japanese History*, 8.

6. Runkle, *Japanese History*, 9.

7. H. Byron Earnhart, *Religion in the Japanese Experience* (Belmont, Calif.: Wadsworth, 1997), 47.

8. Earnhart, *Religion in the Japanese Experience*, 103.

9. This is true of the early Taoists, in the period that concerns us. I must acknowledge, however, that later neo-Taoists became obsessed with prolonging human life and at the same time adopted beliefs about life after death that cannot be traced to any traditional Taoist teachings, such as the *Tao Te Ching*. Most agree that this movement was a gross corruption of Taoism.

10. Lewis M. Hopfe and Mark R. Woodward, *Religions of the World* (Upper Saddle River, N.J.: Prentice Hall, 1998), 194.

11. This is sometimes regarded more broadly as "parent and child."

12. Runkle, *Japanese History*, 11.

13. Milton W. Meyer, *Japan: A Concise History* (Boston: Allyn & Bacon, 1966), 49–50.

14. William Scott Wilson, trans., *Budoshoshinshu: The Warrior's Primer of Daidoji Yuzan* (Santa Clara, Calif.: O'Hara, 1984), 19.

15. Wilson, *Budoshoshinshu*, 21.

16. Wilson, *Budoshoshinshu*, 81.

17. Wilson, *Budoshoshinshu*, 19.

18. Wilson, *Budoshoshinshu*, 40.

19. Wilson, *Budoshoshinshu*, 40.

20. Wilson, *Budoshoshinshu*, 23, 24.

21. Stephen F. Kaufman, trans., *The Martial Artist's Book of Five Rings: The Definitive Interpretation of Miyamoto Musashi's Classic Book of Strategy* (Boston: Tuttle, 1994), xv.

22. Wilson, *Budoshoshinshu*, 30.

23. Wilson, *Budoshoshinshu*, 25–26.

24. Wilson, *Budoshoshinshu*, 72.

25. Wilson, *Budoshoshinshu*, 48.

26. Wilson, *Budoshoshinshu*, 49.

27. Wilson, *Budoshoshinshu*, 49.

28. Wilson, *Budoshoshinshu*, 49–50.

29. Wilson, *Budoshoshinshu*, 50.

30. Wilson, *Budoshoshinshu*, 28.

31. Wilson, *Budoshoshinshu*, 66.

32. Wilson, *Budoshoshinshu*, 119.

33. Wilson, *Budoshoshinshu*, 100.

34. Wilson, *Budoshoshinshu*, 41.

35. Wilson, *Budoshoshinshu*, 92.

36. Wilson, *Budoshoshinshu*, 94.

37. Wilson, *Budoshoshinshu*, 94.

38. Wilson, *Budoshoshinshu*, 80.

39. Wilson, *Budoshoshinshu*, 55.

40. Wilson, *Budoshoshinshu*, 102–3.

41. Wilson, *Budoshoshinshu*, 71.

42. Wilson, *Budoshoshinshu*, 104.

43. Wilson, *Budoshoshinshu*, 104.

44. Wilson, *Budoshoshinshu*, 60.

45. Wilson, *Budoshoshinshu*, 127.

46. Oscar Ratti and Adele Westbrook, *Secrets of the Samurai: The Martial Arts of Feudal Japan* (Edison, N.J.: Castle Books, 1999), 91.

47. Ratti and Westbrook, *Secrets of the Samurai*, 90.

48. H. Paul Varley, *Samurai* (New York: Delacorte, 1970), 36.

49. Varley, *Samurai*, 34.

50. Varley, *Samurai*, 34.

51. Ratti and Westbrook, *Secrets of the Samurai*, 116.

52. Mary Midgley, "Trying Out One's New Sword," in *Vice and Virtue in Everyday Life: Introductory Readings in Ethics*, ed. Christina Sommers and Fred Sommers, 3d ed. (New York: Harcourt Brace College Publishers, 1993), 175.

53. Ratti and Westbrook, *Secrets of the Samurai*, 316.

54. Jay Sensei, *Tiger Scroll of the Koga Ninja* (Boulder, Colo.: Paladin, 1985), 10.

55. Sensei, *Tiger Scroll*, 1.

56. Ratti and Westbrook, *Secrets of the Samurai*, 316.

57. Thomas McClatchie, "The Sword of Japan: Its History and Tradition," *Transactions of the Asiatic Society of Japan* 3 (1873–74): 55.

58. Varley, *Samurai*, 128.

59. Nitobe, *Bushido*, 97.

9

The Warrior's Code Today: Are Terrorists Warriors?

Warrior's codes can be construed in a wide variety of ways to reflect the core values of diverse cultures, as we have seen in the preceding chapters. In chapter 1, "Why Warriors Need A Code," I argued that the purpose of a code is to *restrain* warriors, for their own good as much as for the good of others. Therefore the essential element of a warrior's code is that it must set definite limits on what warriors can and cannot do if they want to continue to be regarded as warriors, not murderers or cowards. For the warrior who has such a code, certain actions remain unthinkable, even in the most dire or extreme circumstances.

The great Homeric warrior Achilles forfeits his honor when he abuses the corpse of the noble Prince Hector of Troy. A soldier in a Roman legion suffers permanent disgrace (and risks communal punishment) if he breaks from his formation and abandons his fellow warriors to their fate. Fabled Viking king Volsung cannot run from an unworthy, deceitful opponent, even to regroup and fight on his own terms. A legendary Round Table knight must grant all requests for mercy and must defend those weaker than himself. A Cheyenne peace chief will keep his word and abide by the terms of any treaty he has signed, even after the other side has violated it. War chiefs such as Sitting Bull and Chief Joseph of the Nez Perce will do what is best for their people, even if it means surrendering both their power and their personal pride. The martial monks and nuns of Shaolin spend their days perfecting deadly arts but refuse to employ them except in a purely defensive capacity. And a samurai would sooner die a slow and agonizing death by his own hand than permit someone else—such as his master or the members of his clan—to pay for his mistakes.

Modern warriors can forge admirable models for their own behavior by picking and choosing the best from among these historical and mythical warrior ideals. It makes little difference whether the men and women they hope to emulate ever lived and breathed. Some warriors of today may even feel that they have more in common with fictional figures such as Sigurd or Sir Gawain than with certain of their real-life civilian counterparts.

Some educators, politicians, and members of the media fear that encouraging young warriors to associate themselves with the warrior traditions of the past will somehow lead them to become mindless, Rambo-like brutes with various outrageous bigotries and out-of-date values. Granted, some of the qualities that ancient warriors or warrior archetypes possess do not play well in the twenty-first century. But is it really so great a challenge to separate the wheat from the chaff? The key is to select for preservation only what is consistent with the values cherished by contemporary warrior cultures. Modern American warriors should only resurrect those traditions that cohere with the letter and spirit of the Constitution they have sworn to uphold and defend. For example, they can emulate the humility, integrity, commitment to "might *for* right," courtesy, and courage of a Round Table knight without taking on board his acceptance of an undemocratic, stratified society (where most of the population is disenfranchised and women and serfs are treated as property) or his determination to "pursue infidels."

Far from being outmoded, the genuine, emotional connection of today's warriors to an intentionally idealized warrior tradition and their sense that they must not betray that legacy is more important than ever. That connection and devotion may help them summon the will to show restraint in situations that will sorely tempt them to throw self-control out the window, for the world is no longer arranged in such a way that conflicts are likely to arise among great powers that are fairly evenly matched. When two nations with similar strength and resources battle one another, it is relatively easy for their leaders to establish mutually beneficial rules of engagement. It is rational for them to reach agreements about such matters as the identification of noncombatants and the treatment of prisoners of war, because doing so will serve the interests of both parties without giving a disproportionate advantage to either one. This is not the case, however, in the so-called asymmetric conflicts that have become the norm in recent years, which feature lopsided distributions of military might. When weaker forces take on stronger ones, any restrictions on the conduct of war that the former accept can only limit their arsenal of potential means to overcome their opening handicap.

Picture a boxing match between Muhammad Ali in peak physical condition (i.e., between his matches with Joe Frazier) and Woody Allen (in his physical prime . . . whenever that was). In a fair fight, Woody will get pulverized. Therefore, if he has any interest in winning, he should not (with any sincerity) agree to a set of rules that will limit his options in the ring.

His hope is to find a way to "fight dirty." The only way Ali will hit the mat before him is if Woody can, for instance, smuggle in a hypodermic filled with a strong sedative and inject the Greatest before his first swing.

You may argue that even in such a mismatch, the underdog has a motive to endorse at least minimal restrictions on the combatants' conduct. After all, Woody would want there to be a rule against Ali beating him to death just for fun. Might not the weaker party voluntarily give up the chance to use underhanded tactics if it meant it could guarantee its own survival in the event of its defeat?

The answer is that it depends on the stakes. It may be hard to picture Woody Allen (a man who once said, "I don't want to achieve immortality through my work, I want to achieve it through not dying") so devoted to a cause that he would willingly risk death just to hold on to the slim possibility that he might be able to defeat a more powerful opponent if there are no holds barred. However, many people are sufficiently dedicated to their side of an asymmetric struggle that they would sooner see themselves martyred than surrender the slightest edge.

The privileged warriors of today, like my students who are soon to be military officers in the service of what some call "the sole remaining superpower," will increasingly find themselves pitted against adversaries who fight without any rules or restraints. Because they see no other way to advance their objectives, these desperate men and women are likely to employ methods that are rightfully viewed as horrific and appalling by the rest of the civilized world, such as terror attacks on civilian populations. They will take fighting dirty to unimaginable depths, and since they are already willing to die, they will not be deterred by any threat of punishment for continuing to disregard the laws of war.

As Ariel Merari, director of the Project on Terrorism at the Jaffee Center for Strategic Studies at Tel Aviv University, points out in his essay "The Readiness to Kill and Die: Suicidal Terrorism in the Middle East," old ideas about tit-for-tat and the applications of rational decision theory are worthless when dealing with those who are ready, if not anxious, to sacrifice their lives for the cause. Merari quotes Lord Chalfont, an authority on counterterrorism:

> The whole time that I have been involved in terrorist operations, which now goes back to 30 years, my enemy has always been a man who is very worried about his own skin. You can no longer count on that, because the terrorist [today] is not just prepared to get killed, he wants to get killed. Therefore, the whole planning, tactical doctrine, [and] thinking [behind antiterrorism measures] is fundamentally undermined.[1]

How should the stronger side in an asymmetric conflict respond when its weaker opponents resort to terrorist tactics? One perfectly understandable reaction would be for the stronger side to want to take off the gloves, too, especially when the terrorists seem to be banking on the fact that it will not. It seems natural to say, "If they will not respect the rules of war and use some restraint, then neither will we." I remember sitting in a crowded wardroom with my "Code of the Warrior" students and a group of mostly junior officers on the morning of September 11, 2001, watching the collapse of the Twin Towers of New York's World Trade Center, seeing black smoke billowing out of the Pentagon, and hearing about the crash of a fourth hijacked plane into a Pennsylvania field. Waves of shock, grief, rage, pride, and patriotic fervor overwhelmed me. If I could have gotten my hands on the man responsible for planning the attacks, I know that a part of me would have wanted to at least consider the pros and cons of bringing back the practice of drawing and quartering.

Of course, one of the most serious cons that a country like the United States must consider before taking the gloves off is that it would be a violation of our own values for us to engage in a war with no rules. It is beyond infuriating that some of the people who claim to hate who we are and what we represent are yet able to benefit from our commitment to restraint. The more they push us and the more suffering we endure, the harder it is for us to fight with one hand tied behind our back rather than unleashing the full extent of our power to wipe them from the face of the earth. But if we give up who we are in order to destroy our enemies, what sort of victory will we have secured for ourselves?

In the spring semester following the 9/11 attacks and the start of President George W. Bush's "new war against terrorism," I gave an unusual assignment to the students in my advanced "Knowing Your Enemy" seminar (a sequel to my "Code of the Warrior" course). I asked them to write essays detailing exactly "Why I [meaning each of them] am different from a terrorist." The midshipmen were to spell out as clearly as possible how the roles they intended to fill as future naval and Marine Corps officers were distinct in morally relevant ways from that of, say, an al Qaeda operative. They immediately dubbed the assignment "creepy" but gamely agreed to do it (since it was, after all, for a grade). After they had read their efforts aloud, I gave the project an even creepier twist. I had them exchange papers and told them each to write a critical response to their classmate's paper from the point of view of a terrorist. When the responses were complete, I had them read those aloud, as well.

The class found the entire exercise very disturbing, because it forced them to reflect upon that thin but critical line I described in chapter 1 that separates warriors from murderers. In their initial essays, several of them stressed the fact that as members of the U.S. military they will not intentionally target innocent people. Here is a segment of an argument from Nick Nordvall, who was a midshipman in that class:

> It is wrong to kill innocent people even if it does further the cause of the United States. There are rules to war. . . . We learned in Naval Law about the

Law of Armed Conflict and the Rules of Engagement. There are targets that are acceptable and have "military value" and there are targets that are simply killing for the sake of killing. Terrorists see targets of military value as too difficult to strike. They do not have the means to strike these targets. They instead will take out the easy targets for shock value, just to disrupt the lives of those they hate.

Both warriors and murderers take lives. Both cause pain and suffering. Both may even cause the deaths of innocents. But there is a moral difference between intentionally targeting civilians and causing civilian deaths as the result of attacks on legitimate military targets, or what is known as "collateral damage." To illustrate this difference, let me present two very unpleasant scenarios (that I pray will forever remain purely fictional) in which I might shoot and kill an innocent little girl.

In the first case, I just walk up to a six-year-old girl on the sidewalk in front of her school and shoot her in the chest. My motive has nothing to do with anything the girl herself has done (she is, after all, too young even to be considered a moral agent, responsible for her own actions). Rather, I hate her parents or others who will be affected by her death and want to hurt them by killing the girl. Her death is just a means to my ends.

In the second case, I am for some reason the only person who sees a man trying to take a bomb onto a school bus full of children. I happen to have a gun. The man screams out his intention to blow up the bus and the kids and starts to climb on board. I decide to shoot him before he can detonate his explosive device. I fire off several rounds, killing the man but also hitting a six-year-old girl who steps between us. The girl's wound is fatal.

Now, in the two cases, the girl is equally dead, and it was I who killed her. In the first case, she was my intended target, while in the second case I killed her accidentally in an effort to stop what I took to be a greater evil. Yet even my achieving the good result of saving the other children in the second scenario does not somehow transform the little girl's death into a positive or morally desirable event. The girl herself is an innocent victim both times. In the first scenario, she is a victim of my murderous intent, while in the second case she is a victim of the bomber's.

Saint Thomas Aquinas, the medieval theologian who championed the philosophy of Aristotle and supported the union of faith and reason, laid the groundwork for two principles of Natural Law that offer provisions for identifying situations in which it might be morally permissible to take a life. These are known as the principle of forfeiture and the doctrine of double effect. These doctrines have influenced both religious and secular theories of just war and the conduct of war (*jus ad bellum* and *jus in bello*). The principle of forfeiture states that a person can forfeit his or her natural right to life by taking or attempting to take an innocent life. In other words, this principle would permit me to shoot the bomber who threatened the busload of schoolkids.

The doctrine of double effect is somewhat more complicated. It applies to situations in which it may be necessary or unavoidable to take an action that will cause the loss of innocent life in order to achieve some greater good:

> The principle holds that such an action should be performed only if the intention is to bring about the good effect and the bad effect will be an unintended or indirect consequence. More specifically, four conditions must be satisfied:
> 1. The action itself must be morally indifferent or morally good.
> 2. The bad effect must not be the means by which the good effect is achieved.
> 3. The motive must be the achievement of the good effect only.
> 4. The good effect must be at least equivalent in importance to the bad effect.[2]

This doctrine seems to apply in the case where I shoot the little girl unintentionally while acting to prevent the bomber from blowing up the bus full of children. The action of saving the busload of schoolkids is a morally good action. The bad effect—killing the little girl—is not the means by which I saved the other children. My motive was only to save the children, and their lives are at least as important as the life of the girl I accidentally shot.

In a similar way, the doctrine of double effect can be used to justify taking actions that will cause innocents to be killed as collateral damage during the prosecution of a just war. Aquinas wrote "Vengeance is . . . virtuous *to the extent that its purpose is to check evil.*"[3] But, again, the four provisions of the doctrine of double effect must be satisfied. Most importantly, killing innocent noncombatants may be excused so long as their deaths are unintended consequences but cannot be justified if their deaths are the *means* to some further end, even if that end is morally desirable. Suppose that the 9/11 terrorists had chosen only legitimate military targets and their actions were aimed at achieving morally defensible ends. They would still have violated the doctrine of double effect by using planes full of innocent noncombatants—including children, who have the best claim to innocence—as the means to achieve those ends.

Just as noble ends can be tarnished by the base means used to achieve them, what might otherwise be regarded as admirable behavior is no longer praiseworthy if it is directed at ignominious objectives. There has been much debate about the legitimacy of labeling the 9/11 terrorists "cowards." If the issue is whether or not the hijackers showed courage on that day, the crux of the matter is the definition of "courage." The Greek philosopher Aristotle drew a valuable distinction between actually possessing the virtue of courage (which falls in the mean between the excesses of cowardice and foolhardiness) and simply having what we might today call "guts." The former, like all Aristotelian virtues, demands a noble object. The courageous individual is one who displays courage at the right time, to the right extent, and *in the right cause*. It may take guts for a person to plan and execute a murder (or mass murder), but that does not make the murderer courageous in the classical sense.

The second part of the "Why are you different from a terrorist?" assignment required my students to try to get inside the heads of those who commit terrorist acts. It forced them to consider how easy it might be to rationalize crossing the line between warrior and murderer in the interest of what you believe to be a noble cause. As most of them recognized, terrorists do not see themselves as murderers. They believe that they are warriors. They often consider themselves "freedom fighters," struggling against those they have dubbed their "oppressors."

It is clear from studying Osama bin Laden's writings and interviews that he made a careful effort to persuade his followers in his international terrorist organization, al Qaeda, that they are warriors engaged in a jihad, or holy war, against what he called the "Crusader-Zionist alliance." Misappropriating medieval classifications, the crusaders he had in mind are the Americans and their allies, while the Zionists are the Israelis. To grasp the significance of this, it is important to understand the role of a jihad in the tradition of Islam.

The two primary literary sources of Islamic religion are their most sacred text, the Qur'an, and the Hadith, which provides details about the life and teachings of Muhammad. Although the Qur'an speaks of jihad in terms of an internal struggle against evil (battling temptation and sin), Islamic jurists of the eighth and ninth centuries established the tradition of an external form of jihad. These jurists described two types of holy wars: offensive jihad and defensive jihad.. Islamic ideology divides the world into two spheres, the *dar al Islam* and the *dar al harb*. The dar al Islam is the Islamic world, where Islamic law is obeyed and the teachings of Muhammad are followed. The dar al harb is the world of war and includes everything that is not included in the dar al Islam. The dar al harb is often seen as a godless region where Islamic law does not apply. Thus some feel that what a believer does in the dar al harb does not affect his soul as his actions within the dar al Islam do.[4]

Offensive jihad is an attack by Islamic believers from the dar al Islam against the inhabitants of the territory of the dar al harb for the purpose of expanding the dar al Islam. There are very strict rules associated with an offensive jihad. Foremost among these is the restriction that an offensive jihad can only be declared by an extremely high-ranking Muslim religious authority. The view that many Muslims hold is that only an imam or a caliph, religious leaders believed to be directly descended from Muhammad, has sufficient authority to declare an offensive jihad. However, according to most versions of Islam, there are no such imams or caliphs alive today. Nor will there be another such leader until the arrival of a messianic figure known as the Mahdi. In a Muslim vision of the Final

Battle (the Islamic equivalent of the events described in the Christian Bible's Book of Revelation) the Mahdi, or last imam, will return to earth, purge the dar al Islam of all apostates and unbelievers, and declare offensive jihad against the whole of the dar al harb, initiating a war that will result in the conversion of the entire planet into the dar al Islam.[5]

In addition to rules about how an offensive jihad can be declared, there are Islamic conduct of war rules that apply in the case of an offensive jihad. There are strict prohibitions against the targeting of noncombatants and specific restrictions concerning the use of weapons and tactics. For example, a Muslim leader fighting an offensive jihad is not allowed to use fire or weapons that harness fire against his enemies unless and until those enemies use such weapons first. (This is because fire is seen as a weapon reserved for God's use.)[6]

A defensive jihad is understood by some to be a very different matter. Defensive jihad need not be declared by a legitimate religious authority— or by any authority whatsoever. It may not even need to be declared at all. Defensive jihad is simply the defense of the dar al Islam against an invasion from the dar al harb. Therefore, participation in a defensive jihad is the individual duty of every Muslim.

The original idea behind the concept of defensive jihad seems most likely to have been that if invaders from the dar al harb entered the dar al Islam, it would be desirable for every Muslim, regardless of his occupation or status, to take up whatever arms he had at hand and attempt to repel the attackers without waiting for orders or permission to do so. Defensive jihad would therefore be a desperate response to a threat against the very existence of the dar al Islam. It may have been believed that some of those who fought would not be capable of understanding or complying with rules of engagement, which would explain why there are no rules associated with defensive jihad.

Perhaps followers of Osama bin Laden and other radical Islamic fundamentalist terrorists convince themselves that they are engaged in an ongoing defensive jihad against the United States and its allies (citing past events such as the deployment of U.S. troops on Saudi Arabian soil, near the Islamic holy cities Mecca and Medina, as evidence of "invasions" of the dar al Islam by the dar al harb). They would then consider themselves free to fight without restraint, to use whatever weapons they can devise against the inhabitants of the dar al harb, making no attempt to distinguish combatants from noncombatants. However they may justify their actions to themselves, if they refuse to accept any rules of war, they forfeit the right to be regarded as warriors by the rest of the world. In international law, they will be termed "illegal combatants." We may view such men (and women) as fighters, killers, or murderers, but they are not warriors.

Individuals can fight for an objectively bad cause or a corrupt regime and yet still be warriors, so long as they have a warrior's code that requires them to observe the rules of war. For example, most of the ordinary German soldiers who fought against the Allies in World War II were warriors, even though many (if not all) of their SS brethren were not. Although slavery in the American South was an unqualified evil, there were Southern warriors in the U.S. Civil War who fought honorably over what they perceived to be an issue of states' rights. But there can be no honor in any conflict for those participants who, because they think they are engaged in a defensive jihad or for any other reason, believe that they have no moral obligation to restrain their behavior in any way.

While they were working on the second half of their "Why I am different from a terrorist" assignments, some of my students reported having trouble understanding how anyone, no matter what his convictions, could agree to take part in terrorist operations that were not limited by moral constraints and involved intentionally targeting innocents. They wondered, Are the people who can do these things inhuman monsters? Can they really create meticulous plans to slaughter unsuspecting civilians without being stopped in their tracks by impossible-to-ignore pangs of conscience?

Albert Bandura, the David Starr Jordon Professor of Social Science in Psychology at Stanford University, explains how ordinary people can be persuaded to see killing as morally acceptable:

> People who have been socialized to deplore killing as morally condemnable can be transformed rapidly into skilled combatants, who may feel little compunction and even a sense of pride in taking human life. . . . The conversion of socialized people into dedicated combatants is not achieved by altering their personality structures, aggressive drives, or moral standards. Rather, it is accomplished by cognitively restructuring the moral value of killing, so that the killing can be done free from self-censuring restraints.[7]

It is probably not the case that those who have been bewitched by the rhetoric of bin Laden and others like him feel no revulsion at the thought (or in the act) of killing unarmed, helpless civilians. Rather, they have most likely been convinced, or have convinced themselves, that any apparent pricks of conscience they may feel are not the screams of their precious humanity hoping to be heard but rather their human weakness battling against their will to perform their sacred duty. They would therefore consider it a triumph of the will to accept the charge to kill without mercy or discrimination.

In *A Report on the Banality of Evil: Eichmann in Jerusalem*, Hannah Arendt describes how Heinrich Himmler, one of the chief architects of the Holocaust, responsible for arranging the slaughter of millions of innocent people, found himself at times made physically sick by horrors he helped orchestrate. Nevertheless, he refused to interpret his distaste for the gruesome details of his job as an indication that what he was doing was morally reprehensible. Instead he took pride in the fact that he maintained his dedication to the duties assigned to him despite his disgust for them:

> The member of the Nazi hierarchy most gifted at solving problems of conscience was Himmler. . . . [P]hrases, taken from speeches Himmler made to the commanders of the *Einsatzgruppen* and the Higher S.S. and Police Leaders, [include]: . . . "We realize that what we are expecting from you is "superhuman," to be "superhumanly inhuman." . . . What stuck in the minds of these men who had become murderers was simply the notion of being involved in something historic, grandiose, unique ("a great task that occurs once in two thousand years"), which must therefore be difficult to bear. This was important, because the murderers were not sadists or killers by nature; on the contrary, a systematic effort was made to weed out all those who derived physical pleasure from what they did. The troops of the *Einsatzgruppen* had been drafted from the Armed S.S., a military unit with hardly more crimes in its record than any ordinary unit of the German Army, and their commanders had been chosen by Heydrich from the S.S. elite with academic degrees. Hence the problem was how to overcome . . . the animal pity by which all normal men are affected in the presence of physical suffering. The trick used by Himmler—who apparently was rather strongly afflicted with these instinctive reactions himself—was very simple and probably very effective; it consisted in turning these instincts around, as it were, in directing them toward the self. So that instead of saying: What horrible things I did to people!, the murderers would be able to say: What horrible things I had to watch in the pursuance of my duties, how heavily the task weighed upon my shoulders![8]

It is truly disturbing to consider how easy it may be for a person to rationalize the terrible transition from warrior to murderer. An individual may be persuaded to become a murderer by a single charismatic person, by a group or movement that answers some psychological need, or by the effects of a traumatic event (such as witnessing the death of a close friend or family member). Here again I must stress that the line between a warrior and a murderer is profoundly important, but very thin. Once it has been crossed, the harm to the individual may be irrevocable.

Ben Hobbs, a student in my 2002 "Knowing Your Enemy" seminar (who had at the time the distinction of being the only person to have taken all three of my warrior ethics courses), raised the issue in class of whether a warrior who had crossed the line and allowed himself to become a murderer could ever find redemption and, in a sense, regain his warrior status. My response, which is influenced by the work of psychologist Jonathan Shay (whose research on combat stress is discussed in chapter 1), is that it depends a great deal on the individual's own reaction to having crossed that line. If he refuses to examine the immorality of his actions, he may start down a slippery slope from which it might not be easy to escape. He may try to tell himself that it was naïve ever to have clung to a code—that there is no real difference between, for example, killing an enemy combatant in the thick of a firefight and killing an unarmed civilian in cold blood. On the other hand, if he rejects his ignoble behavior rather than excusing it, he may be able to restore his sense of honor and renew his commitment to the path of restraint.

The main reason I made my students do the "creepy" assignment that required them to explain why they are different from terrorists is that they need to understand how the line between warrior and murderer can be crossed so they can avoid crossing it themselves. Unfortunately, it is most difficult for warriors to keep from slipping over that line when they are fighting against those who have already crossed it.

In 1989, my father had a conversation with a World War II fighter pilot who knew firsthand what it feels like both to see an enemy cross the line from warrior to murderer and, in response, to cross that same line yourself. He described the experience that had haunted him for over forty years:

> "Three ME-109s came at us from out of the sun. It was one hell of a dog-fight. Jimmy Craig was hit and bailed out. He was up there in his chute, settling down easy, when this Kraut pulls away and takes dead aim at Jimmy. I couldn't believe it. You never shoot a guy hanging in a chute. But that's what he did. He cut him in half. I swung round on that bastard's tail and picked at him until he bailed out. His chute opened. I watched him floating there just like Jimmy. I wanted to see his eyes. But he had goggles on. Then I shot that son of a bitch out of the sky."
>
> "How'd it feel?" My father asked him.
>
> "It felt good."
>
> "Really? . . . Well, you were there."
>
> "No. . . . Okay, . . . I cried."[9]

It is easier to remain a warrior when fighting other warriors. When warriors fight murderers, they may be tempted to become the mirror image of the evil they hoped to destroy. Their only protection is their code of honor. The professional military ethics that restrain warriors—that keep them from targeting those who cannot fight back, from taking pleasure in killing, from striking harder than is necessary and that encourage them to offer mercy to their defeated enemies and even to help rebuild their countries and communities—are also their own protection against becoming what they abhor.

Legend has it that when a Spartan mother sent her son off to war she would say to him, "Come back with your shield or on it." If a warrior came back without his shield, it meant that he had laid it down in order to break ranks and run from battle. He was supposed to use his shield to protect the man next to him in formation, so to abandon his shield was not only to be a coward but also to break faith with his comrades. To come back on his shield was to be carried back either wounded or dead.

Thus the adage meant that the young warrior should fight bravely, maintain his martial discipline, and return with both his body and his honor intact.

The warriors' mothers who spoke this line were not heartless monsters—far from it. It was spoken from great love. They wanted their children to return with their sense of self-respect still with them, feeling justifiably proud of how they had performed under pressure, not tortured and destroyed by guilt and shame. To come back with their shields was to come back still feeling like warriors, not like cowards or murderers.

The Spartan mothers' message is timeless. Everyone who cares about the welfare of warriors wants them not only to live through whatever fighting they must face but also to have lives worth living after the fighting is done. Consider the postwar sentiments expressed in the closing lines of the poem "Old Airfield," written by World War II veteran Andrew H. Hines Jr.:

> The crescendo built—a war was won and men came home,
> Came home to lives completely changed—
> as they were changed.
>
> Came back to love and warmth and the prospects of a life stretching
> beyond a day or two.
> So life resumed its pace—
> different, but still within their knowledge of its ways.
> The years went by, the burdens were assumed, the responsibilities grew
> And seldom did they stop to think of the intensity and commitment they
> had known.
>
> But on occasion, as lightning brightens the sky, some word or headline
> brought it back
> And they knew for a moment the heightened stress—
> and then relaxed and resumed their way.
>
> And, like old airfields, found in new ways the fulfillment of dreams
> And the sense of being part of a larger plan—
> as once they were so long ago.[10]

"Come back with your shield or on it." Andy Hines came back with his shield. But for many reasons, not all warriors do. Some are never able to leave the horror of war behind them. Their bodies come home alive, but their faith in themselves, their dreams, and their hopes for the future are long dead. Had they been given the choice, they might have preferred not to come home at all.

The warrior's code is the shield that guards our warriors' humanity. Without it, they are no good to themselves or to those with whom and for whom they fight. Without it, they will find no way back from war. My students are the warriors of the future. When and if they go into combat, I want them to be able to return from it intact in body *and* soul. I want all of them, every last one, to come back with their shields.

NOTES

1. Ariel Merari, "The Readiness to Kill and Die: Suicidal Terrorism in the Middle East," in *Origins of Terrorism: Psychologies, Ideologies, Theologies, States of Mind*, ed. Walter Reich (Washington, D.C.: Woodrow Wilson Center Press, 1998), 193.

2. Ronald Munson, "An Overview of Aquinas' Natural Law Theory," in *Ethics for Military Leaders*, ed. George R. Lucas et al. (New York: Simon & Schuster Custom Publishing, 1998), 397.

3. Saint Thomas Aquinas, *Summa Theologica*, vol. 2, trans. Fathers of the English Dominican Province, 1911; my emphasis.

4. I am grateful to Laurent Murawiec, philosopher and senior security analyst, for helping me understand the difference between the dar al Islam and the dar al harb and the implications of that distinction.

5. James Turner Johnson, "Jihad and Just War," *First Things* 124 (June/July 2002), 12–14.

6. I am indebted to just war theorist James Turner Johnson for clarifying these points and offering this specific example in a lecture on the difference between defensive and offensive jihad delivered at the U.S. Naval Academy in the fall of 2001.

7. Albert Bandura, "Mechanisms of Moral Disengagement," in *Origins of Terrorism*, ed. Reich, 163–64.

8. Hannah Arendt, *A Report on the Banality of Evil: Eichmann in Jerusalem* (New York: Penguin Books, 1963), 105–6.

9. Peter A. French, *Responsibility Matters* (Lawrence: University Press of Kansas, 1992), 29.

10. Andrew H. Hines Jr., "Old Airfield," in *Time and The Kite* (St. Petersburg, Fla.: author, 1986).

Index

About the Author

Shannon E. French teaches in the ethics section of the Department of Leadership, Ethics, and Law at the United States Naval Academy in Annapolis, Maryland. She earned her B.A. from Trinity University (San Antonio, Texas) in 1990 and her Ph.D. in philosophy from Brown University in 1997. She joined the USNA faculty in June 1997. Her main area of research is military ethics. She has published articles and book reviews (including a book discussion series for the *Journal of Military Ethics*), presented papers at international conferences, and coedited textbooks in this field, including *Ethics for Military Leaders*. At the Naval Academy she teaches "Moral Reasoning for Naval Leaders" (the core ethics course), "The Code of the Warrior," "Advanced Warrior Ethics," "Philosophy of Religion," and "Knowing Your Enemy." In 2000 she was awarded USNA's campuswide Apgar Award for Excellence in Teaching for demonstrating "effectiveness in teaching the qualities of leadership, with special emphasis on character, responsibility, and integrity."